The Archaeology and Early History of the

CHANNEL ISLANDS

The Archaeology and Early History of the

CHANNEL ISLANDS

HEATHER SEBIRE

For my three Guernseymen, Phil, Jonathan and Joshua
and all my dear friends in archaeology – you know who you are!

First published 2005
Revised and reprinted 2011

The History Press
The Mill, Brimscombe Port,
Stroud, Gloucestershire, GL5 2QG
www.thehistorypress.co.uk

British Library Cataloguing in Publication Data.
A catalogue record for this book is available from the British Library.

ISBN 978 0 7524 3449 0

Typesetting and origination by The History Press
Printed and bound in Great Britain by
Marston Book Services Limited, Didcot

CONTENTS

PREFACE

Guernsey, Jersey and Alderney, collectively known as the Channel Islands since the nineteenth century (Hocart 1995), lie just 25km off the western coast of the Cotentin peninsula of Normandy in France and some 120km from mainland Britain. Strategically placed in the western channel, but subject to very large tidal ranges and strong currents, the islands have been home to people who have come and gone from the islands from the early prehistoric period to the present day. This book describes in some detail the archaeological record of the Channel Islands from early prehistory to the Middle Ages, which I hope will be of interest to the general reader. I have drawn on many previous sources but also have brought the reader up to date with the last 20 years or so of research and rescue excavations that have taken place, particularly in Guernsey. As archaeology is such a wide-ranging discipline today, it would be impossible for one author to do the in-depth surveys of the past such as those of Kendrick (1928) and Hawkes (1937). More recently the volumes of Johnston (1981), Kinnes and Grant (1983), Bender (1986), Johnston (1986) and Patton (1987) all paid particular attention to the prehistoric monuments in the islands. This was largely due to the fact that at the time of their writing there was little settlement evidence available. Also, those volumes with particular reference to Guernsey draw heavily on the original manuscripts of Frederick Corbin Lukis, a nineteenth-century archaeologist and polymath, who excavated many of the extant burial monuments on that island (Sebire 2003). There is also a diverse range of specialist papers on Guernsey which was published as a festschrift to Bob Burns (Sebire 1998). Dr Mark Patton's important review of the Neolithic Communities of the Channel Islands (1995) was a synthesis of the material from the relevant museum collections and the excavations to that date presented in a theoretical framework. Following on from all those publications it seemed appropriate to attempt in this volume to synthesise the considerable body of material that now exists on the archaeology and early history of the Channel Islands, some published and some as yet unpublished, alongside all the exciting new finds of the last decades.

THE ISLANDS TODAY

The islands today are dependencies of the British Crown and Her Majesty the Queen is represented by Lieutenant Governors in both Guernsey and Jersey, who stay in the island for a three-year term of office. The islands retain their independence to levy taxes (at an attractive rate for the offshore finance market) and custom duties, and are self-governing. Islanders are also free to elect their own parliament and the leaders are Bailiffs who also preside as Chief Judge. They are divided into parishes each with their own identity, 10 in Guernsey and 12 in Jersey, and in the descriptions that follow the relevant parish will be cited.

In recent years the finance industry has taken over as the main upholder of the economy of the islands, bringing in its wake, among other things, an inflated rise in house prices, and the demand for more and more services, as staff for the industry are brought in from the UK and elsewhere. This has inevitably brought with it a boom in building and redevelopment. The centres of St Helier and St Peter Port in particular, where new office accommodation is constantly in demand, have changed considerably over the last 20 years. Many of the more rural outlying areas have also been used to provide out of town housing of an executive quality, despite an attempt by the local planning authorities to control development. This has, of course, had great effects on the preservation of archaeology, as sites are being disturbed at an alarming rate, and has necessitated many rescue excavations, in an attempt to record some of what is being destroyed.

The tourist industry, however, which relies heavily on the attraction of Heritage sites, continues to be important and in the summer months the populations virtually double. The islands boast a long and interesting history, from prehistoric times to the present day. One major event in recent memory was the Occupation by German forces during the Second World War, from 1940 to 1945, when the islands were fortified as part of Hitler's Atlantic Wall. During this time, the landscape changed dramatically, as the islands were fortified with bunkers, lookouts and gun batteries, particularly around the coast, many of which were on sites previously fortified in Napoleonic times and earlier.

Channel Islanders pride themselves on their quality of life, although many people who now live in the islands are not native born. An outstanding heritage, which will be outlined below, is but one aspect of that quality of life. I have been privileged to hold the post of Archaeology Officer at Guernsey Museum since 1995, taking care of part of the islands' heritage and hope I can convey to the reader what a remarkable archaeological record the islands have – never forgetting that it was people such as ourselves, with families and friends, lives and loves whose remains we are studying; real people, reflecting every aspect of the human condition. My only complaint is that every time I tried to have a clear session on writing this book yet another site would need attention. In fact, at the time of writing, a rescue excavation is underway at King's Road, in Guernsey, on an area alongside that previously excavated in the 1980s, where an Iron Age settlement and warrior cemetery were found (see Chapter 5). To date further evidence of the settlement has been located and seven graves have been excavated. Two of the graves contain grave goods. In one there was a sword, fibula and other objects and in the other, several bronze rings and items of jewellery.

There seems no end to the exciting archaeological discoveries that the Channel Islands produce.

Heather Sebire
Guernsey
August 2005

NOTE ON DATES

Dates used to describe geological periods are written as bp (before present). More recent dates which have been produced by radiocarbon dating have been calibrated where possible and are written as BC or AD.

ACKNOWLEDGEMENTS

The book would not have been possible without the help and cooperation of many people. In the first instance Tim Schadla-Hall encouraged me to write this general survey and John Renouf persuaded me that it would be more useful to cover all the islands. My thanks are due to Peter Kemmis Betty for agreeing to publish it. I have drawn on the published work of many people from, in particular, the Transactions of La Société Guernesiaise and the Bulletins of La Société Jersiaise, which are an invaluable source of information. I wish to pay tribute to all the scholars who published their research therein. The Bulletins of the Alderney Society and the Guernsey Society have also been useful.

In Jersey I wish to particularly thank Margaret Finlaison for generously supplying unpublished information and offering advice. Her contribution to Channel Islands archaeology is considerable. Thanks also to Olga Finch of the Jersey Heritage Trust for help with images and information generally and in particular La Hougue Bie. Mark Patton, Ann Spencer, Peter Roberts and Chris Aubin all helped with information gathering as did the Director of the Jersey Heritage Trust, Jonathan Carter. Warwick Rodwell kindly supplied me with information on his work at Mont Orgueil in advance of publication and an image of the Écréhous brooch.

Peter Arnold on Alderney supplied invaluable information and help with access to material in the collections of the Alderney Society. I am also grateful to him for the use of his reconstruction drawing of Les Huguettes.

In Guernsey I wish to thank the Director of Guernsey Museums and Galleries, Peter Sarl, for support over many years during the many rescue excavations that the museum has sponsored and for permission to use images from the collections. My colleagues at Guernsey Museum have been very supportive, but my thanks are due in particular to Paul Le Tissier for help with images and Lynne Ashton, for general encouragement. Tanya Walls also helped with information from the Guernsey SMR.

Mark Wood kindly supplied information on the Roman period in advance of publication. I wish to thank Brian Byron and Barbara McNee for the use of their superb art work. For general support and discussion I am very grateful to my predecessor at Guernsey Museum, Bob Burns, who, during his time, also made a considerable contribution to local archaeology. I am grateful for the assistance of the librarians and staff of the Guille Allès and Priaulx Libraries in Guernsey. The library and photo archive service of La Société Jersiaise were also of great help. My research outside the Channel Islands took place in many institutions and I am grateful to the librarian at the Society of Antiquaries of London, for permission to use images from their collections. As ever the members of the Guernsey Museum Archaeology Group have supported me throughout the duration of the project; their work has added greatly to the archaeological record of Guernsey.

Philip de Jersey kindly read my text and made useful comments as did Barry Cunliffe and Brendan O'Connor. I wish to thank the many colleagues whose interest in Channel Islands archaeology over many years has been invaluable, and with whom I have had many discussions, namely: Ian Kinnes, Barry Cunliffe, Ken Barton, Philip de Jersey, Tim Schadla-Hall, Bob Burns, Margaret Finlaison, Olga Finch, Mark Patton, Bob Thomson, Duncan Brown, Jon Adams, John Renouf, Mark Wood, Jason Monaghan, Michael Batt, Rick Schulting, Alison Sheridan, Tim Champion, John Robb, Mick Atha, Barrie Cook, Darryl Ogier, Marion Archibald, David Bukach, Warwick Rodwell, Jim Campbell, Bob Jones, John McCormack, Seán McGrail, Wendy Childs, Richard Keen and, laterally, Anne Tresset, Emanuel Ghèsquière, Cyril Marcigny, Jean-Noël Guyodo, Gwenäelle Hamon and Chantal Conneller.

Finally thanks to my long-suffering family for love and support throughout.

I

THE RISING TIDE: THE FORMATION OF THE CHANNEL ISLANDS

Les Îles de La Manche sont des morceaux de France tombés dans la mer et ramassés par L'Angleterre…. Des Quatres îles, Serk. Le plus petite, est la plus belle; Jersey la plus grande, est la plus jolie; Guernsey, sauvage et riante participe des deux…

The Channel Islands are fragments of France that fell into the sea and were gathered up by England…. Of the four islands, Sark, the smallest, is the most beautiful; Jersey, the largest, is the prettiest; Guernsey, wild and charming shares their characteristics… (Victor Hugo 1883)

…nothing is still; everything around us is in the process of change, from what was to what will be and our islands no less than we who look at them. (Renouf 1977)

INTRODUCTION

The group of small islands which lie off the northern French coast now collectively known as the Channel Islands have, since their origin about 8000-9000 years ago, been a microcosm of human settlement (*colour plate 1*). Crucial to their existence is the fact that the water surrounding the islands is so shallow that a drop in sea level of some 20-30m would leave them on the edge of the landmass now known as France. The islands came into being in the Holocene period after the last great ice age but for much of the last million years the sea level was so low that the islands were in effect part of the French mainland, in the great Bay of Mont St Michel. Today they are thriving communities, albeit with small populations, who have established themselves in the modern global world, as centres of tourism and high finance, each with their own characteristics. Collectively they provide evidence of human occupation over 250,000 years (*1*).

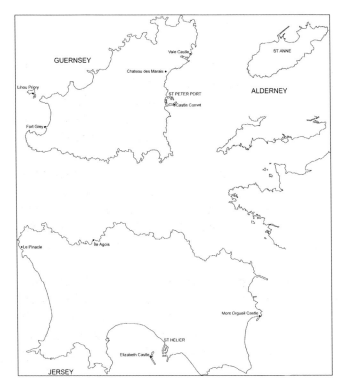

1 The location of the Channel Islands

The archaeological story begins a very long time ago, however, with Homo Neanderthalensis finding an 'offshore' residence in a cave off the south-west tip of what is now Jersey; in fact, at the time of the discovery in 1912, temporarily taking the name Homo Breladensis (after the parish in which it was found). Since the beginning of prehistory people (both friendly and not so friendly) have been coming from and going to the islands, some settling and establishing themselves, others trading or just passing through, but all leaving visible traces of themselves and their successive generations on the landscape. The strategic position of the islands and in particular the good harbours off the east coast of Guernsey, ensured that trade routes were established early in prehistoric times and continue to be important today.

THE FORMATION OF THE ISLAND GROUP

In order to tell the archaeological story it is necessary to begin with the formation of the island group, before considering the people whose material remains we now study as the archaeology of the Channel Islands. The small archipelago today comprises the islands of Jersey, Guernsey, Alderney, Herm and Sark, the smaller islets of Lihou, Burhou, Jethou, and Brecqhou, and the offshore reefs of Les Minquiers, Les Écréhous and Les Casquets.

BACKGROUND GEOLOGY

Before the time of the first human appearance in the islands their formation is a geological story. The geology visible in the islands today is a combination of very old rocks on one hand and more recent processes on the other. These have produced both the surface deposits that are presently visible in the cliffs, bays and headlands that characterise the islands, and the sea level changes occurring as a result of the recent ice ages (Renouf 1977).

The hard rock geology on Guernsey consists of two main bands (Roach et al. 1991). The southern and largest band consists of metamorphic gneiss and schists cut by minor igneous intrusions. The northern band is a complex of plutonic igneous rocks including granites and diorites and gabbros. Both groups of rocks are cut by thin intrusions or dykes of dolerite, which were important as a source of stone for axes in the Neolithic period.

Jersey has similar granites, diorites and gabbros with dolorites which cut across the north-western, south-western and south-eastern corners. It has sedimentary shale in the central area and the only evidence for volcanic rocks in the islands on its eastern side. The west of Alderney has metamorphic rocks largely similar to Guernsey and a central plutonic igneous complex similar to both Guernsey and Jersey. To the east, a reddish-purple sandstone forms a softer deposit similar to the north-east corner of Jersey.

Of the smaller islands Sark is part of an old metamorphic complex with many dolerite dykes. Lihou Island off the west of Guernsey is part of the southern metamorphic complex of Guernsey, whereas Herm and Jethou to the east of Guernsey belong to the plutonic group of rocks. Burhou and the Casquets, just off Alderney, are composed of sandstone. The extensive reefs of Les Minquiers and Les Écréhous are mainly old metamorphic rocks.

SEA LEVEL CHANGES AND RECENT GEOLOGY

It is difficult not to over-emphasise the importance of the range of changes in sea level around the islands over time, because this factor is crucial to both their physical development and to the interplay of human events that have taken place in them.

During the Pleistocene period from about 200,000 years ago the rise and fall of the sea level and periods of glacial and interglacial climate had dramatic effects on the plateaux that become the islands, which stood out as hills on a coastal plain of shallow river valleys. Although the islands were never covered by ice, the area was cut by a river system based around the valleys of the Seine and the Ay. These would have caused the erosion processes which are visible in the islands today. During the interglacial periods raised beaches and associated fossil cliffs and wave-cut platforms were formed (Campbell 2000). By the time of the period known as the Palaeolithic, covering at least the last 250,000 years, the islands stood out on a plain on the edge of the French continent jutting out into the western channel. The climate in the area that is now Brittany and Lower Normandy was intermittently sub-arctic, and tundra-like conditions prevailed on the land. The site of La Cotte de Saint Brelade in Jersey (see Chapter 3) has provided valuable evidence about the Pleistocene period in the Channel Island area.

The events of the last 12,000 years or so in the more recent Holocene period are the ones that will mostly involve us here (2). By the end of the period of the last glaciations, the continental ice sheets began to melt and as water returned to the sea, the sea level began to rise. Around 13000 BC melting ice and also the release of pressure on the land masses caused sea level rises in different ways. By the nominal close of the ice age at some 10,000 years ago, the shoreline had moved up the Channel from its furthest position, well out in the Western Approaches from -100m to c.-40m. The Channel Islands' shelf was now outlined though all individual 'islands' were still fully connected by land with each other and the adjacent continent. The rise to this date had been rapid; around 1m per century, and this rate was sustained until well towards 8000 years ago at c.6000 BC. By this time Guernsey and the smaller islands, and also Alderney, were surrounded by water and were true islands (3).

Latest research under way is refining the picture of island separation (Renouf & Sebire forthcoming) but it is clear that the Mesolithic inhabitants of the area had to contend not only with a continuing reduction in the land available to them but with the whole relationship of land, coast and sea (see Chapter 3). Jersey remained an island linked to the adjacent Cotentin peninsula of the French mainland for perhaps another 700 to 1000 years until more or less the beginning of the Neolithic period.

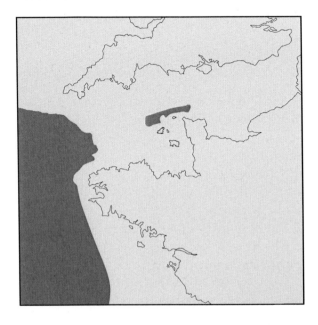

2 Sea levels in the Western Channel c.16,000bp. *After Renouf & Urry, 1976*

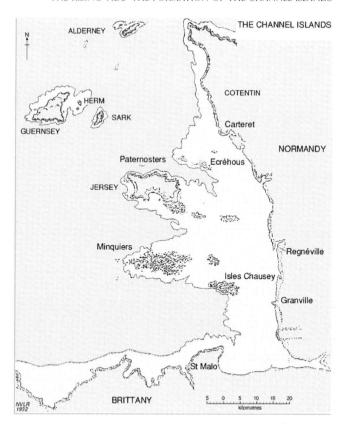

3 The Channel Islands
showing the 10 fathom
(± 10m) marine contour.
After Rybot 1932

So by 5000 BC, Guernsey, Sark, Herm and Alderney had become islands,
whereas Jersey may still have been accessible from the French mainland (Cotentin
peninsula) during exceptionally low tides. The present day sea level was reached by
3000–2500 BC but it is difficult to say whether it hovered below this at any point.
It is clear also that up to the Neolithic period the land masses would have been
considerably larger than they are today (Renouf & Urry 1976, Jones et al. 1990).
Once the islands came into being the formation processes left each with individual
features. Although formed from the edges of the same land mass, the main islands
have very different characteristics and orientations (see below).

TOPOGRAPHY, SOILS AND VEGETATION

Even though the islands were never actually covered by ice the effect of being on
the edge of the ice sheets is visible in the more recent geology, and the glacial and
interglacial periods caused dramatic effects, not least due to the sea level changes
described above. The improving temperatures that brought the ice age to an end
were also responsible for changes to the nature of the seasons, the weather, the
climate and thus the fauna and the flora. The landscape was transformed overall

from the open tundra-like steppe of the late ice age to a mid-latitude open forest that would be our present environment if it were not for the changes induced by human activities over the millennia.

The plateaux that became the Channel Islands were eroded by powerful glacial streams and there was also deposition brought by cold easterly winds carrying silt material from beneath the ice sheets. This wind-borne dust or loess was deposited on the islands, in some places just a few centimetres and in others up to 1m and more thick, giving a very fertile soil cover. The freezing temperatures during the glacial periods had another effect: rock fragments from exposed outcrops were broken off and moved down the surrounding slopes, mixing with silt and loess to form the characteristic orangey-yellow rubble deposit known as 'head' which is visible in the eroding cliffs today. Although the highest points on the islands are relatively low (130m), they are characterised by central plateaux traversed by small streams. The plateaux slope to coastal plain and marsh areas. Guernsey in particular has relatively high cliffs to the south which rise to around 100m above sea level. The central high ground drops to coastal plains in the north and west.

Three studies that focused on vegetational developments are particularly relevant to the Channel Islands and immediately adjacent areas. The work of M.-T. Morzadec-Kerfourn on the palynology (the study of ancient pollen) of the Baie de Mont St Michel marshes led the way (1974). Later, a more diversified team approach from Coventry University (Jones et al. 1990) covered not only the palynology but also diatoms (fossil plankton) and other faunal evidence; this work was confined to the coastal embayments and some inland valley deposits of Jersey. J.Campbell (2000) examined the palynology of many of the coastal plain deposits of Guernsey and Alderney. Combined with other studies on both the original and evolved soils found in the islands, it becomes possible to present a moderately detailed picture of the evolution of the landscapes of the islands since the close of the ice age (Renouf pers. comm.).

A soil survey of Guernsey identified several different soil types based on the underlying geology and drainage characteristics (A.D.A.S. 1989). The soils on the plateaux areas consist of deep deposits of the fertile loess brought in during the last glaciations with fine, sandy, silty loams above. These soils are where most present-day cultivation takes place. The fertile loess deposits are a crucial element of the islands' archaeology as the first farmers found good soils to grow their crops. Research that is in progress in some tidal areas of the islands is revealing the presence of residual loess that is saturated with saltwater. In Jersey, at La Rocque, a mammoth tooth has recently been found on top of the silt (John Renouf pers. comm.), and off Guernsey's east coast, worked flint has been found in a similar deposit by Crevichon (see Chapter 3). On the coastal headlands thin, sandy loams are found which drain well and are rarely cultivated.

A soil survey of Alderney (Hazelden 1992) identified fine, sandy loess and calcareous dune sand. In Jersey the plateaux are covered in thick deposits of loess whereas the headlands have extremely thin deposits characteristic of the underlying granitic subsoil (Jones et al. 1990). Peat deposits are present on the three major islands formed behind barriers of sand dune during the periods of changing sea levels indicating brackish coastal marsh. These can be found at Vazon and Bordeaux on Guernsey, St Ouen's and St Brelade's on Jersey and at Longis on Alderney. Artefacts have been found in these deposits which will be discussed later.

FLORA AND FAUNA

The mild oceanic climate enjoyed by the islands today largely affects their flora and fauna. Several species of plants and animals just reach as far north as the Channel Islands but no further in the British Isles (Jee 1977). The larger islands of Guernsey and Jersey have a variety of habitats with topographical differences, acidic soils and the degree of shelter being main factors in producing characteristic assemblages of plants and animals today. The evidence of Jones et al. (1990) suggests a dominance of birch woodland, with elm and beech in the post-glacial period on higher ground, and birch and willow on the valley bottoms and coastal marshes. Later, at the beginning of the Atlantic period c.6000 bp, oak and hazel are present with alder in the wetlands by the coast, with grassland and scrub woodland in the drier areas. Campbell's research (2000) documented the human impact on the vegetation of sites in Alderney and Guernsey. At Vazon Bay in Guernsey evidence suggests that there were human induced changes to deciduous woodland during the Late Mesolithic-Early Neolithic period, c.6800 bp, as will be discussed later.

TOPOGRAPHICAL FEATURES OF THE ISLANDS RELEVANT TO THEIR ARCHAEOLOGY (4)

Jersey, the largest of the island group, is formed of a plateau some 130m above sea level which slopes to the south. It measures 16 x 7km (9 x 5 miles) and is just 22.5km (14 miles) distant from the coast of Normandy in northern France. On a clear day the coast of the Cotentin peninsula seems very near. The island is high in the north (130m) and slopes to coastal cliffs (60m) and bays in the south. The north coast has precipitous cliffs interspersed with small coves. The area to the east is low-lying and at low tide reefs are laid bare for some distance, on occasions for up to 2km. The west coast is characterised by large sand dunes which stretch for approximately 6km with large rolling waves crashing to the shore, making this area unsuitable for landing vessels. In contrast to Guernsey, there is no natural roadstead anchorage and it was not until the late nineteenth century that major harbour works at the capital, St Helier, produced a properly sheltered harbour.

Guernsey is very different in form, being roughly triangular in shape. The south coast has the highest cliffs (100m) and small coves which probably appeared unapproachable by sea and are now accessible only by steep cliff paths (5). The island slopes to the north where there are sweeping bays and promontories, also characteristic of the west coast. It measures 14.5 x 8.5 km (9 x 3 miles) and is nearly 50km (30 miles) west of Normandy and 120km (75 miles) south of Weymouth on the southern British coast. Guernsey was, in fact, two islands until the mid-nineteenth century. A sandy 'braye' separated the two land masses of the low-lying area until the 1800s when it was drained by General Doyle and a 'bridge' created which gives its name to the area today. As a result, as well as natural harbours, the east coast has low-lying marshy areas which may have been navigable in prehistoric times. The island is much further away from the French coast than Jersey but has a major roadstead along the eastern coast between it

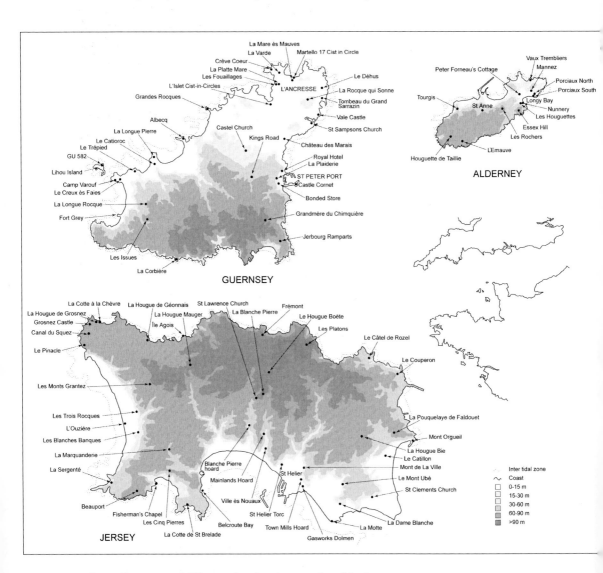

4 Jersey, Guernsey and Alderney showing sites mentioned in the text

5 Typical
Channel
Island scenery
at the south
coast cliffs
of Guernsey.
Photograph:
Guernsey
Museums and
Galleries

and Herm and Jethou, with sheltered natural harbours at the site of present day St Peter Port and at Bordeaux further north. The modern capital of St Peter Port is located in the middle of the east coast between two natural valleys.

The island of Alderney is the third largest and most northerly of the group of islands and lies just 13km (8 miles) from the Cotentin opposite. The island is approximately 3km (1.5 miles) wide and almost 6km (4 miles) in length along an axis lying in a north-east to south-west direction. High cliffs rise to the south and west, whereas the eastern coast which faces France is low-lying. The islet of Burhou is situated some 3km north-west of Alderney across a stretch of water called the Swinge and rises just a few metres above sea level. Some distance to the north-west lies a rocky outcrop known as the Casquets which has been home to a lighthouse since the early eighteenth century. The original harbour was at Longis Bay on the north-east coast, but a new modern harbour, complete with an extensive breakwater, is now situated in the centre of the north coast. However, it is worth noting that the waters between the island and the Cotentin are home to a dangerous fast moving current making navigation for small boats extremely hazardous.

THE SMALLER ISLANDS

Like Alderney, Herm, Jethou and Sark all belong to the Bailiwick of Guernsey. Herm lies opposite Guernsey's east coast just 5km distant across an expanse of water known as the Little Russell. The island is just 2km long and physically resembles Guernsey with low cliffs to the south and a low-lying sandy plain to the north.

Jethou lies next to Herm but is different in form as it rises sharply to a flattish summit of *c*.100m high with little low-lying ground at sea level. The smaller islets of Crevichon and La Grande Fauconnière alongside it rise to some 30m and 32m respectively above sea level. Both are accessible from Jethou at low tide. Crevichon was quarried extensively, not least for the building of Castle Cornet, which has left it rather asymmetrical. Off the west coast of Guernsey, the small tidal islet of Lihou is the most westerly part of the island group.

Sark has a plateau-like form which rises some 110m above sea level with dramatic cliffs on almost all its edges. The island lies some 12km off Guernsey and 17km north-west from Jersey. Sark is nearly split in two by a narrow isthmus known as La Coupée. The larger part is known as Great Sark which is just over 4km in length and is joined to Little Sark, just over 1km in length, by the narrow isthmus. The islet of Brecqhou lies off its west coast and is a similar size to Little Sark.

Another group of islands named Chausey are geographically part of the same range although now belong politically to France. They are a group of low-lying islets rarely more than 10m above sea level which lie off the south-east coast of Jersey close to the coast of France.

THE OFFSHORE REEFS

Les Écréhous are a small group of islets which lie to the north-east of Jersey between the island and the Cotentin coast of France. The reef covers some 700ha at low water. The largest island, Maître Île, rises some 18m above sea level and the smaller Blianque Île and Marmotière are only separated at high water. To the south of Jersey the reef known as Les Minquiers is, amazingly, larger than Jersey itself at low tide, extending up to 28km (18 miles) east/west and 22km (14 miles) north/south. Of this great plateau only nine islets are not submerged at high water and only Maîtresse Île has structures standing which were used for people quarrying stone in the eighteenth century. For at least part of the Neolithic period these reefs would have been extensive tracts of good land.

THE ISLANDS TODAY

The formation of the islands back in geological time continues to influence life today. One of the major factors, that is difficult for people who do not live near the sea to understand, is how that element of nature continues to dominate island life. The huge tidal range within the Bay of St Malo is a constant factor which, while easily accepted by islanders whose lives it dictates, to a certain extent remains a mystery to visitors and incomers who do not have experience of the sea. In Guernsey the 10m tidal range increases the land mass at low water mark by 15 per cent. In Jersey tides up to 12m expose huge expanses of tidal reefs particularly on the spring tides. Currents are very strong and local knowledge of the island waters is essential to ensure safe passage between the islands. This factor has influenced the development of the Channel Islands over thousands of years.

2

ON THE SHOULDERS OF GIANTS: THE HISTORY OF ARCHAEOLOGICAL RESEARCH IN THE CHANNEL ISLANDS

We are all shaped by the past. The discovery of that past is therefore a voyage of self-discovery. (Lord Renfrew of Kaimsthorn 1996)

I now with pleasure resume the pen, which … records a work of much interest and excitement, known only to those who enter into the pursuits and joys of the antiquary and historian! (F.C. Lukis 1843)

It is well documented that our ancestors were curious about their past and revered it in much the same way as we do today. The voyage of self-discovery that Lord Renfrew talks about in the Preface to the *Cambridge Illustrated History of Archaeology* (1996) is something that we all embrace in different ways. Certainly an innate human trait of curiosity seems to play a part in humankind's general interest in the past. An early record of this curiosity is of Nabonidus, who was King of Babylon in the sixth century BC. He is reputed to have excavated the floor of a temple down to a foundation stone laid some 2,000 years previously (Bahn 1996). In Guernsey, it is quite probable that the people who lived in the village community at Les Fouaillages during the Bronze Age, in the lee of the earlier burial mound which dominated their immediate landscape, would have regarded the monument with awe and reverence. On Jersey, the great monument of La Hougue Bie has acted as a marker on the landscape for generations that followed the building of this tomb, and curiosity about its origins and function is documented. When considering the archaeology of the Channel Islands today it is interesting to see how the bank of knowledge has built up over generations and how many of our interpretations of the past have changed as new discoveries are made.

EARLY VISITORS AND OBSERVERS OF MONUMENTS IN THE CHANNEL ISLANDS

One of the earliest written observations of the Channel Islands is a description included in William Camden's *Britannia* written in 1565. Camden was a teacher who became Master of Westminster School and published his *Britannia*, first in Latin and then later in English editions. This was a record of his travels around the British Isles and included descriptions of Hadrian's Wall and Stonehenge. Camden described the waters around Jersey as having 'shallow places, dangerous for such as saile that way.' He remarked on 'a most strong castle seated on the East-side with a haughty name called Mont Orgueil'. On Guernsey he noted St Peter Port harbour and the castles of Cornet and the Vale, which would have been standing at the time, and on Alderney he remarked on 'an ancient fort [now known as the Nunnery] and a dwelling house built at the charge of the Chamberlans [Essex Castle]'. The remaining comments are mostly historical and a description of the main pursuits of the people at the time, reading more like a guide book than an historical survey (Stevens-Cox 1969).

A century later Jean Poingdestre, who was Lieut. Bailiff of Jersey, writing about the island in 1685, described three sorts of ancient reminders or monuments of antiquity: 'the first and doubtless the most ancient are those wee call Poquelayes' (Nicolle 1889, 8). He remarked that there were half a hundred of them in the island. Poingdestre's second class of monument were Hougues or 'sepulchres of eminent persons' and his third class were castles but rather in the form of earthworks such as Le Câtel de Rozel, 'It is a great work raised in the manner of a Bulwarke with a deep ditch without it, making a square whose length is neere an aker and the breadth about half an Aker' (see Chapter 5). He had much else to say about the island including remarks about the encroachment of the sea in many areas of Jersey in the mid-fourteenth century.

Peter Heylyn was an English antiquary and geographer, who had travelled to France and 'the adjacent isles' in 1629. He was not at all impressed by the island's antiquities, as an account of his excursion about the same time as Poingdestre reveals (1656, 280):

> It was also the last part of my intention, to do something in honour of the islands by committing to memory their Antiquities, by reporting to posterity their Arts of Government, by representing, as in a tablet, the choicest of their beauties; and in a word, by reducing these and the Achievements of the people, as far as the light of Authors could direct me, into the body of an history. But when I had a little made myself acquainted with the place and the people, I found nothing in them which might put me to that trouble.

One can only assume that Heylyn did not take the time or trouble to get fully acquainted with the islands, for if nothing else local legend and folklore would have pointed to the existence of burial monuments.

In Falle's *History of Jersey*, published in 1694 with later editions, the following account is given:

> There are still to be seen in this island some old monuments of Paganism. They are great
> flat stones or rag-stones of vast weight & bulk, raised 3 or 4 feet from the ground and borne
> up, by others of a less size. We call them Pouquelayes, a word, I can hear of no where, &
> therefore take it to be purely local.

Pouquelaye in fact is a local Jersey word which probably meant 'stones of the fairies' from 'Pouque' being fairy and 'laye' being stone.

THE EIGHTEENTH CENTURY

In the eighteenth century there are more references to local antiquities. The notion that the megalithic burial chambers were in fact Druid's altars was prevalent, as many of the early illustrations show. F.C. Lukis of Guernsey was the first to dispel this notion (see below).

Francis Grose included the Channel Islands in his masterly account of the *Antiquities of all the regions of the British Isles* (Grose 1785). On Guernsey the antiquities he considered of note were 'Cornet Castle, Marsh Castle (Château des Marais), Michael's (St) or Vale church and Sampson (St) Castle'. In Sark (which he describes as 'fortified on all sides by cliffs which render it almost inaccessible') he noted the convent of St Maglorius and on Jersey, Elizabeth Castle, Gowray or Mont Orgueil Castle and the Chapel of Notre Dame de Pas (Grose 1785). He also published some fine engravings of sites in the islands including the megalith at Le Mont de la Ville in Jersey which was discovered in 1785 during levelling of an area of high ground above St Helier for a new parade ground. As the monument was somewhat in the way and the Governor of the day, Marshall Conway, had taken great interest in it to the extent of having a model made, the townspeople of St Helier decided to present it to him. The result was that Conway had it dismantled and re-erected on his estate at Henley-on-Thames where it can still be seen today (*colour plate 2*) (Hibbs 1985).

A few years later the megalithic tomb of Le Faldouet appeared in the *Gentleman's Magazine* as part of an article entitled '*Remarkable antiquities of Jersey*' written by someone with the initials 'MS'.

Samuel Bonamy, who became Bailiff of Guernsey in 1758, had been aware of megalithic remains. He wrote *A Short Account of the Island of Guernsey* (Add. Mss 6523, 1749) describing three megalithic monuments. At the end of the manuscript he drew a map showing their positions. He had interpreted the tombs as pagan altars:

> For it appears that the ancient inhabitants were pagan by their altars; three of which remain
> at this day, upon which they used to offer sacrifices to the gods of the sea. They consist of

flat ragstone, of a vast bulk and weight, supported three or four feet above the ground by three or four lesser stones, on which they are so artfully laid, that they seem hardly to touch them, and where they do touch the diameter is scarce two inches wide; and yet, which is very surprising, they have remained in that position above seven hundred years. Of the three which are yet left in Guernsey, two are in the Vale and one in St Saviour's parish. This last was being destroyed by the owner of the ground, to prevent which I purchased the land.

This is a very early example of monument protection in the islands and was followed by the actions of John de Havilland, also a Guernseyman. He purchased the 'land on which was situated' the chambered tomb at Le Déhus in the Vale parish to the north of Guernsey in 1775. He appears to have saved the monument, just before it was to be broken up for building stone. De Havilland may not have been fully aware of the significance of his actions, but there can be no doubt that he recognised the antiquity of the construction (Hocart, 1998).

According to an anonymous author writing about Jersey in 1840, who gives a discourse on Druid Temples and then describes the megalithic tombs of Faldouet, Le Couperon and Mont de la Ville, Falle's history of Jersey in 1734 paid little attention to the island's antiquities. He goes on to discuss the 'Roman works' namely a wall or earthwork known as La Petite Caeserée in the north of Jersey from which he states that 'Roman bricks and tiles were found in demolishing this immense rampart' (Anon 1840, 219).

Joshua Gosselin of Guernsey is best remembered for his painting and recording of natural history, but he also took great interest in archaeology and made the earliest technical sketches of Guernsey's monuments. These were published in the journal *Archaeologia* (Gosselin 1812). He also painted La Hougue Bie in Jersey in 1775 and the 'Druidical Altar' at the Catioroc in Guernsey from both north and south in 1783 (the latter in the collections of Guernsey Museum). He had examined Le Déhus in 1809, which he sketched, and also the tomb on the Catioroc which is now called Le Trépied. In 1811, he heard about the new discovery of what was then called a Druid's Altar, at La Varde 'on a height near the shore, on the left of L'Ancresse Bay' (Gosselin 1812). As a result of this he wrote to the famous naturalist Sir Joseph Banks with a description of what had been found. This letter was read to the Society of Antiquaries of London in December 1811 and published in their proceedings (ibid. 1812). More importantly, on the day that Joshua Gosselin visited the site at L'Ancresse, he was accompanied by his much younger cousin, Frederick Corbin Lukis, (see below). When Gosselin and Lukis arrived at the site, soldiers who had been working on the common to make a redoubt thought they had discovered an artificial cavern and were digging through pottery and bones. They had in fact uncovered what is now known to be the largest Neolithic passage grave in Guernsey (6). Lukis reported that after examining the tomb, he and Gosselin went away with a human skull each, and it was this field trip that appeared to have begun Lukis' lifelong fascination with archaeology.

6 Sketch of the passage grave at La Varde, Guernsey, by Joshua Gosselin. *Photograph: Guernsey Museums and Galleries*

THE NINETEENTH CENTURY

Archaeological discovery and recording in the nineteenth century in the islands was dominated by the remarkable Lukis family of Guernsey but developments also took place in Jersey later in the century and in both islands learned societies were formed. There was a consolidation of general and scientific interest in the remains of the past and a much greater accuracy in the recording of sites. Also, by the close of the century a number of entirely new discoveries had been made.

Fredrick Corbin Lukis (7) was born in St Peter Port, Guernsey and became an antiquarian and natural historian. As a young man Lukis became interested in a wide variety of pursuits including natural history, botany, geology, conchology and science but it was archaeology that held his attention throughout most of his long life. He was elected a Fellow of the Society of Antiquaries on 28 April 1853, and communicated many letters to the Secretary and other members. Lukis married his first cousin, Elizabeth Collings, in 1813 and they had six sons and three daughters.

Lukis was progressive in outlook, looking beyond the confines of his native Guernsey and Channel Islands to where the major advances in thinking about the past were being made. He established contacts in Denmark, France and America, alongside those in Britain. His importance stretched far beyond his own region of the Channel Islands as he entered the main intellectual debates

7 Frederick Corbin Lukis of Guernsey. *Photograph: Guernsey Museums and Galleries*

of his era, considering the past in the context of the Three Age system, the establishment of mankind's antiquity, and the institutionalisation of the study of archaeology. Although Lukis' work was mostly on Guernsey and Herm he spent a considerable amount of time on Sark as his daughter married the Seigneur. He also spent time in Jersey, not least rescuing material from the monument at Mont Ubé in 1846. Lukis recorded all his work on paper, the majority of which was bound into seven volumes entitled the *Collectanea Antiqua* which he put together about 1850. The work is now part of the Guernsey Museum collections (Lukis 1850).

Four of his children became archaeologists in their own right. The eldest son Frederick Collings Lukis MD FSA lived in Guernsey and practised medicine. However, he became interested in his father's archaeological work and published a type series for megalithic monuments (Lukis 1851). The second son, John Walter Lukis, moved to northern France. He became a mining engineer and through his work collected geological samples, many of which are now in the collections of Guernsey Museum. He also carried out many archaeological excavations in Brittany. The third son was the Rev. William Collings Lukis MA FSA. He entered the church and lived in England, first in Wiltshire and later in Yorkshire. He is the best known of the Lukis family outside of Guernsey, particularly for his very accurate plans and sections of megaliths in Britain, France, the Netherlands and the Channel Islands. Lukis' youngest surviving son, Capt. Francis du Bois Lukis excavated in the neighbouring island of Alderney. He lived with his father and inherited his museum which, on his own death in 1907, he bequeathed to the island of Guernsey in accordance with his father's wishes. Of Lukis' three daughters Mary Anne Lukis was the most involved in archaeology. She lived with her father and devoted much of her time to illustrating his work. Lukis himself excavated widely on Guernsey particularly at the important megalithic sites of La Varde and Le Déhus, showing remarkable skill in excavation technique for his time, including the use of sieves and drawing sections of his work to show the stratigraphical detail of the site.

SIGNIFICANT FINDS IN THE LATER NINETEENTH CENTURY

In 1861 some of the earliest discoveries were made in Jersey, when Joseph Sinel and Samuel Dancaster, both just 16 years old at the time, found a flint chipping site at La Cotte a la Chèvre on Jersey's north-west coast. They were observant enough to realise that it was unusual to find flint because of the geology of the island (Callow & Cornford 1986, 15). The date of their find was significant as it was only two years after the publication of Darwin's *Origin of Species*. Dancaster, who was a local farmer from the north end of St Ouen's Bay in Jersey, went on to discover the more important site of La Cotte de St Brelade with T. Saunders in 1881.

Just before that event, however, there was a growing awareness of the national importance of monuments and the Society of Antiquaries of London decided to prepare a list of 'all historical and regal monuments requiring protection throughout the country'. Lieutenant S.P. Oliver RA was to be quartered in Guernsey, and so it placed him in an ideal position to survey not only Guernsey but all the Channel Islands. He volunteered his services and as a result he published two papers (Oliver 1870, 1870a) which list all the sites known at that time. These papers also include drawings and plans which he drew up with the assistance of John Walter Lukis. Oliver's report was very important as it drew together all the known information at the time and is still of use today.

LOCAL SOCIETIES

An important development on both the islands of Guernsey and Jersey towards the end of the nineteenth century was the formation of learned societies, La Société Jersiaise in Jersey in 1873 and La Société Guernesiaise in Guernsey in 1882 (known initially as the Guernsey Natural Science Society). These two bodies are still thriving today and their publications are full of local reference work that is a fitting testament to the amount of interest that existed, not just in archaeology, but also in the natural sciences and local history.

After the inauguration of La Société Jersiaise by 'une dizaine de Messieurs qui s'intéressent à l'étude de l'Histoire, de la langue, et des Antiquités de l'Île' an archaeological sub-committee was formed (Green 1973,18) led by E.K. Cable, a retired civil engineer. Five excavations were undertaken, the first of which in 1874 was at Les Cinq Pierres, St Brelades, which was under threat from quarrying and in fact no longer exists today. The detailed report and plan is now the only record of this site, highlighting the importance of these early records for present day study. The next was near Beauport, La Moye, which was a site, also in a ruinous condition, but for which the excavators left careful notes including the immortal phrase 'trowel now substituted for the shovel' (Cable 1877). This work was followed by an excavation at La Hougue de Vinde and a re-examination of Le Ville-ès-Nouaux which, along with Le Mont Ubé, Faldouet and Le Couperon, had been discovered previously. In 1878 a small museum opened for members in which some of the finds from the excavations were displayed and in 1893 the present building in Pier Road, St Helier, was gifted to the society.

A second phase of work in the early 1900s began with an excavation at Le Mont Grantez undertaken by Edmund T. Nicolle and Joseph Sinel. Sinel had been manager of the furniture department at Voisins, a local department store, but later became self-employed so he was able to pursue his interests in natural history and archaeology. In 1907 he became curator of the Société Jersiaise Museum. Sinel was a very important figure in Jersey archaeology because of his great contribution to the study of early man. He published nationally on natural history, and he wrote and published a geological account of the island in 1912. He also wrote a book on the archaeology of the islands which, for the first time, created an in-depth portrayal of the importance of sea level changes in the area (Sinel 1912). His map of the river system below the present waters around the islands is still the most useful there is. But he also contributed much to the study of early man with excavations and discoveries at La Cotte de St Brelade.

Edmund T. Nicolle was a barrister who became the Honorary Secretary of La Société Jersiaise in 1901 and drew Sinel and others into the Archaeology section. Further excavations were undertaken. In 1922 the site of the Ossuary was excavated by Captain Darrell Hill and Major Norman V.L. Rybot. Rybot had spent his leave on Jersey until he was invalided out of the army after the First World War; he used his military training to become a skilled archaeologist and fine draughtsman. The Ossuary excavation was followed in 1923 by the excavation at Le Sergenté jointly by H.J. Baal, Capt. Hill, Major Rybot and E.T. Nicolle.

In 1919, another important event had taken place. La Société Jersiaise bought the site of La Hougue Bie in the east of Jersey, which was a huge circular mound on which a medieval chapel had been built. Shortly after this the first investigation of the mound, which it had long been suspected contained a Neolithic tomb, began (see Chapter 4).

THE TWENTIETH CENTURY

The twentieth century was a period of major figures and major discoveries all playing a part in increasing knowledge about the islands' past.

In Guernsey a summary of the 'Archaeological remains in Guernsey' was produced early in the century (Derrick 1907). Then Spencer Carey Curtis, a London-trained architect, became president of La Société Guernesiaise from 1919-1920. When attention was drawn to a site at L'Islet in the north of the island, 'with very large stones appearing', he offered to excavate it for the Society with the help of a 'volunteer working party of members' and Lieutenant Colonel Thomas William Mansell de Guérin. The excavation revealed the site to be a megalithic cist-in-circles complex. A delightful contemporary photograph (Carey Curtis 1912) records a visit to the site by members of La Société Guernesiaise (8), later satirised in G.B. Edward's novel, *The Book of Ebenezer Le Page* (Edwards 1981). The site was consequently left half-exposed and protected by a fence, forming an early example of monument preservation in Guernsey. Later, in 1920, de Guérin bemoaned the fact that the States of Guernsey were allowing the monument to be encroached on by houses and greenhouses. Under public pressure the States did actually buy up some land to ensure that there

8 La Société Guernesiaise visit the excavations at L'Islet in 1912. *Photograph: Guernsey Museums and Galleries*

would always be a right of way up to the monument. It is interesting to note that the site is now almost enclosed by a post-war, States of Guernsey, housing development.

Primarily an historian, de Guérin specialised in the medieval period, but he also took an interest in the earlier phases of the island's development, contributing some 10 articles on archaeological subjects to the Transactions of La Société Guernesiaise from 1910-1927. He produced a catalogue of the material in the Lukis Museum in 1912, following on from the work of the Rev. G.E. Lee, and he also compiled a useful list of dolmens, cists and menhirs on Guernsey from records and place names recorded in the local land deeds, Extentes and Livres de Perchage (de Guérin 1921). The following year de Guérin and A. Collenette carried out a small excavation at Le Déhus following in Lukis' footsteps, and first noticed some carvings on one of the capstones. It was later, in 1918, however, when a fuller examination of the capstone was made with the use of artificial light, that the full extent of the carving was realised. This still remains one of the very few pieces of megalithic art in the island. No original archive from these early excavations survives, but they are reported on in the proceedings of La Société Guernesiaise.

A MAJOR DISCOVERY IN JERSEY: LA COTTE DE ST BRELADE

In Jersey, after the discovery by Dancaster and Saunders of the cave at La Cotte de St Brelade, systematic work began in 1905 and the history of work at this important site warrants a brief summary. Due to the nature of the cave (see Chapter 3) the work was threatened throughout by the possibility of falls from the roof and so in 1910 La Société Jersiaise employed quarrymen to clear the overburden and make the excavation safe. No plans of this early work were published but descriptions of the deposits were included in a report by Nicolle and Sinel (1911, 17). Also in 1910 the important discovery of nine human teeth was made, followed two years later by four more, arguably the most important find from the site, placing it with the comparatively few in the British Isles and adjacent French mainland from which human remains are known. These were identified as from a Neanderthal hominid by Sir Arthur Keith of the British Museum. (Keith & Knowles 1912).

Only 11 square feet of deposit to a depth of 3–4ft was excavated at this time, but the finds included bones, horns and teeth of rhinoceros, reindeer horse and bovidae, but by 1911 the layers of overlying ice age head deposit were considered a problem and stopped the work (Callow & Cornford 1986, 16). In 1913, the British Association for the Advancement of Science, who had been approached by Jerseyman, R.R. Marett, formed a committee to sponsor further work, the result of which was that by the end of 1915 some 1200 square feet had been excavated and the number of flints found had risen to over 5000 (9).

9 Hand axe from La Cotte de Saint Brelade. *Photograph: Guernsey Museums and Galleries. Courtesy of the Jersey Heritage Trust/Société Jersiaise Collections*

Work continued throughout the war years including a session with boys from Victoria College under the supervision of their master A.J. Robinson, who showed Arthur Mourant the site in 1921. Mourant went on to contribute to the archaeology and geology of the islands. All the material from La Cotte up to this point was thought to have come from one level and had been merged together, thus making it impossible to distinguish different deposits. This inevitably caused the loss of valuable information.

Work resumed on the site later in 1936 after an inspection. This coincided with the completion of work at the site of Le Pinacle by the team of Burdo, Lomax and Godfray. Father Christian Burdo was a Jesuit priest who returned to Jersey in 1924 after teaching in France and the Middle East. He was initially interested in geology but was then drawn to archaeology and carried out excavations at the important site at Le Pinacle (see Chapters 3 and 6) and then was involved with La Cotte de St Brelade for many years. Some clearance to obtain new deposits then took place and an attempt to carefully record the stratigraphy as accurately as possible was made. In 1938 the site was visited by Professor F.E. Zeuner, the renowned Pleistocene geologist, and he also visited La Cotte à La Chèvre and Belcroute cave. Zeuner recognised two peat deposits at La Cotte de St Brelade and advised Burdo to look below them. The Second World War intervened but when Burdo resumed in 1953 he dug through the loess into a bank of solid ash.

He recovered a considerable amount of material in situ which he described in a short monograph (Burdo 1960). The work at the site comes up to date with the series of excavations from 1961-1978 by Professor Charles McBurney from Cambridge University which will be discussed in Chapter 3.

T.D. KENDRICK AND THE BRITISH MUSEUM

In 1928 a milestone in Channel Islands archaeology was reached. T.D. Kendrick, from the Department of British and Medieval Antiquities at the British Museum, was invited by Dr R.R. Marett, who was by then Reader in Social Anthropology at Oxford and from Jersey, to write a book on the archaeology of the Channel Islands.

Kendrick's work was intended to be published in two volumes as *The Archaeology of the Channel Islands*, Volume One of which was to be on the Bailiwick of Guernsey (1928), and Volume Two on The Bailiwick of Jersey. However, by the time of the later volume he had passed his work on Jersey to Jacquetta Hawkes who published it in 1937. In the preface to the Guernsey volume, Kendrick belittles his work as merely 'a thin and reluctant trickle of information'. However, these volumes are still regarded as standard works and Kendrick's masterly overview has largely remained unsurpassed. In the Guernsey volume Kendrick draws heavily on the Lukis archive resulting in a scholarly yet readable tome. Speaking as a Jerseyman, Marett had been magnanimous in his praise of Lukis particularly as he felt that there was no one equivalent in Jersey (1941, 180):

> But during the nineteenth century the sister-island of Guernsey had produced in the Lukis family a band of archaeologists quite on a level with the best of British authorities at that time concerned with the far past.

Further research into the original Lukis material (Sebire 2003), however, has highlighted some inaccuracies due to confusion of place names. Kendrick had visited Guernsey in 1923 and excavated a small cave at the bottom of La Grande Hougue called L'Ancresse, situated in the north of the island. This visit presumably coincided with an opportunity for him to carry out research on the antiquities of both islands for his forthcoming work.

Two years after the publication of Kendrick's work, in 1930, a major excavation took place at Le Déhus dolmen, sponsored by Sir Robert Mond and supervised by V. Collum for the States of Guernsey, the results of which are published in a special section of the Transactions of La Société Guernesiaise (1932). Some repair work was carried out at this time on the interior of the tomb and on the outside encircling wall. Collum had some very unusual ideas following the excavation, not least that she considered it had been built in the Roman period. These findings were reported and commented on in 1935 by Carey Curtis in an extended annual report.

In Jersey important work had been carried out at La Hougue Bie and in 1924 Major A.D.B. Godfray was the first person to enter the tomb since it was sealed many thousand of years previously (see Chapter 4). Other important early work included excavations and observations by Major Rybot on menhirs at Quennevais and other sites. In 1930 a series of excavations began at the important multi-period (Neolithic, Bronze Age and Roman) settlement site of Le Pinacle by Godfray, Lomax and Burdo, which ran for six years. Rybot then turned his attentions to Mont Orgueil castle in 1930 and later in 1940 during the time of German occupation.

THE EFFECTS OF WORLD WAR II

The years spanning the duration of the Second World War brought most local research to a halt as the islands were occupied by German forces for five years from 1940-1945. Once the occupying forces were established, however, La Société Guernesiaise was given permission to hold meetings (Symons 1946), and La Société Jersiaise continued to meet.

THE POST-WAR YEARS

The Prehistoric Society visited the islands in 1957. The party included Dr Glyn Daniel, from England, Dr P.R. Giot, (who became the doyen of Breton archaeology) from France, accompanied by Dr A.E. Mourant from Jersey, all of whom had a particular interest in megaliths and knew of the work of the Lukis family in the islands. Dr Daniel apparently asked for a reappraisal of the Déhus site, but unfortunately this has not been attempted to date. Some 26 years later, in 1983, the islands again played host to the Society for its annual Spring Conference.

After the golden years of these major discoveries, the 1950s and early 1960s saw some spasmodic work being done, including an examination of a megalith uncovered in Jersey at the site of the new gas works but the next major phase of work in both islands was a response to the loss of archaeology due to increased development in the early 1970s. This phenomenon, known as 'rescue archaeology', was increasing throughout the British Isles as a building boom caused massive amounts of earth moving on development sites up and down the country and, in a way, reflected the major discoveries that were made in the nineteenth century during the great periods of the development of roads, railways and canals.

EXCAVATIONS BY VISITING DIRECTORS

Visiting archaeologists who came to carry out work in the islands led to many locals taking up the banner of 'rescue archaeology'. Ken Barton, then Director of Hampshire County Museum Service, carried out excavations at Mont Orgueil on Jersey in 1972. Barton was then invited by the States of Guernsey Ancient Monuments Committee, through the museum curator, the late Mrs Rona Cole, to excavate at Château des Marais (or Ivy Castle) on Guernsey. This he did for three seasons. Barton was particularly interested in medieval ceramics and had worked extensively in England, and had studied French ceramics, particularly from the Saintonge area.

In 1982 Barton began a series of excavations at Vale Castle (1984a) and in 1982 he began a series of excavations at Castle Cornet, which were to run for almost 10 years (Barton 2003). Other visiting directors included Philip Holdsworth who, with Margaret Finlaison, carried out excavations at the Île Agois, Jersey in 1979 (see Chapter 7).

TRAINING EXCAVATIONS

Training excavations were then set up for interested locals. David Johnston from the University of Southampton led an excavation at the Beauport dolmen site in Jersey in 1972 (Johnston 1972) whereas in Guernsey a similar exercise was carried out at Château des Marais (Barton 1980a); as a result La Société Guernesiaise formed an archaeological excavation group under the leadership of Bob Burns. Burns (*10*) became, from that time on until his retirement in July 1995, the driving force behind archaeology in Guernsey.

In Jersey this role was taken up by Margaret Finlaison (*11*), who carried out many rescue excavations around the St Helier area with dedication and enthusiasm and took a very active role in trying to set up a system for protecting Jersey's Heritage.

Work continued apace in both islands from the 1970s when the period of excavations increased as more and more rescue sites needed work. Since then major work on all the archaeological periods has taken place and will be described in the following chapters. In Alderney a society was not formed until 1965 and the driving force behind it was Peter Arnold, who wanted to form a society which had as its major objective 'the safeguarding of the island's natural beauty and unique way of life'. The Society resolved to set up a museum and Peter Arnold was one of its first curators. The Society grew in strength throughout the 1970s and 1980s with varied activities including lectures and fieldwork and provided facilities for visiting researchers. The Alderney Society today is thriving and its excellent museum was awarded the Gulbenkian prize for a small independent museum in 2003.

10 Bob Burns excavating in Guernsey in the 1970s. *Photograph: Guernsey Museums and Galleries*

11 Margaret Finlaison excavating in St Helier in 1979. *Photograph: Margaret Finlaison*

La Société Serquiaise was formed in Sark in 1975 for the same reason and was run for many years by botanist Marcia Marsden, although a small archaeology section was active at various times recording archaeological finds from the island. A new headquarters was established in 2005 which has brought new focus to the activities of the society.

The tradition of research that has built up over the last 150 years is still very much to the fore today. Guernsey has an Archaeology Officer in the Museum Service who curates the collections but also carries out rescue fieldwork. In Jersey there is a Curator of Archaeology who takes care of the collections but there is no one actively carrying out fieldwork on a regular basis at present although La Société Jersiaise often have small research excavations. There is no tradition of developer-funded archaeology in the islands due to the islands' planning legislation, although at the time of writing both Jersey and Guernsey have new legislation on the statute books which will hopefully address this problem in the near future. However, research and rescue excavations, the latter particularly in Guernsey, have continued to add new material to the archaeological record up to the present day.

3

FORAGERS AND FARMERS: THE EARLIEST INHABITANTS OF THE CHANNEL ISLANDS

One day we took a boat
And the reeds welcomed us.
Geese were hoarse but we ducked

And where the darkness started
We decided to cease
All quarrels with the sky

And sleep. Mammoths roamed
in our dream, contented
with their lot. When we awoke

what absence of tusks crowded around us!

Adam Thorpe, 'From the Neanderthal' (1999)

THE FORAGERS OF THE LOWER AND MIDDLE PALAEOLITHIC

The islands in the Palaeolithic period, as we have seen in Chapter 1, were on the edge of the French mainland with the sea level changing at different periods between the glaciations. A drop of 20m was all that was required to make Jersey accessible on foot from the mainland of France. Most likely because of this, the oldest human artefacts so far recovered from the Channel Islands are several unstratified hand axes from Jersey. Two from Havre des Pas (St Helier) were found on the modern beach and are very worn and patinated (Hawkes 1937, 35). They are likely to have been washed out from the 25m raised beach and belong to the latest period of the Lower Palaeolithic as they are Acheulian in character. The Acheulian industry is characterised by hand axes and scrapers and evidence from other sites in Europe has shown that large mammals such as mammoth and rhinoceros were hunted and that the people had learnt the use of fire (Bordes 1968).

Two other axes were also found on beaches on Jersey, one from La Crête Point (St Martin) and one from below Belcroute cliff. At both of these places the 8m raised beach is overlain by head material (Hawkes 1937). Two hand axes were also found at Le Pulec, (*colour plate 3*), one in 1948 by Rybot (1949) which had a light grey patina on grey flint and one by Finlaison (1976) which was less diagnostic but showed ancient rolling. These may date to *c*.120,000bp.

A geological survey of the Channel Islands was carried out by David Keen in the 1970s, who noted that most of the Palaeolithic finds were from the cave sites and were rare elsewhere (1978). He recorded a Palaeolithic flake 450m from Noirmont point in the south-west of Jersey. It was in situ some 2.2m above the base of head material north of the Point. The flake is pale grey flint with a large area of cortex remaining, and because of its location Keen considered that it dated from the early part of the Devensian (late) glacial stage (Keen 1978a). It is possible that the artefact was made by someone who had inhabited the cave at La Cotte de St Brelade (see below) during the similar phase. In 1980 an Acheulian-type axe was found during bait-digging on the beach at Le Dicq, Havre de Pas, Jersey, which still had clay sticking to it (Finlaison 1980). It is possible that it had been exposed by exceptional tides which swept the overlying sand from above the deposit it was in.

In Alderney a recent survey of over 10,000 flint and stone artefacts identified material from the Palaeolithic period, particularly from a storm beach at Longis on what is now the south-east coast (Jenkinson et al. 1991). The area that is now Alderney was even closer to northern France than Jersey and is not far from a source of flint. There is an outcrop of Cretaceous deposits some 10km north of Jersey and also between Guernsey and Alderney. A sea level fall of 25m would be needed for access to this material or up to 50m for access to the deposits in the English Channel which would only have been achieved when the ice was at its maximum.

Jenkinson et al. (1991) identified three cores, two scrapers and three unretouched flakes which they considered were from the Middle Palaeolithic. All were heavily patinated and the flakes showed use of the Levallois technique. The area that became Alderney may have been part of a much larger hunting area.

The most spectacular Palaeolithic finds in the Channel Islands, however, come from two cave sites in Jersey which have most recently been studied by the late Professor Charles McBurney and Dr Paul Callow both of Cambridge University.

LA COTTE À LA CHÈVRE, JERSEY

The first of these cave sites, now known as La Cotte à La Chèvre, was discovered on Jersey's north-west coast by Dancaster and Sinel in 1861 (see Chapter 2). Some 20 years later the two excavated in the cave and among the finds was the only known hand axe from the site, which was for some time in the Lukis collection in Guernsey but has now been returned to Jersey. The site was examined again in 1911 by Marett (*12*) (1912), and Nicolle and Sinel (Sinel 1911). This work showed that although the cave is now 18m above sea level it was formed as a sea-cave (Callow & Cornford 1986). It is now about 9m long and only about 3m wide. Professor Charles McBurney examined the cave in the 1960s and found that most of the surviving deposits had been disturbed. However he managed to retrieve a small series of artefacts from deposits he felt were in situ. A layer of sand and pebbles and large sea-worn boulders on the cave floor are probably contemporary with its formation. These are overlain with a white sandy loam layer which, in turn, is overlain by loess. Based on a comparison with deposits and geology at La Cotte de St Brelade the cave is likely to be a quarter of a million years old. The 'white loam' contained occupation debris from at least two hearths. Sixty-six flint tools were identified from McBurney's work, dominated by denticulates and notches. The Levallois technique of tool manufacture was used to remove flakes of a predetermined size and shape (Timms 1980). Two Levallois tortoise cores were also found in the assemblage and Levallois flakes in the loess layer, with one fine rejuvenation flake similar to one from La Cotte de St Brelade (see below). Dr Paul Callow considered that because of the height of the cave and the material recovered, that it must pre-date La Cotte de St Brelade and that the first major occupation corresponds to the base of the sequence at La

12 A diagram showing deposits at La Cotte à la Chèvre on the north-east coast of Jersey. *By kind permission of the Society of Antiquaries of London*

Cotte de St Brelade (Callow 1983). Later visits were made to the site by users of different flint technologies such as the Levallois debitage and perhaps the hand axe. The northerly aspect of the cave would have favoured occupation during warm periods.

LA COTTE DE ST BRELADE, JERSEY

The second cave site is located on Jersey's south-west coast and is really quite exceptional as it is one of the most important Palaeolithic sites in Europe (*colour plate 4*). This is not just for the deposits that were found within the cave but also for the contribution that the research on the cave has made to both Pleistocene and Palaeolithic studies, as the occupation in the cave spans a quarter of a million years. The site is important for several reasons, partly linked to its location. As Jersey is on the continental shelf, a drop in sea level of just 20m made the area accessible from the French mainland. Its present coastal location gives us an indication of how sensitive the area would have been to sea level changes. Accessibility to the mainland had implications for the possibility of human occupation as access to raw materials for tools became possible. The cave has not only produced archaeologically rich deposits but has given a unique opportunity to study certain aspects of the relationship between early man and a changing environment (Callow 1983).

The fissures in the rock where the cave is situated are up to 50m deep which has allowed deposits of great depth to build up over a very long period of time. The geographical position of the site is also crucial. It is on a promontory, making it an ideal place to trap animals feeding on the plateau above and indeed was exploited by hunters before the Ipswichian interglacial (120,000bp). The history of the discovery of the cave in 1881 is described in Chapter 2 up to the time of the most recent excavations. These were undertaken, from 1961 onwards, by Professor Charles McBurney of Cambridge University, who used La Cotte de St Brelade as a teaching excavation for many years.

MCBURNEY EXCAVATIONS 1961–1978

The Cambridge excavation phase, from 1961–78, produced 130,000 stone artefacts which rose to over 200,000 when earlier finds were included. In 1961-2 a deep sounding was excavated in order to get a satisfactory stratification and to aid this process latex 'peels' of the sections were made. In 1966 bone layers were discovered which appeared to be deposits of deliberate accumulation of woolly mammoth and rhinoceros. These had not been known before in deposits of this kind. This gave La Cotte a new importance and the British Museum Natural History Department conservation staff helped devise techniques for the delicate task of excavating the bones from the loess.

After McBurney's untimely death in 1979 the responsibility for the excavation and the report fell to his research student Dr Paul Callow (Callow & Cornford 1986) who, in 1981, took further soil samples from the cleaned sections at the site to check various deposits and their stratigraphy. This was followed in 1982 by the re-opening of the deep sounding. The bottom of the sequence has not yet been reached, leaving some deposits intact.

THE LA COTTE DE ST BRELADE SEQUENCE

The location of the site on the south-west tip of Jersey is in an area of granite characterised by extensive cooling fractures which have been eroded by the sea into deep fissures. At La Cotte de St Brelade cave the fissure is T-shaped. The sea enters the west ravine today which has been completely scoured clean by sea action. Head deposits which date to the last glaciation are still just visible where the stem of the 'T' joins the arms. This head deposit once filled the cave to a height of some 40m. The main interest however is in the north ravine where most of the archaeological discoveries were made. After the final season in 1978 a decision was taken by La Société Jersiaise to wall up the exposed sections to protect them for future generations but some deposits are still visible on the east side of the cave (Callow 1983).

The stratigraphy here is very complex so McBurney grouped the phases and linked them to the underlying geology and corresponding environmental stage. Dates were correlated by reference to isotopic stages, calibrated from deep sea cores. The most important environmental stages are listed below (after Callow 1986):

Stage 0: the formation of the ravine itself when beach pebbles and sea rounded boulders would have been deposited at the base of the cave (this stage was not proven by excavation).

Stage I: the deposition of loess followed by the formation of ranker soils (humus accumulation) during a cold period. In a later warmer period the loess was washed into a pond. This material was layer H in the excavation which contained the earliest finds.

Stage II: the earliest interglacial in which there were temperate conditions has been dated by thermoluminesence on burnt flint to approximately 238,000bp (OX-TL 222) and is associated with a soil formation period (pedogenesis) in Layer E. The earliest archaeological deposit is part of layer H in the stratigraphic sequence (loess) but layers F-C are also in this loess deposit. These layers were deposited during a glacial period meaning that sea levels were much lower so the Jersey area was accessible on foot from what is now the French mainland. The archaeological layers were a dark grey brown in colour and contained ashy deposits. They are very rich in artefacts.

Stage III: formed during a very cold period and has a predominately loessic matrix. There are rich occupation layers including the lower bone heap.

Stage IV: is marked by encroachment of the sea which caused partial destruction of the cave but also a laying down of deposits at about 9m above sea level. The equivalent raised beach at Belle Hougue on Jersey's north coast is dated to around 121,000bp.

Stage V: The deposits here were mostly removed during the early excavations and so are poorly understood, but the greater part of the deposits were laid down under extremely cold conditions

Stage VI: This represents the Flandrian or most recent interglacial and was essentially a temperate (warm) phase. This is the recent soil layer which has been dug away.

LIFE IN THE CAVE AT LA COTTE DE SAINT BRELADE

In simple terms there were two main periods of activity in the cave, one in the Lower Palaeolithic and later in the Middle Palaeolithic, separated by long periods of time. The site was first occupied during cold periods when large tracts of the present sea bed would have been dry, giving access to flint deposits that are now submerged. The cave would have given shelter from the bitterly cold climate and the cliff above would have provided a vantage point from which to follow animal herds roaming the low-lying land below. The stone and flint tools from the cave suggest that it was used intermittently from around 250,000 years ago to about 150,000 years ago by bands of hunters, possibly when there was some remission from the rigours of the freezing climate. These hunters were the early hominids known as Homo Erectus, who evolved from their predecessors Homo Habilis, with larger brains and the capability to manufacture the classic Acheulian axe type (Renfrew & Bahn 1996). There are no Homo Erectus human remains from this phase at La Cotte but two layers contained bone heaps with remarkable preservation, one of which comprised nine mammoths and one rhinoceros. The bones had been arranged in such a way as to suggest that this may have been a cache of meat which the hunters might return to (13). The second bone heap comprised at least eight mammoths and three rhinoceroses. One suggestion is that these represent single hunting exercises and that the animals would have been herded to the edge of the cliff and forced off, giving the hunters a substantial catch in one go.

The second phase of occupation of the cave took place in the Middle Palaeolithic. This was after the sea had risen, invading the cave and eroding some of the lower deposits. The conditions would have been dry but very cold with fauna, including woolly mammoth, woolly rhinoceros and reindeer. It was during this phase that the humans whose teeth were recovered had occupied the cave. When the teeth that had been discovered in 1910 were re-examined (see Chapter 2) it was found that ten were genuine and three others were casts: there is no record of what happened to the originals. C.Stringer and A. Currant who examined the teeth agreed with the original report that they showed Neanderthal characteristics and 'fell within the expected ranges of variation for

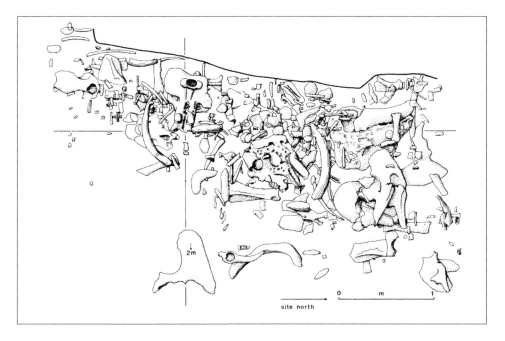

13 Bone deposits at La Cotte de Saint Brelade. *After Callow & Cornford, 1986*

European Upper Pleistocene Neanderthal samples' (Stringer & Currant 1986). Of the other skeletal material recovered in 1912 they considered that the small piece of child's skull that was recovered also had neanderthaloid features as there was evidence of protruding 'occiput' or back of the head (ibid. 156). One other interesting factor was that flint analysis demonstrated the occurrence of left-handedness in the La Cotte population which bears on the question of the development of speech. Homo Sapiens Neanderthalensis lived in Europe from *c.*130,000 to 30,000 years ago and their role in the evolutionary process is still poorly understood (Renfrew & Bahn 1996, 156). Some researchers think they may have developed into our own subspecies, Homo Sapiens Sapiens, and others consider that they were the end of an evolutionary line. Whatever the case, can we imagine life in the cave all those millennia ago and how the people kept themselves alive in such conditions?

One of the most interesting aspects of the discoveries at La Cotte à La Chèvre and La Cotte de Saint Brelade is to consider the 'catchment' areas of the caves and what are called 'site exploitation territories'. The concept of the catchment area (SC) was developed in the 1960s (Callow 1986a) and concerns the terrain covered by occasional forays out from the cave to look for raw materials for tools. The site exploitation territory (SET) is the area constantly used from a single site for hunting. The SET is based on an estimation of how far people would travel for their regular needs. For the sites on Jersey there are many elements that have to be taken into consideration, such as the position of the caves in relation to the wider landscape and its limitations and also the micro-environments of the caves which may not be apparent to us today. For example, we know that the sea has destroyed everything outside the caves at La Cotte de Saint Brelade and so we need to try to imagine a wider area than the present headland as part of the site. However it is possible to estimate with some confidence that a two hour travelling time from both the cave sites is reasonable. For La Cotte de Saint Brelade this would cover a wide area giving vantage points for hunting. For La Cotte à La Chèvre the area would have been much more restricted particularly in periods of high sea level when fresh water was not as readily available. This may have been a factor in the length of time that the cave was occupied.

LA COTTE DE SAINT BRELADE TODAY

In his summing up of the work by Cambridge University Dr Callow points out that (1986a, 389):

> La Cotte is of much greater interest than the archaeological finds alone would suggest.
> Certainly the richness of its industries and faunal remains place it high in the ranking of
> Middle and early Upper Palaeolithic sites.

He goes on to list his conclusions and the significance of the site including: the contribution to study of Pleistocene deposits and sea level changes; evidence for early hominids and their exploitation of the area; evidence for single hunting episodes; a range of lithic industries from the Acheulian to the Mousterian with Levallois technique employed, with evidence of reuse of tools reflecting the paucity of raw material (*14*). As with many sites the potential for further research on the finds is vast and the physical remains within the cave, which is not suitable for public access, continue to be a challenge for La Société Jersiaise in whose care it remains.

THE UPPER PALAEOLITHIC PERIOD

Evidence of the Lower and Middle Palaeolithic still remains elusive in Guernsey although the Jersey evidence from the cave sites detailed above is largely applicable to the whole Channel Islands region (Callow & Cornford 1986). The Upper Palaeolithic period brings us closer to the time when the islands were formed after the last ice age.

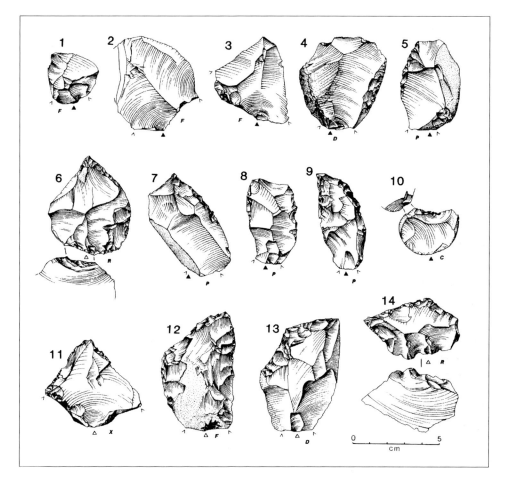

14 Levallois technique flint implements from La Cotte de Saint Brelade. *After Callow & Cornford, 1986*

CREVICHON LANDING, GUERNSEY

Although there is some evidence of Upper Palaeolithic material from the cave at La Cotte de Saint Brelade, this period in general has not been well documented in the Channel Islands. However, material recently presented for identification to Guernsey Museum has helped to illuminate this time in the archaeological record. In 2000, a local postman contacted Guernsey Museum, as he had collected some very unusual flints which he was sure would be of interest. In his spare time he dived and fished from his own boat around Guernsey and the neighbouring, smaller islands of Herm, Sark and Jethou. For many years a favourite landing spot of the Corbet family had been an area between the islands of Jethou and Crevichon which lie due east of St Peter Port on Guernsey itself. Most of this area is only accessible on very low spring tides and is otherwise submerged. Several finds of 'eoliths' (very ancient stone tools) are recorded in the antiquarian records of Guernsey Museum but no convincing evidence from the Upper Palaeolithic period had been identified. Corbet's material was identified as 'Palaeolithique finale' by visiting French colleagues (Ghesquière pers. comm.) in June 2002, after which arrangements were made for a visit to the site. It soon became clear that flint was eroding from a buried land surface from before the islands were separated from France and dated to around 12,000 bp. This surface survived as a sand bar forming the land bridge between the islets of Crevichon and Jethou. Flint was collected from an area of about 200m x 50m although it centred around a low-lying pond-like depression in the middle of the area between the two islets c. 60m x 40m. The flint has recently been examined by Dr Chantal Conneller who reported that the small collection of 220 worked flints was Upper Palaeolithic in character. The condition of the material varied as some were sea worn, although one had some chalky cortex remaining, suggesting it was obtained from an outcrop of chalk, the nearest of which is 11km to the north or 17km to the south-west. A small axe rough-out was made from darker flint material. The industry was based on blade technology with the largest 109mm long. A backed bladelet is unfinished but may belong to the late Magdelenian series; burins and scrapers are also present. Further work at this site is ongoing and may yet produce more diagnostic material (*colour plate 5*).

Several possible Upper Palaeolithic waste products from blade manufacture were also present in the flint assemblage in later deposits from the Royal Hotel site on the east coast of Guernsey (Ghesquière pers. comm.) (see below). As with the earlier material from Alderney and Jersey, these finds represent occupation on the edge of the land mass of the continent of France while the islands were still part of the mainland and existed as small, flat-topped plateaux rising above flat plains crossed by shallow, broad river valleys running in a generally west to north-westerly direction.

THE MESOLITHIC PERIOD: THE FIRST ISLANDERS

So when did the islands finally become cut off by the sea? Did people actually witness the inundations and pass the stories down to their children and grandchildren? Was the event within living memory of the generations of people who hunted and fished on the edge of the land? Was it slowly progressive, as we are witnessing now in parts of eastern England, or was it speedy flooding? These are all questions which largely remain unanswered but which are being addressed by work on a Guernsey site, on Lihou Island (see below). As mentioned above, recent work on sea level changes suggests that Guernsey and Alderney were first isolated from the French mainland sometime between 10,000-8000 years ago and Jersey some time later. At this time a period of adaption by the hunter-gatherers would have been necessary and bands of people may have retreated from the coastal edge of the islands to areas still accessible to the hinterland of the French mainland. If, as the evidence suggests, the straits between the islands were formed in the Mesolithic period, the people living on the areas of land that became the islands would have been surrounded by a deep and at times hostile sea. These bands of people must have adapted to the new smaller land masses by exploiting the rich marine resources that were now available to them both through coastal shore-gathering and deep-sea fishing (Bender 1986). It appears that by the seventh millennium BC the first people on the islands had established themselves on sites near the present coast. Until current work that is ongoing on Guernsey started, the most recent summary of Mesolithic material on the islands was by Dr Mark Patton, who examined the unstratified collections in the museums of Guernsey, Jersey and Alderney (*15*) (Patton 1994). He also presented the evidence from systematic work at Le Canal du Squez on the north-west of Jersey. Here material had been collected by local amateur archaeologist Brian Phillipps over many years and Dr Patton supplemented this with fieldwork in 1989. He concluded that the assemblage collected from Canal du Squez represented a Mesolithic community living on the plateau now called Les Landes, located near a source of fresh water. The flint assemblage consisted of flakes, blades, cores, microburins, scrapers and backed bladelets and could be paralleled with sites on the Cotentin of northern France. Dr Patton also pointed out that as Jersey was still attached to the mainland at this time, the resources available to the community at Le Canal du Squez would have been varied. They would have included resources from the nearby coast, alongside fowl and fish from the estuary of the River Ay just to the north and terrestrial resources such

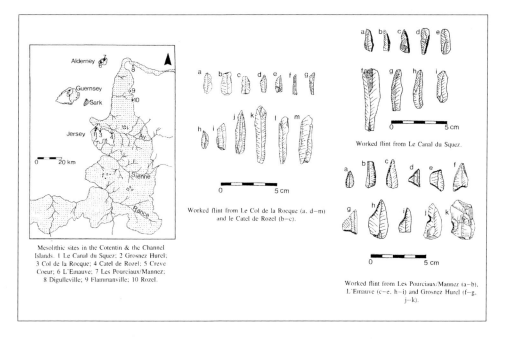

15 Flint microliths from Channel Island sites. *After Patton, 1993*

as deer and wild boar in the forested areas, supplemented by aurochs on grassland areas. These are indicated by palaeoenvironmental evidence from the area (Jones et al. 1990). A fine Mesolithic axe was also found at L'Ouziére in Jersey (*colour plate 6*), perhaps an early indication of woodworking for the construction of shelters or for transportation.

GU 582: A MESOLITHIC COMMUNITY ON LIHOU ISLAND

New information is coming to hand, however, as recent excavations on the north-east coast of Lihou Island, a tidal islet off the west coast of Guernsey, have produced evidence of a stratified middle Mesolithic activity site (Schadla-Hall 2001). The site was mentioned by Kendrick (1928) and Keen (1976) and was very likely first discovered because of modern day coastal erosion. It had been monitored for some years by David Lane and members of the Guernsey Museum Archaeology Group who had spotted a line of flints eroding out of the present bank and had retrieved both flint cores and finished tools. The site was designated GU 582 from the Guernsey Museum Sites and Monuments Record number and a small scale excavation planned to establish the stratigraphy, to assess the extent of the deposit and to recover a sample of material to understand the nature of the Mesolithic period in Guernsey and by comparison, the other islands. This was directed by Tim Schadla-Hall of the Institute of Archaeology, London.

An area of some 30m was examined in section and over several seasons 8m² were excavated on the main area of activity and several 1m² test pits were dug to try to establish the extent of the site. It soon became clear that the flints were concentrated in a clearly defined layer of windblown sand associated with pebbles and stone which had been brought to the site (*16*). In the Mesolithic period the site would have been some way from the shoreline, indicating that the beach pebbles used as raw material were being transported some distance to be worked. Full analysis of the material is ongoing but suggests a full range of flint working is present from the preparation of cores to tools. This is known by archaeologists as the chaîne d'operation. Microliths are the most common tool type, mainly consisting of obliquely blunted points and basally-modified forms. Other tools are rarer, but included scrapers, burins, borers and some heavy-duty retouched pieces (information C. Conneller). The density of material is surprising, over 4,000 finds in the small area that was excavated. Several hammer stones and bevel-ended tools were also recovered. Soil analysis showed that there has been very little disturbance on the site which indicates that the material is almost definitely in situ and therefore represents a 'real' distribution. Wood, charcoal and a few hundred fragments of hazelnuts from a hearth area were recovered after flotation of the material (Stevens 2002). This is when a soil deposit is mixed with water and the lighter organic material floats to the surface and is recovered

16 The Mesolithic site GU582 on Lihou Island, Guernsey, under excavation and showing flints eroding out of the section. *Photograph: Tim Schadla-Hall*

for analysis. Hazelnuts (*Corylus avellana*) are a common feature on Mesolithic sites and they must represent food remains. Stevens also makes the point that the presence of the nuts suggests that hazel would have been growing on the island in this early post-glacial landscape and that they must have recolonised rapidly. Jones et al. list hazel along with some oak as being present in the dryer areas of Jersey at this period (1990 Table 7, 116). What is of even greater interest is that the hazelnuts have produced a Carbon 14 date of 7483-7299 BC at 95 per cent probability (OxA-14198). This date is very interesting because on present estimations Guernsey and the islet of Lihou would still have been attached to the mainland of France. The implications of this are still being considered but might help to explain why the flint industry appears similar to the Middle Mesolithic sites of Brittany including 'lamelles Berthaume' (Ghesquière pers. comm).

The results from this site will help to put into context the unstratified collections that exist in the various Channel Island Museums, particularly in Guernsey, from sites at Creve Coeur on the north-east coast and La Corbière on the south coast (Keen 1976). Some Mesolithic material was also found under the first phase of the long mound at Les Fouaillages (Kinnes & Grant 1983). Here the sub-soil consisted of a raised beach of sand and pebbles, on which had accumulated a deep forest soil with tree-holes marking the existence of dense woodland. A few flint tools characteristic of the later Mesolithic period were recovered. The groups of people who made them would have lived on hunting and fishing in the area. The miniature blades have secondary chipping to produce precise geometric shapes, and evidence from elsewhere indicates that such microliths were set in rows or groups in wooden hafts as knives and harpoons (ibid.). The tool kit of the big game hunter was no longer needed. These smaller flint tools were most likely rapidly made and rapidly discarded (Bender 1986).

On the site of the Royal Hotel (Sebire forthcoming) two particularly fine backed blades, and two bone points from the middle Mesolithic period (M. Patton pers. comm.) were found redeposited in Early Neolithic contexts (see below), also suggesting a continual use of the same area. Random collection of material from present day coastal erosion has produced flint assemblages with confirmed Mesolithic tools from several other areas of Guernsey's coastline. All the flint industries are based on local beach pebble and therefore by their very nature restricted in size.

Patton (1993) identifies three sites on Jersey, Le Col de la Rocque, Le Catel de Rozel, and Le Canal de Squez, along with L'Emauve and Les Porciaux on Alderney, all represented by surface collections, which he considers are Late Mesolithic industries. Of particular interest in the Alderney collections Jenkinson et al. (1992) identified a blade assemblage at L'Emauve on Alderney and in fact suggested that there was in situ tool making at the site. There were backed blade artefacts but the assemblage was dominated by microliths, although there was some later material that was typologically Neolithic. At Porciaux/ Mannez on Alderney out of c.800 artefacts 57 were worked and included burins, microgeometric points, scrapers, both thumbnail and end scrapers, points and awls, suggesting a Late Mesolithic/Early Neolithic assemblage.

The accumulated evidence suggests, then, that the islands were able to support a successful Mesolithic population who very likely were exploiting a wide range of wild foods. These might be gained in different ways: gathering seeds, nuts, fruits, roots and shell fish, hunting and trapping small and large game, and fishing (Bender 1975, 4; 1986, 24). The role of the sea and its effects on this population, as the low-lying tracts of land between the islands and the French mainland flooded, is also crucial and is currently being addressed as further research is carried out on sea level changes relevant to the Islands' formation.

We can imagine the lives of the people from their material remains but we have little tangible evidence of their belief systems or social hierarchy from our evidence in the Channel Islands. However, nearby on the coast of Brittany Mesolithic shell middens have been found which are substantial in size and reflected elsewhere in the British Isles (see Chapter 4). In these shell middens burials have been excavated which had been inserted into the middens in a monumental fashion. Although midden material is often seen washing out of the banks of the various islands no evidence of burial at this early phase has been found.

SEA CHANGE: THE FIRST FARMERS OF THE NEOLITHIC

So, do the island dwellers carry on collecting and hunting their food? Yes, to some extent, but they also adapt to farming at the beginning of the Neolithic period. The Neolithic is the general term used by archaeologists to describe the time when people settled into communities and began to provide for themselves through the introduction of farming practices, including the domestication of animals and plants. Domestication of crops first took place on the grassy uplands of the Middle East between 10,000-8000 years ago (Cole 1970; Smith 1998). In the Channel Islands evidence of the first farmers survives from their settlements and spectacular burial monuments (see Chapter 4) although, as outlined in Chapter 1, vast tracts of land which would have been used by the Neolithic farmers have been lost to the sea.

One of the questions that continues to challenge archaeologists is how the skill of domesticating crops and animals, and the seeds and animals themselves, were transported from the Fertile Crescent in the Middle East across Europe, to arrive in Britain sometime in late fifth or early fourth millennium BC. Also a subject of great debate is how the transition from the Mesolithic way of life took place, which, as Caroline Malone puts it, 'has tended to focus on artefact procurement and technologies, subsistence and the environment that people lived in', to the Neolithic period, 'in which the peoples are more tangible through their settlements and burial traditions' (Malone 2001). Evidence now suggests that the techniques and skills associated with agriculture arrived in the Channel Islands by the beginning of the fifth millennium BC, i.e. just after 5000 BC. This may have been through people arriving on boats from the French mainland, perhaps island-hopping across the reefs, or by way of a landbridge to Jersey. Alternatively, people from the islands travelling to the neighbouring 'mainland' would have interacted with people on the coastal zone and in defining the coastal zone it may be sensible to include the islands within it.

Kinnes (1998) suggested an interaction zone between Mesolithic groups along the North Sea and Atlantic coasts and two Neolithic groups on the French mainland. The initial group were those first farmers in the Atlantic coastal areas of France and the second group were the Bandkeramik peoples who settled on the low-lying plains of the Paris Basin and Normandy. This interaction may have been through both deep sea and coastal fishing. Rather than the old idea of the Neolithic 'revolution', Neolithic 'evolution' seems to be more appropriate. The first of these two groups were people with pottery making skills, who used pots known by archaeologists as cardial or impressed wares, decorated with impressions made by a cardium shell, who originated from the coastal zone of the Mediterranean. Further north the Bandkeramik peoples who colonised from the Danube valley across the great European plain were spreading into the Netherlands, Belgium and northern France as far as the Paris Basin. This group used a distinctive type of pottery with linear decoration known as Linearbandkeramik. Communities were introduced to the skills of farming and a whole new cultural tradition that went with a more settled way of life. It was thought that as the farmers progressed across Brittany the indigenous people, with their Mesolithic way of life and microlithic industries, had been pushed to the marginal areas of land by the ocean. But Mesolithic sites are now being found inland in Brittany, suggesting a more direct interaction with the first farmers. Similarly in Normandy and the Cotentin recent work has also provided evidence for a coastal zone and an inland zone in the Mesolithic period (Ghesquière et al. 2000).

Evidence from rescue excavations on sites in Guernsey will help to give a context for the Early Neolithic material from Jersey which, apart from Barton's excavation at Mont Orgueil in the 1970s, was mostly excavated in the early part of the last century. Material from the earliest phase of the long mound at Les Fouaillages on Guernsey is also comparable (see below).

THE FIRST FARMERS IN THE CHANNEL ISLANDS

When the first farmers reached the Channel Islands, the land would not have been as it is today. Due to the sea level rise after the Neolithic period much of the good agricultural land, probably enough to double the size of the island, has been eroded by the Atlantic waves. We know from Kinnes' work in the early 1980s at Les Fouaillages that Guernsey was colonised by sea at the end of the first wave of movement across Western Europe (Kinnes & Grant 1983). More recent excavations on Guernsey have provided evidence of a very early introduction of farming. The seeds of domestic crops and animal breeding stocks must have been imported during difficult sea voyages as the waters and currents around the islands are dangerous. The first farmers arriving in the Channel Islands would have found them densely wooded except along the coast which the Atlantic winds kept treeless but, as Jones et al. reported (1990), alder thrived in the wetlands by the coast with grassland and scrub woodland in the drier areas. New research on Guernsey and Alderney (Campbell 2000) has produced evidence of major burning of vegetation c.5000 BC with the removal of elm and clearance of alder carr probably for pastoral purposes c.4800 BC.

In northern France an early farming settlement has recently been excavated at La Haut Mée (Ille-et-Villaine) not very far inland which revealed a settlement with a large, timber-framed house. Among the finds was pottery similar to that from the Paris Basin from the type-site of Villeneuve-Saint-Germain (Cassen et al. 1998). The site is situated on loessic soil with underlying granite. The fertile soils and geology of the Channel Islands and Guernsey in particular are very alike. At the former Royal Hotel site, in a coastal position on the east of Guernsey, similar material has now been found. Several rescue excavations, some because of urban development and some due to coastal erosion on Guernsey, have added to our knowledge of these early farmers.

EARLY NEOLITHIC SETTLEMENT ON GUERNSEY

Camp Varouf, L'Erée is situated on Guernsey's west coast. In 1998 a small research excavation was carried out directed by Professor Barry Cunliffe of the Institute of Archaeology at Oxford University. This coastal site, on the south-west of Guernsey facing the Atlantic Ocean, was first noted by geologists Dr John Renouf and Dr Jim Urry from Jersey while carrying out a geological survey of the islands (Renouf and Urry 1976). They noted prehistoric pottery and flint eroding from the exposed low cliff. Subsequently the site was monitored for many years by local archaeologists, under advice from Dr Ian Kinnes following the major excavation at Les Fouaillages. This work took place after particularly severe winter storms which caused visible erosion to the cliff and among the finds were pottery, flint, a stone bracelet fragment and part of a polished axe. Two main phases of occupation had been indicated from the surface collections, Early Neolithic and Early Bronze Age, which appeared to have been separated by a long period of inactivity. This was confirmed by excavation. The settlement was towards the upper end of the loessic plain and would have been some 100m from the sea (Cunliffe & de Jersey 2000). It is situated in a natural amphitheatre giving shelter, although directly facing the sea, with fresh spring water nearby. The underlying soils are the fertile loess, which would have been easily worked and the resources of the sea were very close to the site. Charcoal was retrieved from a gully containing pottery which gave a date of 5270-5060 BC (Ox A-8328) at 95 per cent probability, which suggests that the settlement began around 5200 BC with pottery in use at this very early date. The associated pottery was not able to be identified as the fragments were too small. Charcoal sealed in a hearth from a different area gave a second radiocarbon date of 4230-4190 BC (Ox A-7977) (ibid. 2000). Fabric analysis on pottery from the site suggests that there were two compositional types, both from the island; the local L'Erée granite-derived clays and the other from Icart gneiss, which is someway off to the south-east (Bukach 2002). In his discussion Cunliffe suggests that the activity may have been started by a group of indigenous hunter-gatherers who had begun to adopt some of the Neolithic cultural elements from western Normandy. The passage grave of the Creux ès Faïes which is situated on the hill above the site may have been built by their successors who were still active into the Early Bronze Age.

Important Neolithic material has been recovered from the former Royal Hotel site in St Peter Port, Guernsey. This rescue excavation was carried out over a three-year period from 1999-2001 in difficult conditions (Sebire forthcoming). The site was very disturbed but features and artefacts connected with the earliest Neolithic were recovered. Post and stake-holes located suggest that small structures stood on a shelf on the northern side of a wooded valley bottom, spreading out down to the shoreline several hundred metres distant at about 5m lower than the present Guernsey Datum. Boats, whether skin boats or dug out canoes, could easily have beached in the vicinity of the site. About a mile inland in low marshy ground, a portion of a dugout canoe was found at the beginning of the twentieth century. (Anon. 1908). This has not been dated but could be from the Neolithic period.

One of several small scoops excavated at the Royal Hotel appeared to have stake-holes set at an angle perhaps indicating a shelter of some kind. Associated with the earliest Neolithic phase a further grouping of post-holes, severely cut by modern disturbance, suggested that a rectangular house structure *c*.5m x *c*.2.5m is likely to have been present on the site (*17*). An extensive area of burning indicating a hearth from the inside of this structure provided a charcoal sample which has been dated to 5370-5200 BC (OxA-12996) similar to the date from L'Erée and had associated Early Neolithic pottery. The pottery from this earliest phase of the site is similar to that of sites in neighbouring France at Villeneuve-St-Germain and Augy-Ste-Pallaye in the Paris Basin (Constantin 1985; Hamon forthcoming). These wares are the earliest pottery types recovered on the islands and represent influence from the Linearbandkeramik groups mentioned above. The Augy group is now considered to be in the latest phase, dated in France to around 4800 BC. So the radiocarbon date from the hearth material is somewhat early. The earliest types of pottery previously identified have been called the Le Pinacle/Fouaillages group (Kinnes 1982; Constantin 1985; Patton 1995) linked to the northern French Cerny group which is also represented at the Royal Hotel site. Other pots with lugs typical of the Cerny tradition (Constantin ibid.), have also been identified and provide additional links to Castellic wares of Brittany. This simply means that in the earliest Neolithic period when the first farmers were becoming established on the islands they were part of a triangular network linking Normandy and beyond to the western Paris Basin, the Morbihan

17 An artist's reconstruction of a Neolithic farming community based on information from the Royal Hotel site, Guernsey. *Photograph: Guernsey Museums and Galleries*

and Brittany. As more information becomes available these links may become clearer.

Recent work by Bukach (2002) on the mineralogical inclusions in pottery from a number of the sites on Guernsey (although not specifically the Royal Hotel site) suggests that the majority of pottery was made from clays taken from within a 2km radius. Thus it would seem that the pottery was made locally in Guernsey, but based on the latest imported styles from France, perhaps indicating a movement of ideas rather than peoples.

Also on Guernsey, at Clos du Pont, Route de Carteret, Castel, rescue excavations ran from 1998 to 2000, some 850m inland from the west coast. The work revealed the presence of a raised, sandy beach with embedded boulders, at a height ranging between 8-9m above sea level (Walkington et al. 2001). This deposit represents the last interglacial (Ipswichian) beach sand with sub-rounded boulders. Above the ancient beach deposit a loessic layer had formed and was sealed by a more recent soil. People were living on the fertile soils in the Neolithic period and later in the Bronze Age. Although no radiocarbon dates are available for this site at present, arrowheads, both hollow-based and leaf point, were found with other flint tools and pottery. Ceramic sherds similar to the Early Neolithic material found on the Royal Hotel site were recovered, albeit small in quantity and very abraded, indicating a small settlement. Kinnes has suggested that the leaf arrowhead may be linked to the prestige of archery (Kinnes 1988, 2004a). A later Bronze Age phase was also represented (see Chapter 5) but there seems to have been a similar period of inactivity here as at L'Erée between these two phases of occupation.

JERSEY AND THE OTHER ISLANDS

Settlement evidence for the very earliest period of the Neolithic has been elusive in Jersey but recently Dr Mark Patton and Margaret Finlaison published sherds from a pottery vessel similar to those at the Royal Hotel site. It had come from peat deposits south of L'Ouzière slip on the west coast of Jersey in the area of St Ouen's Bay (Patton & Finlaison 2001). The peat deposits had been exposed in 1990, revealing preserved roots and stumps of alder (see above). Flint and stone objects were recovered along with pottery sherds. Among the pots was a distinctive sherd decorated with repoussé boutons. This decoration is typical of the Early Neolithic period and the boutons (or buttons) are made by the potter pushing through the clay with the point of a shell or bone to raise the surface of the pot. Three sherds from another vessel had applied cordons and bosses similar to the Villeneuve St Germain pottery from the Paris Basin. A settlement from the earliest Neolithic may have been in the area but is now lost beneath the waves.

LE PINACLE

The first farmers may have also occupied Le Pinacle on Jersey, but this complex site may have been significant for other reasons. It is visually spectacular, named after a stack of granite which towers over the narrow col of land that connects it with the cliffs of Jersey's north-west coast (Patton 2001). The first major period of activity of this remarkable site has occupation from the Early Neolithic, the final Neolithic and the Bronze Age. Fine pottery with Cerny associations is recorded from excavations in the early 1900s (*colour plate 7*). Claude Constantin, a French archaeologist and pottery researcher grouped this material with the material from Les Fouaillages in Guernsey which he has designated 'Pinacle/Fouaillages' style (Constantin 1985). The Cerny style of pottery is considered by French archaeologists to be from the slightly later middle Neolithic group. Extensive excavations at Le Pinacle in 1930–1935 revealed a complex of features including groups of hearths and other occupation debris. There were also interlinked stone walls in the form of stone and earth banks which span the western end of the col. These walls have been given a range of possible interpretations, as either domestic, industrial or ritual in nature. Large quantities of finds were made, particularly from the Early Neolithic levels and this has allowed a more comprehensive analysis than usual. Although it is difficult to make sense today of the early stratigraphy, the site is a very rare example of a stratified Neolithic and Bronze Age occupation area, (Patton 2001). The faunal remains from the site gave important evidence of the domestication of animals. The pottery is fine and thin walled, very often with burnishing on the surface and rounded bottoms. Some are decorated with lines of boutons or knobs and others with lines of decoration made with a bone point as described above (*18*). In his reassessment Dr Mark Patton argues that the importance of Le Pinacle is not the evidence for early domestic settlement but that it represents a stone axe production centre exporting to Guernsey, Alderney and Sark, where examples of axes made from rock from Le Pinacle have been found (Patton 2001). This hypothesis is relatively untested and further evidence in the form of debitage would support the argument. The quantity of animal bone recovered has allowed a proper analysis and the presence of saddle querns may indicate early farming practices and a more domestic role.

Other sites on Jersey which have produced an Early Neolithic phase include Mont Orgueil, the medieval castle on the east coast (Cunliffe 1984). During excavations by Ken Barton in the 1970s (see Chapter 8) Early Neolithic pottery with repoussé boutons was recovered. The forms are different to those of Le Pinacle where vessels with narrow mouths and upstanding rims are the norm whereas at Mont Orgueil a simpler hemispherical style of bowl is present, (Cunliffe 1984).

On the Écréhous reef, which may have still been attached to the mainland of France at the time, evidence of the Early Neolithic occupation survives in the form of pottery and stone tools. During excavations by Dr Warwick Rodwell in

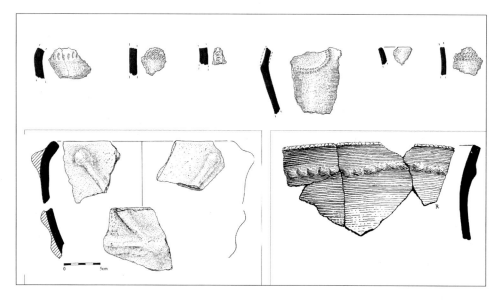

18 Early Neolithic pottery from the Channel Islands. Top, Les Fouaillages; left, L'Ouziére, Jersey; right, Le Pinacle, Jersey. *After Kinnes, forthcoming, Patton & Finlaison, 2001 and Godfray & Burdo, 1949*

the late 1980s, mainly to examine the archaeology and ecclesiastical structures that survive at Les Écréhous, Neolithic pottery and flint were recovered from what survived of the loessic deposits on the reef. On La Maître Île a sherd of pottery with three rows of repoussé buttons was found, similar to vessels from Le Pinacle and Les Fouaillages (Patton 1996). The flint assemblage includes scrapers and retouched flakes.

Other than finds of flint, no Early Neolithic material has been recovered from Alderney.

LAND MANAGEMENT

Two other as yet undefined sites on Guernsey have been examined recently and may be associated with land management as a result of early farming. At 1-2 Les Canichers, St Peter Port, part of a large stone-built cairn was found. The size and scale of this monument is surprising and no parallels are immediately apparent. An area of some 12m² has been examined and this appears to be only a small proportion of the cairn. Two smaller, circular cairns were present at Les Fouaillages (Kinnes & Grant 1983; Kinnes 1988) and there are elements of cairn construction at La Hougue Bie in Jersey (Patton et al. 1999) but neither of these are very similar. It appears to be a clearance rather than a burial cairn, associated with prehistoric land management, on a terrace some 200m above the low-lying coastal fringe and the Royal Hotel site. Evidence of early agriculture is present in the form of plough marks running alongside the cairn.

At Pré du Galet, Perelle, a row of stones which seemed to suggest a boundary of some sort or alternatively part of the kerb surrounding a much bigger structure, such as a burial chamber, were uncovered during gardening landscaping works in the south-west of Guernsey in 2001. No specific dating material was recovered although the absence of modern material at the lowest level is indicative of a prehistoric date for the monument. The site is located some 100m from the present coastline. This may be another example of land division and management in the Neolithic.

All of this material evidence gives us an idea of how the early farmers in the Channel Islands would have lived, probably in long houses, with a few animals and crops growing nearby, using cooking pots on their hearths. But what do we know of their burial practices and belief systems?

EARLY NEOLITHIC BURIAL AT LES FOUAILLAGES, GUERNSEY

Before this recent settlement evidence on Guernsey was discovered, a tomb for the first farmers, c.4500-4000 BC, had been excavated in the early 1980s by Dr Ian Kinnes of the British Museum. This was at Les Fouaillages (which means furze break) on the sandy plain to the north of Guernsey, on what is now common land. The site had miraculously survived the ravages of agriculture, sand extraction by troops in World War II and landscaping for a golf course. The excavation results were surprising in that the site did not turn out to be a passage grave or local variation as predicted (see chapter 4), but was, in fact, a long mound built by people from a group using Linearbandkeramik pottery. This type of pottery was bound within the earliest phase of the monument and still represents the only evidence for it, or people who knew how to make it, crossing over the sea. This fact alone forces us to ask the question – if the Danubian farmers spread their culture as far west as Guernsey, why did they not cross the Channel to mainland Britain at the same time? The technology and maritime knowledge would not have been a problem under the right conditions (J. Adams pers. comm.) so were there other factors preventing the first farmers crossing the Channel? It would appear so. Anyhow this remarkable monument at Les Fouaillages pre-dates most of the other megaliths in the islands. At the time of the excavation the site produced the first radiocarbon dates for the initial Neolithic in Guernsey and, indeed, the Channel Islands. Three samples of charcoal calibrated to 4600-4880 BC (BM 1892R) 4700-4930 BC (BM 1893R) and 3930-4760 BC (BM 1894R) were from the earliest phase of the long mound (Patton 1995). After the Mesolithic period there was evidence that the forest was cleared from the area and a particular site chosen for the monument, perhaps close to a yet undiscovered Neolithic settlement. Ian Kinnes describes the earliest phase of the monument thus:

Four separate structures were built along a line from north-east to south-west, and were surrounded by a triangular mound of cut and stacked turves some 20m long and 10m wide. Each side of the mound was defined by a kerb wall of granite boulders and slabs with some dry-stone infill, and the wall was especially well-built on the northern side. At the eastern end was an impressive façade of monumental flat-faced slabs which focussed attention on a narrow entrance gap just south of the centre. Behind this point of access lay a small D-shaped forecourt which was defined at one side by a large upright slab.

At the rear of the forecourt was a small slab-built chamber with three capstones on three uprights. To the rear of this lay a second stone chamber, but of a completely different form. To the west of the second chamber lay a sub-rectangular cairn of tightly packed slabs and boulders, 1.9m long, 1.8m wide and 1m high. This covered a small cist, or open space, with boulder walls forming a semi-dome roofed by a single capstone. At the east end of the cairn stood a shouldered marker slab, perhaps chosen for its distant resemblance to a human figure (Kinnes & Grant 1983).

Kinnes considered that all these structures were built at the same time (*19*), but they are visibly of quite different function. The platform and the cairn, which was covered by the mound from the outset, may have been of no more than ritual or votive purpose. The two chambers, however, were clearly left open for continued use, perhaps for several generations of burials and associated ceremonies. The small chamber, though at the focal point, may have been no more than a place of temporary storage, a sort of funeral chapel. The larger, unroofed chamber, accessible only by crossing the mound from a gap left at the front of the southern kerb nearby, may have been the place of permanent internment, a possibility reinforced by the presence of likely grave goods, from nearby settlements. Throughout the mound there were considerable quantities of domestic refuse, broken pottery, discarded flint and animal bones. The elongated form of the mound recalls the long houses of Linearbandkeramik settlements. Around 4000 BC the tomb was deliberately closed, after prolonged use, for what reason we shall never know. Kinnes' description continued:

the unroofed chamber had a boulder wall built across its entrance, and the interior was filled with large stones to the level of the side-slabs. The front chamber was backfilled with clean beach sand, and its forecourt plugged with tightly-packed boulders to the line of the façade. In this state the monument seems to have stood prominent in the landscape for some centuries, still perhaps an object of veneration, but no longer an active place of resort.

The new evidence from Guernsey seems to indicate that a successful Neolithic economy was established in the Channel Islands from early in the fifth millennium BC. The recent confirmation of stratified Mesolithic material on Lihou Island also indicates that this Neolithic settlement was not the earliest successful subsistence on Guernsey or the extremities of the continent if, indeed, the island was still attached. Other new research is suggesting that change from

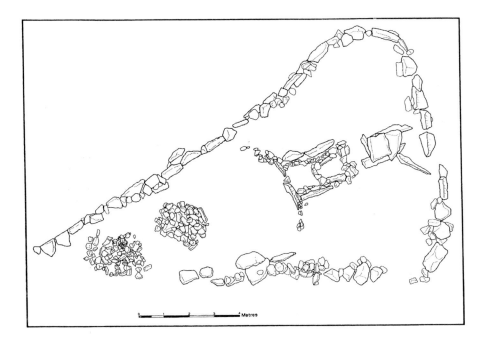

19 Plan showing the earliest phases of Les Fouaillages, Vale, Guernsey. *After Kinnes, 1982*

the Mesolithic to the Neolithic way of life was abrupt and that what people were eating changed considerably (Schulting & Richards 2000; Richards et al. 2003). New research on the isotopes in skeletal material is indicating that people stopped eating fish and started eating dairy produce and animal products or as Kinnes put it so succinctly, the change was 'fruits de mer replaced by meat and two veg' (Kinnes 2004). It seems incredible that inhabitants of the Channel Islands surrounded by the sea would stop using fish as a resource but as we are dealing with what was in effect a 'new world' there may have been other reasons, possibly based on belief systems, that we can only guess at today, why people changed their diet.

The new evidence from Guernsey is also significant when we consider that it is the most westerly of the island group and the most difficult to get to from mainland France. In his 1998 reflection on the excavation of the long mound at Les Fouaillages, Kinnes re-emphasises that for Guernsey the Bandkeramik tradition must have been sea-borne and that the knowledge of agriculture and the animals and seeds necessary for its establishment would have reached the islands (and elsewhere) by a network of experienced fishermen. But if these cultural elements are crossing the sea as far as Guernsey why do they not get across the Channel to mainland Britain until almost a thousand years later? In the next chapter we shall examine the evidence of the burial traditions of these early farming communities.

4

TOMBS OF THE ANCESTORS: THE FIRST FARMERS AND THEIR BURIAL MONUMENTS

Megalithisme, Les pierres de memoire. (Mohen 1998)

The dead are placed in tombs by those that survive them and the monuments can, for that reason, be seen as 'tombs for (the use of) the living'. (Chippendale, in Jossaume 1985)

At last La Hougue Bie has been compelled to reveal its secret. (Nicolle 1924a)

Evidence that the Neolithic was established in the Channel Islands, possibly as early as the fifth millennium BC, has been outlined in Chapter 3. Shortly after this, the inhabitants of the islands adopted a phenomenon which was sweeping across many parts of Europe particularly in coastal areas. This phenomenon was the practice of tomb building with large stones or 'megaliths'. This began the creation of megalithic monuments, some of which survive today, having avoided the ravages of subsequent generations and their farming, quarrying (particularly in the Channel Islands), road building and even incorporation into other buildings. Some 70,000 megalithic structures are known in Western Europe, stretching from Poland across the great European plain and on to Ireland and from Scandinavia in the north to Spain in the south. Each area has its own regional variations and the Channel Islands are no exception.

THE MEGALITH BUILDERS

It had once been thought that the development of these tombs was related to the movement of the first farmers across Europe dubbed 'megalithic missionaries' by Gordon Childe (1925). Others have suggested that the burial practice was spread by communities in close contact through fishing (Kinnes 1982; 1986) or alternatively through farmers arriving independently into different areas at different times (Renfrew cited in Scarre, 2002) perhaps bringing an ideology that transformed the long house for the living into a long mound for the dead. There are many ways to study the phenomenon of megalith building in Europe and indeed across the world (Jossaume 1985). Initially early prehistorians studied the material cultures associated with or incorporated into them, i.e. what was found in the tombs. There were then attempts to understand the sociological aspects of the burial rite and what the function of the tombs might have been to the living communities who built them (Kinnes 1981; Bradley 1998). More recently the settings of the tombs in their surrounding landscapes have been also considered (Bradley 1998; Scarre 2002).

Links back to the Mesolithic in pursuit of the origins of the megaliths have caused academics to look again at the few burials that survive from that period. At Hoëdic and Téviec on small islands in the bay of Quiberon in Brittany, burials cut into shell middens, ensuring a remarkable degree of preservation, were excavated in the 1930s (Péquart et al. 1937) and more recently re-examined by Schulting (2001). The shell middens are of such proportions that they have a monumental dimension of their own. At Téviec a small cemetery of 10 graves contained 23 bodies and at Hoëdic 14 bodies occupied nine graves. What is remarkable for this early period (5500 BC) is that the burial rite was very elaborate with grave goods, such as bone and flint tools and ornaments such as painted stones. One grave at Hoëdic had a covering of antler from red deer. Were the people who built these graves, with their Mesolithic culture, the predecessors of the megalith builders or is there a more direct descent from the early farmers? The evidence to answer these questions is not abundant, particularly in the Channel Islands. This is because a great deal of the excavation on the surviving megalithic tombs was carried out in the nineteenth century by the Lukis family, among others, and in the early part of the twentieth century by those who started the learned societies, at a time when excavation skills were still in their infancy.

General reviews of the megalithic monuments in the islands have been carried out several times since Kendrick's synthesis in 1928 (see Chapter 2), which was largely based on the Lukis archive held at Guernsey Museum and other early records at La Société Jersiaise. However Kinnes' work in Guernsey (1986, 1998) and excavations in Jersey by Johnston (1972), Hibbs & Shute (1984), Rault & Forest (1992), and Patton et al. (1999) and on Alderney by Johnston (1973 & 1974), have enabled some new information to be added. Two separate traditions of monuments are still apparent, placing the islands in an interesting position, juxtaposed between the passage graves of the Atlantic coastal distribution and the long mounds of the North European plain. The early phase of the long mound at Les Fouaillages has already been described in Chapter 3. Other types of monuments in the islands were defined by Kinnes in 1988 and included: passage graves, such as those at La Varde on Guernsey, Les Monts Grantez on Jersey and Les Porciaux North on Alderney; gallery graves such as Le Couperon on Jersey;

closed chambers with just one example at La Hougue Boëte on Jersey; and drystone galleries such as Beauport on Jersey.

These types of monuments are primarily associated with the Neolithic period although many have later phases. Later monuments associated with the Bronze Age include cists-in-circles such as at L'Islet on Guernsey, Le Monceau on Herm and Les Platons on Jersey.

Menhirs or standing stones, such as La Longue Rocque on Guernsey and La Dame Blanche on Jersey, are another form of megalithic monument which occasionally survives in the landscape today. Evidence from Brittany has shown that they were also reused and incorporated into megalithic tombs (Le Roux 1984 and see below). On Guernsey there are also exceptional, carved standing stones or statue menhirs at Castel Church and St Martins Church which will be described below.

PASSAGE GRAVES

The passage grave tradition in the Channel Islands is part of the group that is generally thought to have been distributed along the Atlantic coast from Portugal and western France to as far north as the Orkney Islands possibly being spread by people travelling up the coast. The term 'passage grave' refers to tombs where a narrow entrance leads to a broader chamber. They were built in a variety of ways with megalithic stone upright props and capstones, with drystone walling, cut into natural rock, or a combination of the three. They were often contained within circular mounds, sometimes of stepped or terraced construction.

One example which differs from the majority of graves in the islands is at La Sergenté in St. Brelade's parish in Jersey, which may represent one of the earliest megaliths, contemporary with the initial phases of Les Fouaillages. It is a type of passage grave, but was covered in a round mound, much of which survives. It is the only example in the Channel Islands of a type common in Normandy such as at Vierville and La Hoguette (Verron 2000). It consists of a short passage, entered from the south-east, just over 2m long. The passage appeared to be stepped, leading down to a circular chamber of drystone construction about 3m in diameter, originally roofed by a drystone vault. At the entrance to the chamber stand a pair of uprights with a low slab across. The chamber was paved with close-set slabs apart from the south-west corner where there is an internal setting of low blocks which divides it from the main chamber. The site was discovered in 1923 (Nicolle 1924) when the excavators thought they had found a beehive hut. In 1983 the pavement of the tomb was re-examined (Hibbs & Shute 1984). No buried land surface was found but it appeared that the pavement was integral to the chamber. Four fine pots had been found during the original excavation which were undecorated and had rounded bottoms. The tomb is likely to be Early Neolithic, c.4500 BC.

LA HOUGUE BIE

La Hougue Bie, in the parish of Grouville on Jersey, is the most spectacular of all the Channel Island passage graves (*colour plate 8*). Under a vast mound 12m high and 54m in diameter is a passage grave of middle Neolithic date. The monument is covered by its original mound, and it was not until the 1920s when La Société Jersiaise purchased the site that the suspected chamber was sought after and found.

La Hougue Bie remains one of the most impressive megalithic monuments in Europe (Kinnes & Hibbs 1988). It was a focus of local myth and legend as it was so dominant on the landscape and is clearly marked on the Duke of Richmond map of Jersey, drawn in 1787, as La Houque. In the early medieval period a chapel, Notre Dame de la Clarté, was built, probably to counteract paganism, and later an early Tudor chapel, the Jerusalem Chapel, was erected. In the eighteenth century the Prince's Tower, a pseudo-Gothic edifice which surrounded the medieval chapel, also known as La Tour D'Auvergne, was erected. Later the site boasted a hotel in the grounds but the whole fell into decline until it was taken up by La Société Jersiaise in the 1920s, when the hotel was knocked down and the archaeology of the site was considered.

The Neolithic burial monument consists of an unusually long passage entered from the south-east, which leads into a bottle-shaped chamber with three side chambers opening from it in a cruciform arrangement. In the chamber there are several uprights dividing off significant areas and cists with small standing stones which appear to be very rare examples of ritual activity in a megalithic tomb (*20*). There are 24 circular cup marks carved on the east slab in the northern lateral chamber. Cup marks are also carved on the capstone of this chamber. The interior of the site was first excavated in 1924 by Godfray and other members of La Société Jersiaise including Rybot, Guiton, Keiley, Baal and Nicolle (Baal et al. 1925). They broke into the tomb by putting a trench into the mound until they hit the chamber. They had in fact arrived at the gap between the second and third capstones. And just as Carter marvelled at the entrance to the tomb of Tutankhamen, Godfray saw the chamber for the first time since it had been sealed. Dr Arthur Mourant, who had studied the geology of the tomb, pressed for many years for new excavations. He lived long enough to witness those directed by Mark Patton and Olga Finch in the 1990s for the Jersey Heritage Trust, with additional seasons being directed by Dr George Nash. The following is a brief summary of their results:

> Phase 1: The passage grave in its present form (but with a shorter passage) was constructed c.4000-3500 BC together with the primary cairn [*21*]. It may have replaced an earlier monument.
>
> Phase 1a: The passage was extended by c.2.4m within a short time of the original construction. The geometry of the original cairn was modified to accommodate this extension and the primary terraces were added.

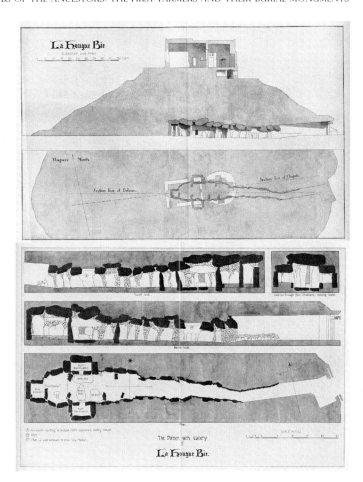

20 La Hougue Bie plan and section. *After Rybot, 1924*

Phase 1b: The secondary terraces were added almost certainly within the fourth millennium BC. The passage grave remained open for a period of between 500 and 1000 years. The ditch was probably dug at some time between 3500 and 3000 BC.

Phase 1c: The passage was sealed and the forecourt area blocked with rubble at around 3000 BC. Prior to the blockage it is likely that some form of de-sanctification of the passage took place involving the displacement of the slab which formed the edge of the 'sanctuary' platform and a partial disturbance of the pebble floor of the passage and chamber. It is possible that the deposit of pebbles found within the forecourt relate to this event. Evidence that came to light during the restoration suggests that one of the orthostats supporting the entrance capstone may have been deliberately removed at this point. Part of the outer stone façade may have been dismantled to provide the material for the blockage. At some time after this a vessel was deposited in the blockage horizon.

Phase 1d: The external structures of the cairn were covered up between 2900 and 2500 BC.

The site seems to have then been completely abandoned until medieval times. Among the finds from the early excavations were the bones of up to eight

21 Section through the mound at La Hougue Bie showing the position of the primary cairn. *Courtesy of the Jersey Heritage Trust / Société Jersiaise Collections*

adults, both male and female, and many ceramic sherds mainly of vase-supports including two complete vessels, also known as the iconic *coupe-à-socle* (Kinnes 1998). Several displayed evidence of burning and may have been used as lamps or to infuse hallucinogenic drugs (Sherratt 1991). Until recently these ceramic wares were associated with burial chambers but some sherds have recently been found in other contexts in France and they now have a much wider provenance (Kinnes 2004a). They are another example, however, of a type of pottery found in the islands with parallels in Brittany (Cassen 2000), which is not found on the British mainland, the other being the Linearbandkeramik pottery from Les Fouaillages. Among the other artefacts at La Hougue Bie were flint tranchet arrowheads, bracelet fragments and part of a stone mace head.

Two other aspects of La Hougue Bie are of great interest. One is the geology of the stones within the tomb which were studied by Dr Arthur Mourant (1933) and the other is the relationship of the tomb to the equinoctial sunrise. The geology shows that material for the tomb was brought from some distance away and from several different places. Stone was brought from Le Dicq some 3.5km to the SSW, Fort Regent some 3.5km to the SW, La Rocque (4km to the SSE) and Le Hocq (4km to the S), diorite from Elizabeth Castle (5km to SW) and porphyry from the area in general. The most striking is a slab and quern from Mont Mado which is 6.5km to the NW (Mourant ibid.). This information about the distance the stone has been brought enables archaeologists to speculate on the social structure necessary to build such a monument. Kinnes and Hibbs (1988) suggested that somewhere in the region of 200 working days for a workforce of 200 would be needed for the construction of the mound material and 160 days for the same workforce for the passage and capstones. As this is such a significant monument it may have been a religious centre for at least half the island and may therefore indicate a population of *c.*1000 people or 200 families.

Speculation that the equinoctial sunrise would have been significant to the tomb builders led the recent excavators to consider the possibility. The entrance to the passage is from the east and in 1996 there was an opportunity to observe whether the equinoctial sunrise would enter the tomb. This was shortly after the demolition of the concrete tunnel which had been built after the 1924 excavations for safety and ease of access to the tomb. The light of the rising sun was indeed seen to enter the chamber and light up the back recess of the terminal cell (Patton et al. 1999). The beam of light was observed first striking the slab of Mount Mado stone mentioned above, some 25cm above the floor of the sanctuary and 60cm from its northern edge. The rays then moved northward to illuminate the back wall and floor. The sunlight then left the terminal cell and started to light up the sanctuary floor and eastern vertical face of the sanctuary threshold stone. After this, light 'streams down the passage for the first time' (*colour plate 9*). Patton and Finch (ibid.) suggest that this emphasises the importance of the sanctuary as a focus of activity within the tomb. This spectacular, complex monument is owned by La Société Jersiaise and in the care of the Jersey Heritage Trust and is well worth a visit in order to appreciate the sheer scale of the construction (see Chapter 10).

Other passage graves on Jersey include La Pouquelaye de Faldouet in the parish of St.Martin, on high ground not far from Anne Port which was first recorded by Poingdestre, Lieut. Bailiff of Jersey, in 1682 (see Chapter 2). It was then drawn by F.C. Lukis in 1839 (*22*). The monument consists of a horseshoe-shaped chamber built of massive stones with an extremely large capstone over a central area which was possibly never completely roofed. This central area contains at least five cists around the walls. The structure is set on an almost east/west axis. Around the monument are two concentric drystone walls and a circle of small upright stones. These walls were broken into and reconstructed in 1868 to allow access to the passage. The western capstone, which is of non-porphyritic rhyolite, is estimated to weigh 23 tons and because of the geology must have been brought from a distance of 300m away. The monument has been extensively excavated (Nicolle & Sinel 1910; Rybot 1932) and restored several times. The finds consisted of pottery vessels including vase-supports, stone pendants and polished axes. The tomb probably dates to the Neolithic *c.*4000-3200 BC.

MONT UBÉ

The dolmen of Mont Ubé in Jersey was brought to F.C. Lukis' attention in Guernsey shortly after it was discovered.

A most interesting discovery has within the last few days been made in the parish of St Clement's near Samarez, in a piece of land belonging to Mr. Ramié. It appears that a few days ago, in uncovering a mound of earth to obtain stone, the workmen employed found some

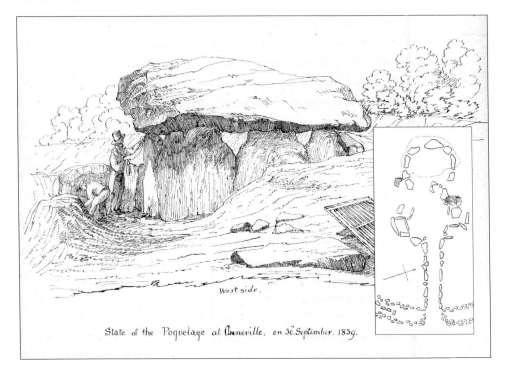

West side.

State of the Poquelaye at Anneville. on 30 September. 1839.

22 La Pouquelaye de Faldouet drawn by F.C. Lukis in 1839 with Rybot's 1932 plan inserted.
Photograph: Guernsey Museum and Galleries

large stones upright, and on closer examination it was found that they continued in succession. At the present moment there are nineteen Stone Pillars uncovered, about seven feet in height and from four to six feet square forming an oval, about fifteen feet wide in the greatest width, and the supposed entrance is about four feet wide. It is presumed that it is the remains of some druidical chapel, as stone pillars of smaller dimensions are found inside upright, about the width of a seat, the floor to which is composed of large flat stones. An earthen Vase was also found in the interior, but unfortunately it was broken in being dug out; small pieces of copper have also been found. The workmen are still employed in clearing away the rubbish, and no doubt when the whole is cleared out, it will be an interesting relic.

Lukis goes on to say that:

I immediately repaired with John W. Lukis (his son) to Jersey, and was much gratified in examining the spot. This structure is entire with the exception of the covering stones, which had been removed some years previous, for building purposes and broken up. One portion on the north side alone, remained in its original place in which, a hole was drilled into it for the purpose of blasting it with gunpowder.

The site had been discovered by quarrymen just before Lukis got there in 1848. It is a horseshoe-shaped chamber just over 7m x 3m with internal stone settings, which are now lost, and a small side chamber on the south side is flanked by two upright stones. The chamber is approached by a passage which is just over 5m long which, as Lukis described, had a number of unidentified stone settings when cleared in 1848. An outer circle of stones and enclosing earthen mound may have been part of the monument. The paving and capstones recorded by the Lukis family were broken up for building material during the dismantling. The finds from the site were numerous and it is possible that the landowner embellished these with antiquities he had himself bought to sell on. Sherds of 10-12 pots were found at the west end of the chamber and three were complete bowls one of which is a grape cup – very rare in the Channel Islands. There were flint implements, an axe, a transverse arrowhead and scrapers. Among the more exotic finds were stones axes, fragments of stone rings and beads, one of which is likely to have been faience (Sheridan 2004). There is also some Iron Age and Roman pottery which is now in the British Museum (Hawkes 1937).

Les Monts Grantez, at St Ouen in Jersey, is also worthy of mention as it is fairly well preserved. It was discovered in 1839 and is described in 1870 by Oliver in a letter to Lukis who describes it as 'a contemporary parallel specimen with the tumulus of Creux des Fées in Guernsey'. It consists of an oval chamber with one side chamber to the north. It is approached by a passage just over 4m long and about 1m wide and the whole is orientated ESE–WNW. It was covered by a mound which at present is elongated *c*.18m long and 6m wide, but this is probably the result of ploughing along both sides of a round mound in historic times. The construction is particularly good with the uprights well grounded and the gaps between them filled in with drystone walling. Six capstones now survive, two having been destroyed. During excavations in 1912 (Nicolle et al. 1913) seven burials were found in the chamber and grave goods with them included animal bones, limpet shells and pebbles. The pottery found is all of one period and included plain bowls and vase-supports. Stone finds included rubbers and hammers, a fine flint pick and a large bead of steatite.

On Guernsey several impressive passage graves survive. La Varde is the largest and most impressive surviving megalithic structure in Guernsey (*colour plate 10*). The site was discovered in 1811 by soldiers of the 103rd Regiment digging a redoubt on the hill (see Chapter 2). Lukis and members of his family excavated the tomb in 1837 (*23*). The chamber is built of large upright slabs with massive capstones. It is 11m in length and just over 3m wide at its greatest extent. It is about 2m high internally and is entered from the east. The largest capstone weighs over 10 tons and although not as large as that at Le Faldouet in Jersey, its positioning is an amazing feat of engineering. The chamber widens from the entrance and this is echoed by an increase in the roof height. There is an oval recess near the north-west corner, which is not a full side chamber but is clearly a deliberate feature. Two layers of paving were recorded by Lukis, indicating successive periods of use, and between and above these were quantities of burnt and unburnt human bone, and many associated finds. The complete pots and

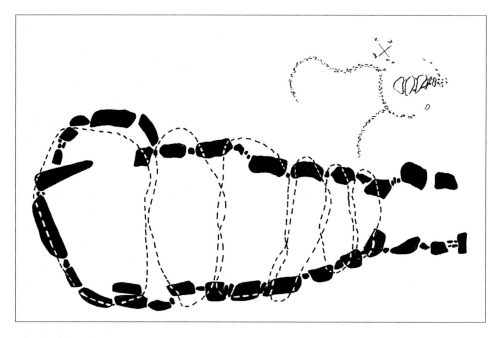

23 Plan of La Varde, Guernsey, (after Lukis) with a sketch of the stone alignments by W.C. Lukis.
Photograph: Guernsey Museums and Galleries

fragments of others are estimated to comprise some 150 vessels (Kendrick 1928), dating from the Middle Neolithic to Early Bronze Age times, and suggesting use as a burial chamber over at least 1500 years from *c.*3500-2000 BC. Flint and stone tools, stone ornaments and bone points were also discovered. Although Lukis' excavations could be criticised as primitive and disorganised his work at this site is remarkable because he recorded the stratigraphy in section drawings. In fact these are some of the the first archaeological sections that were drawn by a British antiquary (Sebire 2003).

La Varde was covered in a round mound, originally some 18m in diameter. A plan present in the Lukis manuscripts at Guernsey Museum indicates the massive stone kerb and lines of stones that radiate out from it.

Another spectacular Passage Grave in Guernsey is Le Déhus in the Vale parish which was purchased by the enlightened John de Havilland in 1775 (See Chapter 2). Lukis and members of his family excavated the tomb between 1837, and 1847. This work was followed by the Rev. G. E. Lee in 1898, Colonel de Guerin in 1915, and V. Collum in 1932, so it is now difficult to unravel the various reports. However, Kendrick (in 1928) gave a summary of Lukis' excavation notes in some detail. This included the discovery made in the north-east side-cell where Lukis considered that bodies of two adults had been placed upright in a kneeling position and packed round with limpet shells and earth. As this was so unusual the drawing was sent to J.A.A. Worsaae the Director of Antiquities in Copenhagen who reproduced it in his own publications (Worsaae 1843). Le Déhus has a basic plan of narrow entrance and broad chamber. At either side of the passage are four small side chambers, while the roofing is of massive capstones. At the centre of the main chamber is the rare feature of a stone pillar, which originally helped to support the second capstone from the rear. This capstone has on its underside a stylised carving of a figure referred to now as the guardian of the tomb (24). The carving features a bearded face, arms and hands, a bow with arrows. The tomb is now lit in such a way as to help the visitor clearly see the carving. The chamber is surrounded by a circular mound with kerb walling, now largely reconstructed but apparently some 18m in diameter originally.

Very large quantities of material were recovered which suggest a chronological range from *c*.3500-2000 BC. The pottery included plain bowls and Beakers, and among other finds were a stone axe, bone points and beads. The human bones were well preserved since the chambers had been filled with limpet shells. Burial deposits were recovered from most parts of the interior, the records suggesting deposition in all states, from complete bodies to bundles of selected bones. A copper axe was also found, one of the few pieces of Early Bronze metalwork from the island.

Le Creux ès Faïes Passage Grave is in the parish of St Pierre-du-Bois, Guernsey. Excavations by Lukis in 1840 produced a few human and animal

24 Carving on the interior capstone of Le Déhus known as 'Le Guardien'. *Photograph: Guernsey Museums and Galleries*

bones, a quantity of Beaker pottery, and two barbed and tanged flint arrowheads. All the datable material is from the period *c.*2000-1800 BC, but this may represent only the final phase of use. The chamber has a narrow entrance but no passage as such and expands to a round-ended space with faces east. The whole is 9m long. Only two capstones survive, but it is likely that the remainder of the structure was originally roofed. The floor level slopes upwards to the entrance, suggesting that the outer passage may have deposits in situ which have never been fully excavated. The chamber appears to be partly cut into the natural slope. A World War II bunker in close proximity is likely to have disturbed some of the deposits associated with the tomb. It was covered with a round mound, originally some 18m in diameter, but now very little is left. Excavations at Camp Varouf on low-lying ground 100m to the south (see Chapter 3) revealed an Early Neolithic settlement that was long lived and was overlain by an Early Bronze Age horizon. It is interesting to speculate that this tomb was the focal point for the early farmers and was actually in use for many generations. No other tombs have been found on the headland. As the settlement site has produced a very early radiocarbon date (5270-5060 BC) (Ox A-8328) (see Chapter 3) it is possible that an earlier form of tomb, perhaps similar to the earliest phases of Les Fouaillages, was in the vicinity.

LA ROCQUE QUI SONNE — PASSAGE GRAVE

This monument, originally perhaps the largest and finest in Guernsey, now survives as two upright slabs and a displaced capstone in the playground of the Vale Infant and Junior schools having provided a climbing frame for generations of Guernsey school children. The site was dismantled around AD 1800 and provided enough stone to load a 150-ton ship with sufficient left over for local building works! There were originally at least nine capstones, but other structural details are not recorded. A circular mound with stone kerb may have surrounded the chamber. The site was excavated by Lukis in 1837 who recorded: 'there were a series of nine Cromlechs in that part of the hougue where we had the good fortune to discover a Dolmen of no mean appearance'. Although the site was already in a ruinous condition the remains produced fragments of Late Neolithic and Beaker pottery, broken stone axes, and part of a decorated jet bracelet of probable Early Bronze Age date. Lukis remarked on the name of the tomb 'the large Cromlech ... said to have consisted of nine Capstones, at least, among which, one hollow surrounding stone, which reverberated when struck with a stone, & which was heard over a considerable space, (said to have been heard over the whole parish)'. The destroyer of the monument, a Mr Hocart, was afflicted by a series of disasters after its desecration. His houses in Guernsey and then Alderney were burnt to the ground, one with the death of two servants. Then two ships in which he was a shareholder were lost at sea carrying, apparently, cargoes of stone from the monument. Hocart himself was then killed in a freak accident on board ship. The story sounds far fetched and certainly would have reinforced local superstitions, but it was substantially verified by the researches of the folklore expert, Sir Edgar MacCulloch (1903). The tomb is likely to date to around 3500-2000 BC.

At Le Trépied, St Saviour, Guernsey, a bottle-shaped megalithic chamber stands exposed on the landscape with slab walls and three surviving capstones (see front cover). There is no trace of a mound or kerb. The tomb is 5.5m in length, with maximum width of 2m. The internal area is 1.3m high. Excavations by Lukis in 1840 produced human bones and Beaker and other pottery. Two flint, barbed and tanged arrowheads were also uncovered. As with Le Creux ès Faïes, the date of the finds need have no bearing on the date of the construction of the monument which is likely to have been around 3000-2000 BC as they probably represent the last phase of its use.

In Alderney none of the megaliths that survive are intact. At Les Porciaux North (see below) and Les Porciaux South there are remains of two megaliths which have been badly disturbed. Les Porciaux South (25) was recorded by Lukis but is now ruinous. It survives as a stone heap and depression although

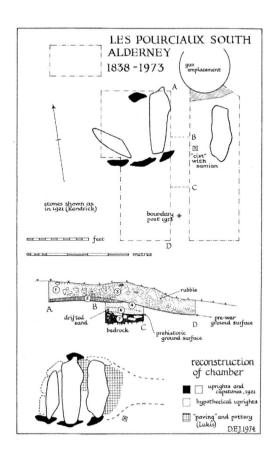

25 Les Porciaux South, Alderney. *After Johnston, 1974*

the site is illuminated by a photograph reproduced by Kendrick (1928, plate XIX) and appears to have been a passage grave with a chamber 4.5m long and 3m wide. Lukis recorded paving with pottery some of which is Roman. This very likely indicates when the grave was first disturbed. It was re-examined by Johnston (1973) who concluded that its form was uncertain.

GALLERY GRAVES

The other main type of monument in the Channel Islands is the gallery grave or the French *allées couvertes*, although there are not many examples locally. These are often beneath long mounds and found in nearby Brittany and north-west France and are thought to be a development from passage graves. These tombs were often made of stone and wood or just wood where stone is in short supply or not easily quarried. Finding timber structures, which may only survive as stains in the earth or traces of post-hole settings, can only be achieved by detailed and careful excavation. Due to the increased sophistication of excavation techniques more timber mortuary sites have been excavated. In the Channel Islands timber mortuary structures have only been identified at Les Fouaillages.

In Alderney Porciaux North was drawn by Lukis in 1853, suggesting it was a gallery grave *c*.8m long with parallel lines of stones *c*.1.5m apart. Three capstones shown are still in place. The monument suffered during World War II as a gun emplacement was built into it. Lukis drew several sections of the tomb, another example of his advanced recording. He recorded three levels, one of blown sand, a middle layer with animal bones and the lowest layer a black soil with human bones. The only finds were in fact two Roman vessels which must indicate a reuse of the tomb perhaps symbolic of its varied use.

The best examples of gallery graves in the islands are on Jersey. Lukis wrote about Le Couperon on Jersey (*colour plate 11*):

The following description of Le Couperon, was received from Mr Thomas Harvey about the year 1839, who visited this Cromlech at my desire:

'The Monument at Le Couperon, is a little curiosity, a perfect little Gem! It is formed of pudding stone, so plentifully found in that part of the island; the Capstones are five in number of which three are still fairly planted in their props, which are 11 number. The stones which form the outer circle (or rather oblong square, with rounded corners) are 22 in number, and seen perfectly to retain their original position. The length of the outer circle is 10 paces, the breadth is 4 paces; there is therefore in this confined space an almost perfect Temple of 5 Capstones, regularly supported on Props. The great western stone, not more than 6 feet in its longest dimension, and the width of the interior, not more than 2½ feet or 3 feet at, most'

During the time employed in making the foregoing sketch of this Cromlech, John W. Lukis, crept beneath the western capstone and near the floor, or, surface of the interior, he found several portions of Urns, of the same character as that of the Pottery & vessels, we have discovered in other Cromlechs.

The observant Lukis family had noticed the difference between this site and the passage graves in the nineteenth century. The monument today is known as a Late Neolithic gallery grave c.3000 BC and consists of a rectangular chamber originally divided into two by the 'porthole' slab now at the east end. There is a rectangular setting of upright stones surrounding the chamber originally set into the long mound which covered the site but which has now disappeared. There have been several restorations of the monument, the first of which was in 1868 before which it was in a poor condition. The present reconstruction is relatively accurate. This type of megalith is very common in France but rare in Jersey and the other Channel Islands. It is therefore of great interest particularly because of the early records.

At Ville-ès-Nouaux in St Helier there is a very complex site which has two monuments and a prehistoric ritual activity area (*colour plate 12*). One of the monuments is a Late Neolithic gallery grave (allée couverte), from c.3250-2850BC. It consists of a parallel-sided chamber with a stone revetment on the north side. The east end is disturbed and its original form can only be speculated. It was excavated by R. Bellis and E. Cable in 1883, who recorded that there were two levels in the monument, the first Late Neolithic with few finds, the second final Neolithic with Beakers, Jersey Bowls and a probable burial (Bellis & Cable 1884). One exceptional find was a fine archer's wristguard, the only complete example from the islands. Oliver (1870) recorded that there were intact Beakers and Jersey Bowls some of which were displayed in Lukis Museum on Guernsey (*26*).

On Guernsey the only possible gallery grave is a ruinous chamber at Delancey. The remains consist of a collapsed megalithic structure with a row of massive slabs. These may belong to some form of elongated chamber some 10m in length. The date is uncertain. The site was excavated by La Société Guernesiaise soon after its discovery in 1919, when finds of probable Late Neolithic pottery were made. More recently Beaker pottery (c.2000-1800 BC) has been found in the adjacent area.

CLOSED CHAMBERS

La Hougue Boëte in the parish of St John in Jersey is a massive bowl-shaped mound 9m high over a closed drystone chamber. It was excavated in 1911 by E. Deyrolle and P. Mauger (1912) who tunnelled into the mound and discovered the stone chamber. Their records are unclear and the finds in the Société Jersiaise collection do not tally with their description. They suggested that a horse skeleton was in the cist with a human skeleton over it. This is unusual although horse remains have been found in Brittany such as at Mané Lud in the Morbihan. The form of this tomb would suggest that this is an early form of megalith.

26 Urns from Ville-ès-Nouaux in Jersey on display in the Lukis Museum in Guernsey.
Photograph: Guernsey Museums and Galleries

The category of tomb known as 'drystone galleries' is known in the Channel Islands only by sites that are very disturbed or have antiquarian records. In Guernsey Le Creux des Fées is described by Lukis in sketch form which shows a D-shaped mound with a façade of flat boulders which gives access to a small rectangular chamber of drystone construction. On Jersey the megaliths at Beauport and Les Hougue de Millais are similar (see Chapter 5).

MENHIRS

> Jacob took a stone and erected it as a monument
> Genesis Ch 3 v35

Menhirs or standing stones remain one of the great mysteries of prehistory. Many suggestions have been put forward for their function, such as territorial markers, the equivalent of totem poles or monuments of religious significance. Individual stones may have had several roles. Dating the stones is difficult, but they are generally assumed to lie within the period *c.*3000-1500 BC. They are especially vulnerable to removal or destruction, and their present numbers in the Channel Islands must only be a small proportion of the original total. Kinnes (1988) recorded one in Alderney, 12 in Guernsey and 14 in Jersey based on what can still be seen and earlier records.

The largest in Guernsey is La Longue Rocque, in St Peters parish (*27*). It is a massive granite block, *c*.4m high. Excavations carried out in 1894 showed that a further 1m extends below ground level for support, but otherwise no artefactual evidence was forthcoming. Fieldwalking recently after the field had been ploughed for the first time for several decades did not produce any convincing prehistoric material. The stone weighs about five tons and as with many of the capstones from other tombs cannot have been easy to erect. It is likely to date to around 3000-1500 BC.

Other menhirs in Guernsey include two at Richmond, La Longue Pierre and Le Crocq. These menhirs stand some 23m apart in an east–west line. La Longue Pierre to the west is a block 3m in height and 1.1m wide, while to the east Le Crocq stands 2.1m high and 1m wide. Excavations by Lukis at the base of La Longue Pierre produced pottery and a stone rubber, but these can no longer be traced. Many other large stones line the road in this general area which might represent other megalithic remains long ago dismantled. These menhirs are also likely to date *c*.3000-1500 BC.

In 1934 Rybot reported that eight menhirs were standing in Jersey. La Dame Blanche, was sketched and painted by Lukis in 1868 (*28*). It stands *c*.2.5m high in a field which is part of Ivy Stone Farm at Samares. It is a block of local

27 La Longue Rocque, Guernsey. *Photograph: Guernsey Museums and Galleries*

Blanche Pierre, St Clement.
(m. leJeune)   8'. 10. high.
.5. 6. wide.

28 La Dame Blanche Jersey by W.C. Lukis. *Photograph: Guernsey Museums and Galleries*

diorite brought inland from the neighbouring coast (Rybot 1934). Excavations by Godfray and Burdo in 1933 showed how the stone was trigged up by small stones. A curious deposit of limpet shells in a stone setting some 3.6m to the south-west was found. The menhir was badly damaged in 1982.

In the St Ouen's Bay area on the west coast of Jersey, four menhirs form a group and are part of a complex prehistoric landscape (Patton & Finlaison 2001). The Broken, Great and Little Menhirs are all of granite and so must have been brought from another part of the island. The Great Menhir is near the Ossuary (a ruined megalith) and now stands *c.*2m high. It was re-erected in 1922 by La Société Jersiaise. No finds were made at the time but trig stones were revealed at the depth of about 1m. The Little Menhir is at the foot of Les Blanches Banques and stands *c.*1.7m above the ground. It was examined in the 1920s also when an old land surface was discovered. The Broken Menhir is so named because the upper part had broken off. During excavations in 1922 a deep socket with packing stones was found for the lower part. The upper section has now been resinstated and so it stands 3m high. Les Trois Rocques appear to be three standing stones which form a semi-circle on the 50ft contour in a flat meadow in low-lying ground behind St Ouen's Bay. Excavation failed to reveal sockets. Also, as two of the menhirs are stumpy blocks both about 1.5m high and the third is a thin slab of 1.7m high, there is some doubt as to their authenticity as menhirs, although they are difficult to explain otherwise.

On the south-east corner of St Ouen's at la Moye a lost menhir, recorded by Plees in 1817 and known as Le Quesnil, stood almost 4m high and had associated ceremonial stones. It disappeared sometime after 1878 due to quarrying. The White Menhir was first recorded in 1933 and is just over 1.7m high some 200m south-west of the Trois Rocques. It has a shallow socket and trig stones but more interestingly it is of a type of granite which outcrops some 3km to the east.

STATUE MENHIRS

One localised form of menhir on Guernsey is worthy of note. Two statue menhirs or carved standing stones survive. Along with the carving on the capstone at Le Déhus, the two statue menhirs are described by Kinnes as exceptional (Kinnes 1980). In a later appraisal (1995) he confirms that the Guernsey examples stand alone in the Channel Islands and only two others are known from Le Morbihan in France. They are anthropomorphic figures, the two statue menhirs representing stylised women, whereas the Déhus figure has been portrayed as a hunter complete with bow and arrows. Kinnes (ibid.) considers it surprising that these exceptional human representations should be found in Guernsey, the most westerly of the islands.

CASTEL STATUE MENHIR

At the Castel church in Guernsey, a menhir has been shaped from a granite slab into a stylised female figure (*colour plate 13*). The entire surface was dressed and the head and body are marked by shoulders and a crown; necklace and breasts are in relief. On the flat back, and towards the base, some form of belt or girdle has been carved. It presently stands 1.65m out of the ground, but its overall height is 2m.

The original position of the figure is unknown. It was discovered beneath the floor of the chancel in the Castel church during restoration work in 1878, and may have been concealed there deliberately in order to rid the church of pagan associations. The figure may have stood in or near a tomb but this uncertain. It is certainly the finest statue menhir of its type and, apart from the damage to the right breast which may have happened in Christian times as an act against idolatry, one of the best preserved. Because of the necklace or lunula it is likely to date to around 2500-1800 BC. In the churchyard another large block of granite is now used as a gravestone and may be a recumbent menhir.

At St Martin in Guernsey a second statue menhir known as La Gran'mère du Chimquière (*29*) stands some 1.65m high just outside the parish church by the gate. This figure was carved at two separate periods. Initially, a granite block was dressed and smoothed to create a stylised human figure, a female. The features

29 La Gran'mère du Chimquière, St Martins, Guernsey. *Photograph: Guernsey Museums and Galleries*

that survive from this earliest carving are breasts above curved arms, both left in relief, and a lower girdle marked by incised lines. Much later, perhaps in the Roman period, the upper part was totally remodelled so that the figure was given pronounced facial features in a frame of curls. There also appears to be some form of hood or ribbed short cape which has a central row of domed buttons. The original location is unknown. Some records suggest that it stood within the churchyard prior to 1815 but was subsequently moved from the sacred precincts. At some point in the past it has been broken in half, perhaps again to deface a pagan object. It is often bedecked with flowers and coins, particularly at marriages in the church, as a token of good luck. The earliest phase is similar to that at the Castel church around 2500-1800 BC

One other piece of megalithic art survives in Guernsey at La Platte Mare (see below). Twelve cup marks are present on the eastern edge of the north-east upright of this small cist-in-circle, excavated by Lukis in 1837. The cup marks along with the Déhus figure are the only example of Neolithic tomb art in Guernsey.

In Jersey cup marks have been identified in La Hougue Bie. There are 24 circular cup marks carved on the east slab in the northern lateral chamber. Cup marks are also carved on the capstone of this chamber. In Alderney a small statuette *c.*18cm high is a small stone carving on a cylindrical pebble which has been pecked and smoothed to give the appearance (almost) of a pair of eyes. Lukis called it an ornamented stone hammer, which is phallic in nature.

LATE NEOLITHIC BURIALS

In Chapter 3 the first phases of the tomb at Les Fouaillages, Guernsey, were discussed as this was very definitely a tomb for the first farmers. However the small slab cists and stone cairns which were covered by a turf mound were not the end of the story. Around 3000- 2000 BC a new cult moved into the area and reused the mound. The eastern end was levelled slightly to provide a flat surface, and extended beyond the line of the façade by the placing of a semi-circle of massive stones. This structure had several courses of tightly-packed beach pebbles, and was overlain by layers of turves. There was then a final sealing of the area by slab and boulders, some of which were of massive proportions. Within this prepared surface, a shrine or mortuary house was built. The excavator Dr Ian Kinnes described it thus: an oval space, about 3.8m across, was enclosed by two concentric settings of boulders weighing up to 1.5 tons individually, and to the east of this were added two semi-circles of similar construction. At the centre were two large sockets for massive wooden uprights set some 2.4m apart. The structure seems to have lasted for a considerable time since the posts required replacement, presumably because of decay. At a later stage, the same zone was redefined by a low boulder wall enclosing a rectangular space about 2.8m long and 1.5m wide. The function of this complex is unknown. Clearly it was not domestic, but whether it was a form of shrine, directly or indirectly associated with the rites of the dead, is not known.

This type of stone circle cannot be paralleled elsewhere in this form, although they are reminiscent of local cist-in-circle sites, especially that at L'Islet. The location of a new monument on top of a pre-existing one is known elsewhere. Whatever the reason for this position, its impressive nature would clearly be considerably enhanced by such elevation.

There were many finds in the foundation material; quantities of flint and pottery, including two near-complete vessels were found. There were many stone tools including a complete stone axe (*colour plate 14*) and fragments of others, as well as hammers and rubbers. There were several *polissoirs* – stones on which axes had been polished with sand and water abrasive – two of which weigh upwards of a quarter of a ton.

Around 2000 BC this structure went out of use and was formally sealed but not before a spectacular deposit of eight flint arrowheads was made at one end of the enclosure. They are of the distinctive barbed and tanged type of the Early Bronze Age, and they were carefully made as matched pairs. Four of a high-quality, honey-coloured flint and likely to have been imported from Grand Pressigny in the Loire valley in Central France some 350km distant. At the same time, the entire structure and the ancient mound below were concealed by a new and even bigger mound some 35m long and 15m wide. This consisted of heaped turves laid on a foundation of rammed pebbles. Visually the mound acts as a permanent memorial to the ancestors within. Domestic material, pottery sherds and flint were incorporated within this mound; these may have been deliberate deposits as part of the burial ritual.

CIST–IN–CIRCLES

This form of megalithic monument is a local regional variation which is mostly found in northern Guernsey and Herm with a few examples in Jersey. There is usually a small stone chamber with a boulder circle surrounding the cist. The best Guernsey example is at L'Islet, St Sampson's (*30*). There is a central D-shaped enclosure with four others attached, all with small boulder walls and overall measuring around 15m. At the centre of the main enclosure is a megalithic cist with a single capstone and a small exterior antechamber; at either side, the western enclosures have small, slab-built cists. The area may have been covered by a low mound. The site was excavated by La Société Guernesiaise in 1912 (see

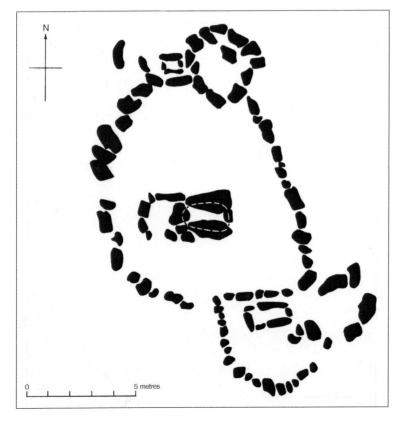

30 Plan of the cist-in-circles, L'Islet, St Sampsons, Guernsey. *After de Guérin*

Chapter two), just after discovery. There were no human remains, as the soil is acidic. The pottery recovered from various contexts suggests a Late Neolithic date around 2500-1800 BC, confirmed by the finding of a complete handled vessel in the main chamber. The outer enclosures may have been added over a period of time. This may have been linked to how the monument was used, with new burials being added around the central cist.

At La Platte Mare, Guernsey, is another less complex cist-in-circle. A small chamber is still visible consisting of seven uprights and a single capstone. What is left to be seen today is misleading (it is 2.1m and 1.8m high), as the original form seems to have been a polygonal closed cist. This was confirmed by excavation in 1981 in tandem with excavations at Les Fouaillages when the chamber and its surrounding mound were re-examined (Kinnes & Grant 1983). As mentioned above a row of 12 cup marks were carved on the eastern edge of the north-east upright (see *32*). Seven of these are now visible above the ground. The chamber is enclosed within a small circle mound, 5m in diameter and with a kerb of large slabs and boulders. The Lukis family excavated the cist between 1837 and 1840, the results being confined to the discovery of Beaker and Late Neolithic pottery, two polished stone axes, and a flint barbed and tanged arrowhead. The chamber had been thoroughly emptied, but most of the mound was undisturbed and pottery of Beaker/Early Bronze Age date was recovered from a primary context suggesting a date *c.*2500-1800 BC.

Two other smaller cist-in-circles are on L'Ancresse in Guernsey but are in ruinous condition. La Mare ès Mauves survives as a rectangular slab-built cist 4.5m in length and 0.6m high with a single capstone, with traces of some form of surrounding slab setting. Lukis excavated here in 1837, but the only finds were stone tools and plain pottery sherds. Near Martello Tower No. 7 the remains were excavated by Lukis in 1837 and 1844. He found pottery fragments, flint flakes and stone rubbers and the structural remains suggest one or more slab-built cists within a circular enclosure of boulders.

In Jersey at Ville-ès-Nouaux, alongside the gallery grave is a cist-in-circle, which was also examined by Bellis and Cable in 1883. It consists of a circle of stone blocks, originally filled in with drystone packing around a megalithic cist. This is formed of four stone slabs, two thin slabs to the east and west with irregular boulders to the north and south which support a large capstone. The space inside the cist is small, 1.2m by 1m and only 0.3m in height. No finds were made by the excavators inside the cist. In the mound that covered it only a few undiagnostic sherds and flint chips were found. From the structure and its position in this complex prehistoric landscape it is likely to date to the Late Neolithic, *c.*2800-2000 BC. Around the sites of the gallery grave and cist-in-circle were found burials of later prehistoric periods – an oval cairn and a small cist – and a menhir was found to the NE (Mont Cochon, now lost having been reburied in 1878).

WHAT CAN THE MEGALITHS FROM THE CHANNEL ISLANDS TELL US ABOUT THE PEOPLE THAT BUILT THEM?

In answer to the question of who built the megaliths Roger Jossaume suggested:

> Surely a population receiving multiple influences from different directions: a process of 'neolithicisation' from the Paris basin, long triangular mounds from northern Europe, and megalith-building from Brittany. (Jossaume 1985, 81)

The megaliths of the Channel Islands can tell us quite a considerable amount about the people who built them even though they are monuments for disposal of the dead and those that survive are only a small proportion of the many that were built (31). The earliest, the long mound at Les Fouaillages, is a monument of such complexity that its structure alone gives us an indication of the social hierarchy that must have been responsible for its erection. But it also reminds us that human nature has probably not changed all that much from the time of the first farmers. Respect for the ancestors, ritual celebration, pomp and circumstance are all suggested by this monument alone and also the nearby passage grave of La Varde with its antennae of stone alignments suggestive of a sacred processional way to the tomb, whereupon perhaps only a select few were able to enter the inner space of the passage and the chamber itself. The early tomb builders at Les Fouaillages with their fine pottery were of a period similar to the users of the site at Le Pinacle – users rather than dwellers as no evidence of habitation has been found with their exquisite early pottery. Was the site used for ritual purposes rather than for living, or as Patton suggests (1991) as an axe manufacturing area? The structural sequence of the monuments on the islands is not easy to follow, but the material culture within them suggests that the development began with La Sergenté on Jersey through the great passage graves found on most of the larger islands with pottery types of simple bowls and vase-supports similar to material from nearby Brittany.

31 Stone De Croze, the original Guernseyman. *By kind permission of the family of Alan Guppy*

Other items associated with this phase are polished stone axes, some of jadeite, imported from the Alps (Bishop & Woolley 1978) and others from Sélédin in Brittany which is somewhat closer. A particularly fine jadeite axe was discovered recently in St Martin in Jersey, most likely imported from Brittany, and now on display at La Hougue Bie Museum (*colour plate 15*). The last phase of the Neolithic in the islands is linked to pottery from the Seine-Oise-Marne group in France and associated particularly with the gallery graves (Kinnes 1988). This group is known as 'flowerpot' as it is coarse and straight-sided with small lugs. All of this material culture enables us to reconstruct the lives of the earliest farmers of the Channel Islands, their belief systems, their engineering skills, their trade networks, their social hierarchy. Advances in scientific analysis now enable us to look more closely at their diet and the consequent implications. Currently research is being undertaken by Dr Rick Schulting who has carried out isotopic analysis on skeletal material from Le Déhus passage grave, and Dr Anne Tresset from the French Archaeology Service (CRNS) in Paris is examining faunal remains from the museum collections. To sum up, the following quote from Ian Kinnes describing La Varde tomb in Guernsey reminds us that the megalith builders were very real:

> Over and around the chamber is a great mound, still visible from half the island. It has no engineering function. It does not support the megaliths, nor does it protect them. It was made to be seen, by its builders and by generations to come. It served as a visible reminder of the community's ancestors, of past achievements, potential and continuity. It stood as a declaration of territorial rights and declared a sense of time and place.
>
> Certainly we are dealing with a lost world, or unidentified and unrecorded people whose very language is unknown, of history recorded only in monuments and artefacts. But the monuments are all around, the artefacts are in the Guernsey Museum: a lost world, perhaps, but not inaccessible. (Kinnes & Grant 1983)

5

NEW CURRENCY: THE COMING OF METAL

The use of metal appeared alongside a new style of pottery; finely made and elaborately decorated beakers. (Parker-Pearson, 2005)

The supply of metal to regions lacking local sources laid the basis for an enduring trade network in a range of commodities. (O'Brien 1996)

…gold shines like fire blazing in the night, supreme of Lordly wealth.
Pindar, Olympian odes. Bk Iii.

As we have seen in Chapter 4 many of the great burial monuments were in use for a long time by generations of people who revered, and in many cases reused, the tombs as a focal point for ritual activity. There seems to be good evidence that many remained in use into the Late Neolithic and Early Bronze Age. The earliest phase of the Bronze Age, sometimes referred to as the Chalcolithic or Copper Age, because copper metal was not yet alloyed with tin, manifests itself on many of the megalithic sites on the islands in the form of Beaker pottery (*colour plate 16*) and the local variants Jersey Bowl and Guernsey Vase (Kinnes 1988). Many of the later forms of megaliths have already been described, such as the cist-in-circles and the menhirs or standing stones, and it becomes apparent that the burial rite changes from one of large communal graves to single burials in smaller cists. The introduction of metalworking was a major development, as this new type of material, and the technology associated with it, enabled more sophisticated weaponry to be made, as well as jewellery and other high-status items. Copper was first mined and worked in south-east Europe in the fifth millennium BC (Parker-Pearson 2005) but it was some thousands of years later before the first metal items made their way into the Channel Islands. New evidence from Ireland and other sites in the British Isles suggests that metalworking was started there by 2400 BC, perhaps before Atlantic France. Beaker pottery, which is known through most of Western Europe and is associated in many areas with the introduction of metal, made its way to the islands around the end of the third millennium BC. The earliest forms of metal objects, from the first centuries of the early 'Bronze Age', were made of copper. Copper is produced from ore which requires melting to a very great heat and the process must have been seen as an amazing innovation to people used to a tool kit of stone, bone and wood. We know from studies on the Neolithic and earlier prehistory that people were aware of the diverse properties of stone, which they procured from some distance if it was seen as valuable; thus, ore-bearing stone would have been much sought after. Bronze is an alloy of copper and tin which produces a versatile metal with greater strength, and was adopted in Britain around 2200 BC, though somewhat more slowly in France. Metalworking changed almost every aspect of life bringing advances in agriculture, woodworking, art and jewellery-making and, of course, warfare (O'Brien 1996). At the same time as copper mining and smelting skills were being developed gold was also being made into highly prized objects, always desired by the rich and famous!

Although there is now a considerable corpus of Early Bronze Age pottery and flint from various sites in the Channel Islands, copper artefacts are quite rare. In Guernsey, Lukis records finding a small copper dagger during his excavations at Le Déhus and recently a small copper flat axe was found by metal detectorists in St Peter's parish, in a hedge bank. One similar is recorded by Kendrick (1928) from the Hougue de Pommier, Guernsey, and one from Little Sark in 1863. At La Rocque qui Sonne passage grave on Guernsey a penannular bracelet was found along with a portion of a decorated jet band. Two flat axes are also known from Jersey but not from megaliths. One is unstratified from La Moye and one from Le Pinacle, associated with Grand Pressigny flint from the Loire valley and barbed and tanged arrowheads. Bronze items do not find their way to the islands until much later although one of the earliest items is a halberd from Alderney. Halberds are large dagger-shaped blades which were fixed to a wooden handle at right angles, like an axe. They may have been sought as status symbols (Parker-Pearson 2005), but recent experimental work indicates that they were functional objects and probably the dominant weapon of the Early Bronze Age in most of Europe. There is also a flat copper axe from Alderney found on high ground to the south-west (P. Arnold pers. comm.)

There is no evidence that metal was mined in the Channel Islands in prehistoric times despite the presence of lead veins and silver-bearing and copper ores in Sark, and possible copper ores in Herm. Copper and tin ores occur naturally in the west of Brittany, which was the closest source of raw material. The only evidence of metalworking from this early time has been found in the islands during rescue excavations at Clos du Pont, Castel (see Chapter 3) which revealed a small crucible with traces of copper residue, suggesting there may have been metalworking at the site. This is awaiting examination.

Settlement evidence for this period is increasing, helping to build up a picture of life in the Bronze Age. Palaeoenvironmental records are also useful for understanding the vegetation and tree cover. The removal of trees and shrubs from around Bronze Age settlement sites has been recorded in Jersey (Jones et al. 1990). There was a growth in wetland vegetation due to the rising water table and coastal vegetation was buried by a covering of sand, indicating a rise in sea levels up to around how they are today. This is confirmed by work at Vazon, in Guernsey, by Campbell (2000). A considerable amount of the fertile land available to the Neolithic farmers was inundated as evidenced by Lukis recording a megalithic burial chamber in 1838 that he located some way down the beach at Les Fontenelles in Guernsey. There is also evidence of climatic change, a deterioration which may have caused a decline in the population in the islands.

At the time of the examination of Les Fouaillages, in Guernsey, an excavation took place in the lee of the burial mound. Evidence of timber-framed buildings, hearths and pits was found. The finds included flintwork and pottery known as Jersey Bowl (so named by Jacquetta Hawkes in the 1930s). These distinctive bowls are sharply carinated with a flat or slightly-hollow base and are ornamented just above the carination with vertical panels of horizontal lines (Hawkes 1937). At Les Fouaillages, Kinnes considered that he had excavated a well-preserved example of a small farming settlement whose inhabitants would have been aware of the great tomb nearby. La Platte Mare (*32*) (see also Chapter 4) some 100m away, was also used during this period, and it is likely, therefore, that this is a rare example for this period of a community and its associated family tomb (Kinnes & Grant 1983). Radiocarbon dates from the excavation suggest a date of *c.*2000-1800 BC.

In the previous chapter we have looked at some forms of Late Neolithic and Early Bronze Age burial such as the cist-in-circles. Another type of funerary monument built at this period were the round barrows, of which there are a few examples in the islands, although many have been destroyed. These follow the development from the large communal passage graves to smaller cists and individual burials. In Jersey a round barrow at La Hougue Mauger was excavated in 1913 prior to its destruction for house building (Baal and Sinel 1915). The mound was 1.8m high and 17m in diameter. Part of the north-east side had been destroyed previously, but the excavators found a displaced slab 1m long. The finds included 22 querns, all but three of which were broken, along with many stone rubbers. The pottery from the mound was distinctive 'flower pot' type, including six complete vessels found along the southern edge of the mound.

In Guernsey, there is strong evidence for a barrow cemetery on the low-lying sandy plane of L'Ancresse common at the north of the island. One of these circular mounds was examined by Percival (1947) and some pottery and burnt human bone was found, along with shells and a partially perforated stone. The excavator was sure the site had been disturbed before, but to date no record in the Lukis manuscripts has been found to confirm this. Many small circular

32 La Platte Mare, Guernsey, by F.C. Lukis. *Photograph: Guernsey Museums and Galleries*

mounds are still visible today from the roadside, at L'Ancresse, and Lukis does record a possible banjo-shaped barrow on the nearby L'Islet Common.

In Jersey, at St Ouen's Bay on the west coast, extensive research, excavation and landscape study has provided evidence for a Late Neolithic and Early Bronze Age (termed Chalcolithic by the authors) ritual landscape (Patton & Finlaison 2001). The Ossuary close by the Little, Broken and Great Menhirs is likely to have been built during this period (*c.*2850-2250 BC). The monument appears to have been a simple chamber in a round mound but is now ruinous. It was excavated in 1922, when the disarticulated bones of at least 20 people were found. A high percentage of the bone material was made up of skulls and long bones suggesting a burial rite which included excarnation and defleshing of the bones, followed by the internment of the significant ones within the chamber. Two Jersey Bowls were found at the site. A site of similar date at La Tête De Quennevais gave evidence of a ritual/funerary complex of Early Bronze Age date. This consisted of a buried prehistoric land surface, a mound faced on the northern side with granite and shale boulders and two stone cists, sealed under a layer of blown sand. A deposition of three Jersey Bowls, which appear to have been broken in situ, was associated with the primary construction of the mound.

At La Moye, in south-west Jersey, two enclosures were found, constructed of earth and stone revetment and built on an ancient land surface. Foundations of three circular structures were revealed, two of which had artefacts in the floor levels. Finds include hammerstones and grain mullers and a possible polishing stone for axes. The pottery was from vessels with broad flattened rims and flat bases. Some had fingertip impressed decoration. The enclosures suggest an agricultural settlement of *c.*1750–1500 BC (Patton 1984).

At the site of Le Pinacle an earth platform with stone revetment was built at the same time, associated with a natural outcrop. This may be an example of living rock being used as part of a ritual monument. In the Early Bronze Age phase at Le Pinacle more exotic items are present, including the flat copper axe mentioned above and a large assembly of flint from Grand Pressigny in France. These are likely to have been a votive deposit. Similar items have not been found at La Tête De Quennevais, however. Although there are Jersey Bowls present, there is no other evidence of domestic activity, and so the site has been interpreted as part of a funerary complex of Early Bronze Age date. Another type of distinctive Bronze Age pot, a vase from Hougues de Millais in Jersey, can be closely paralleled in Armorica. It is biconical and has four flat handles. The upper section is decorated with 12 horizontal hatched triangles (*33*). Nothing similar has been found on the other islands to date.

At La Hougue Catelain, in the north-east of Guernsey, a small rescue excavation was carried out in the late 1980s on a small ridge of land that survived between two quarries. Although few features could be distinguished, a large quantity of Jersey Bowl sherds was recovered, showing all the known types of decoration (Hill 1990). Other finds associated with the pottery included a loomweight, a spindlewhorl and utilised stones and flint, which would suggest a domestic use, as does the density of material from such a small area.

Also in Guernsey, on the Royal Hotel site, a small ditch feature which cut through the earlier Neolithic deposits contained Jersey Bowl. The ditch was

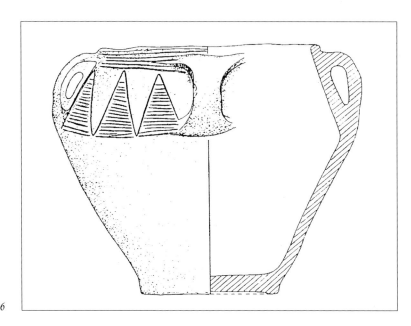

33 Biconical vase from Hougues de Millais, Jersey. *After Briard, 1986*

traced for some 10m across the area and was associated with domestic, rather than burial, features. It appears then that Jersey Bowl can be associated with both settlement sites, as at Les Fouaillages, and burial sites, as at Hougue Mauger and Ville-ès-Nouaux in Jersey (*34*).

Another of the iconic prestige items associated with the Early Bronze Age is the barbed and tanged arrowhead and the Breton examples are particularly fine with elongated barbs. At Kernonen, Finistère, in Brittany, a burial with lavish grave goods includes a bronze dagger with gold studded hilt, an amber wristguard and exquisite ogival flint arrowheads. One such arrowhead has been found at Jerbourg on the south-east tip of Guernsey, where excavations were carried out in the early 1980s on the massive triple-banked promontory earthwork (see below) which had been known since the fourteenth century and first surveyed in the early twentieth century (Derrick 1904). The arrowhead dates to *c*.2000-1700 BC by comparison with examples from sites in Brittany (Briard 1986).

The Early Bronze Age then sees a transition in burial practices from large communal burial mounds into smaller cists, with the introduction of Beaker pottery followed by the local Jersey Bowl and the introduction of metal.

In the later Early Bronze Age, *c*.1900-1500 BC, society changed and in Western Europe small elite groups or chiefdoms developed quite probably because of the new bronzeworking techniques. The Channel Islands has none of the rich burials that characterise Armorica in France and Wessex in southern Britain in the Early Bronze Age. Settlement sites are rare but increasing amounts of undiagnostic pottery from rescue sites in Guernsey may well fill this gap when detailed analysis is carried out. At the prisoner-of-war camp at St Ouen, Jersey, pottery of Middle

34 A group of prehistoric pots from Guernsey. *Guernsey Museum drawn by Barbara McNee*

Bronze Age with flat rims and curving rim and plain cordon was found, which has parallels at Jerbourg on Guernsey (see below) (Patton & Finlaison 2001).

One Middle Bronze Age find from Jersey is exceptional (see back cover illustration). A gold torc was discovered on 17 December 1889 by a workman in Lewis Street, St Helier, in a sandy deposit that was devoid of any other finds (Nicolle 1912). The torc was subsequently restored (Renouf 1974) and its place in Bronze Age goldworking studied by Northover (1989). It is a flange-twisted torc formed from a single gold ingot, with tapered terminals. One terminal was slightly damaged and, in fact, when unrolled there were five pieces that were reshaped into a double loop. It is typical of both the British (Taunton) and French torcs of this type, and might have come from Ireland. It is certainly indicative of connections between the islands, France and England in the area of the western channel in the Middle Bronze Age.

Although Brittany and Normandy continued to be major bronze production areas during the Middle Bronze Age, little material from this period has been identified in the islands. However, a beautifully ornamented bronze bracelet, recently discovered in Sark during building operations for a swimming pool, dates from this period 1400-1300 BC. These decorated bracelets occur on both sides of the English Channel and many palstaves from Brittany and Normandy have been found in southern Britain (O'Connor pers. comm.). At Le Clos de la Sergenté, St Brelade, Jersey, a find of early palstaves and a javelin tip from under a stone buried in a mound was recorded in 1851.

Burial practice changes again in the Later Bronze Age period with cremations under urns being buried in cemeteries or 'urnfields'. At Villes-és-Nouaux in Jersey, in the sand overlaying the megalithic structures, a number of urns were buried in association with cremated remains.

LATE BRONZE AGE METALWORK FROM JERSEY AND ALDERNEY

The situation changes in the Later Bronze Age when, particularly in Jersey, Channel Island metalworkers who were part of a wide network of trade and exchange, began to bury hoards of their metalwork in the ground, suggesting that more metalwork was available than during the Middle Bronze Age. In some cases raw material was included, and sometimes the hoards were in a pot.

Settlement sites of this period are still rare, but in Guernsey a small area of land eroding into the sea at Fort Grey was examined in 1998. A terrace levelled into the natural granite suggested a hut platform on which charcoal, burnt stones and pottery were found. The pottery sherds were from bucket-shaped jars which showed signs of burnishing. Charcoal produced a radiocarbon date of 920-790 BC at 95.4 per cent confidence (OxA-9270) indicating a ninth century BC date for the site.

There is also a Late Bronze Age phase at Le Pinacle, in Jersey, where a basal-loop spear head was found in association with pottery with straight sides and square rims and other vessels with lugs or knobs similar to that from Jerbourg (see below).

Jersey differs considerably from the other islands, however, because of the number of hoards that have now been recovered. In 1836 the first recorded hoard of square-socketed axes was found near the St Helier Town Mills. Out of 88 pieces, two thirds were miniature in size but few now survive. Seven are in the British Museum and one is on display at Guernsey Museum. These Armorican axes belong to the final phase of the Late Bronze Age. Some years later, on 23 November 1871, while a ditch was being dug to plant an apple tree, a hoard of bronzes was found at the property called 'Mainlands' (Hawkes 1937). There were 72 pieces in all, weighing around 24 pounds in weight. The hoard contained socketed axes, socketed spear heads, and a socketed knife. There were also swords and axes, many of which had been broken suggesting either that the pieces were broken ceremonially or that this was a founder's hoard and was raw material for making other products.

A century passed before the next bronze hoard was found, although there had been other finds from the Iron Age throughout the time (see below). On the 28 May 1976 earth moving for the construction of a swimming pool was taking place in the garden of a house named Clos de La Blanche Pierre, St Lawrence, in Jersey. The machining uncovered a pottery vessel containing 'pieces of broken metal which might be swords'. The pot had been damaged by the machine but part survived in situ. Margaret Finlaison's speedy work on the day ensured that sherds of the pot were recovered from the spoil heap including two complete bronze items which were thought to come from the upper part of the pot (35). In total 115 items were recovered. The metal was analysed by Dr J.P. Northover (1987).

The pot was a straight-sided vessel in a coarse fabric with granitic inclusions with the upper edge of rim decorated with pie crust serrations (Finlaison 1981). There were at least two lugs. Pots accompanying hoards are quite rare in Western Europe and quite often pots were not kept when they were discovered as antiquarians prized the metalwork and not the pots. The St Lawrence hoard consisted of weapons, axes, tools and ornaments, casting debris and other miscellaneous items (Coombs 1981). All the objects were broken in antiquity, either deliberately or through wear and tear. Dr Coombs placed it typologically in the earlier part of the Late Bronze Age around 1100 BC; that is before the Mainlands hoard, also from St Lawrence in Jersey, or the hoard found in Alderney at Longis Common (see below). We have no radiocarbon dates yet for hoards from the Channel Islands, so they are dated by similar finds in Britain and France.

In 1995 another hoard was found in Jersey by Brian Cadoret, a member of the Jersey Metal Detectorist Society. It had been scattered across a field due to ploughing and some items had fresh breaks indicating that more material may yet be uncovered. There were 178 pieces of bronze weighing some 11.5kg which were found in a shallow pit, possibly in a leather pot or wooden container. The hoard is of Carp's Tongue type, known after the blade of a distinctive form of

Clockwise from above
1 The Channel Islands from space. *Photograph: Guernsey Museums and Galleries*

2 La Mont de La Ville passage grave by Francis Grose. *By kind permission of the Society of Antiquaries of London*

3 Hand axe from Le Pulec. *Courtesy of the Jersey Heritage Trust / Société Jersiaise Collections*

4 La Cotte de Saint Brelade, Jersey. *Photograph: author*

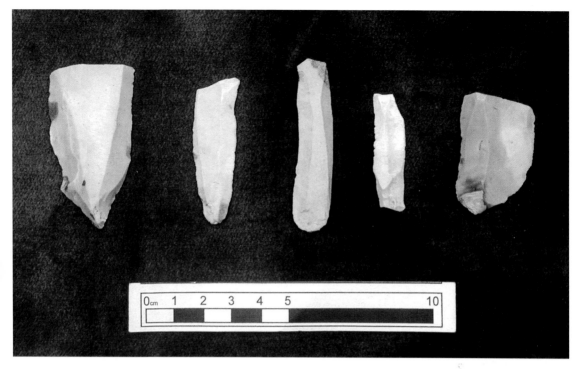

5 Upper Palaeolithic flint blades from Crevichon. *Photograph: Guernsey Museums and Galleries*

6 L'Ouzière (Jersey)Mesolithic axe. *Courtesy of the Jersey Heritage Trust / Société Jersiaise Collections*

7 Above Neolithic Pot from
Le Pinacle, Jersey. *Courtesy of the
Jersey Heritage Trust/Société Jersiaise
Collections*

8 Left La Hougue Bie, Jersey.
Photograph: author

9 Equinoctal sunrise at La Hougue Bie, Jersey. *Photograph: Robin Briault. Courtesy of the Jersey Heritage Trust / Société Jersiaise Collections*

10 Excavations at La Varde, Guernsey, by F.C. Lukis. *Photograph: Guernsey Museums and Galleries*

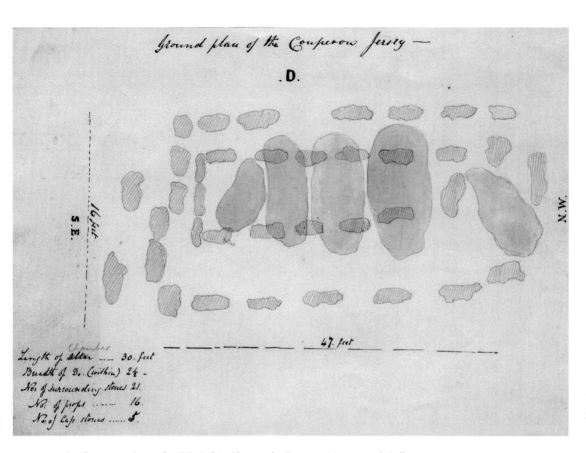

Ground plan of the Couperon Jersey —

.D.

S.E.

16 feet

N.W.

47 feet

Length of altar ____ 30. feet
Breadth of Do. (within) 2¼ -
Nos. of surrounding stones 21.
No: of props ...... 16.
No: of Cap stones ...... 8.

11 Le Couperon, Jersey, by F.C. Lukis. *Photograph: Guernsey Museum and Galleries*

12 Above Ville-ès-Nouaux megalithic complex, Jersey. *Photograph: author*

13 Left Menhir at the Castel church, Guernsey. *Photograph: Guernsey Museums and Galleries*

14 Polished axe in situ at Les Fouaillages, Guernsey. *Photograph: Guernsey Museums and Galleries*

15 Jadeite axe from Jersey. *Courtesy of the Jersey Heritage Trust/Société Jersiaise Collections*

16 Urn from the passage grave of La Varde, Guernsey. *Photograph: Guernsey Museums and Galleries*

17 *Opposite above* A reconstruction of the Iron Age warrior from St Peter Port showing a plan of the grave. *Photograph: Guernsey Museums and Galleries*

18 *Opposite below* An artist's impression of the pottery working site at Les Huguettes, Alderney. *By kind permission of Peter Arnold, Alderney Museum*

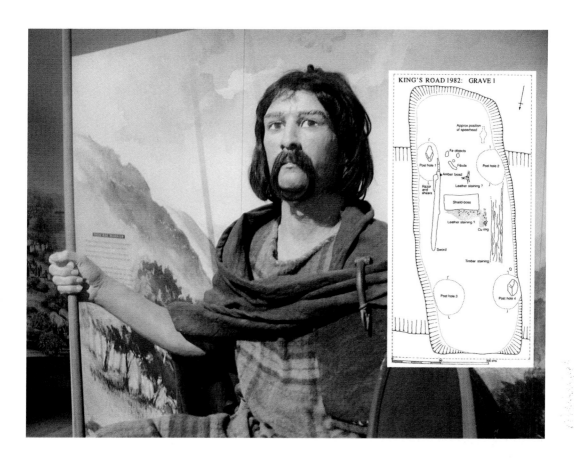

KING'S ROAD 1982: GRAVE 1

19 Artist's impression of Roman ships just off St Peter Port, Guernsey. *Photograph: Guernsey Museums and Galleries*

20 *Opposite above* Lihou Priory excavations looking from the domestic buildings towards the Priory. *Photograph: author*

21 *Opposite below* Medieval brooch from Les Écréhous. *Photograph: Warwick Rodwell. Courtesy of the Jersey Heritage Trust/Société Jersiaise Collections*

22 Castle Cornet, Guernsey. *Photograph: Guernsey Museums and Galleries*

23 Mont Orgueil Castle, Jersey, by Francis Grose 1787. *By kind permission of the Society of Antiquaries of London*

24 Vale Castle, Guernsey. *Photograph: Guernsey Museums and Galleries*

25 Artist's impression of St Peter Port in 1204 based on information from excavations on land and underwater. *Photograph:Guernsey Museums and Galleries*

35 Pot with bronzes from St Lawrence,
Jersey. *Courtesy of the Jersey Heritage Trust/*
Société Jersiaise Collections

sword common in Brittany and used to identify a large group of hoards from
Atlantic France and southern England – similar to those at Mainlands, Jersey, and
Longis, Alderney. It contains ingots, scrap and broken metal, tools and weapons
and most likely belonged to a specialist bronze worker active in the early first
millennium BC. A notable find from the hoard is a fragment of a rotary spit, a
type that probably originated in Portugal and provides evidence of feasting in
the Late Bronze Age (Burgess and O'Connor 2004).

The most recent Jersey hoard was found in 2002 in a field to the south of
St Ouen. It contains some 200 pieces, again found by metal detectorists. It also
contains items of Carp's Tongue type and includes swords, socketed and winged
axes, decorated buckles and buttons, socketed spear heads, socketed gouges and
tanged chisels.

THE ALDERNEY HOARD

A hoard was found in 1832 on Longis Common in Alderney and passed on
to Judge Gaudion who sent it to the Mechanics Institute in Guernsey, whose
President for many years was F.C. Lukis. It was then passed onto the Guille-
Allès Museum which in turn passed it on to Guernsey Museum (*36*). The hoard

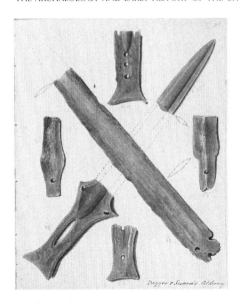

36 Bronzes from the Alderney hoard drawn by F. C. Lukis. *Photograph: Guernsey Museums and Galleries*

contains about 200 objects including broken fragments of Carp's Tongue swords, short-socketed spear points, axes, bracelets, bronze-plated pins and casting debris. These are classic Atlantic items (i.e. typical of material being exchanged along the west coast of France and Britain) (Briard 1986). There are also items that are more British in origin such as barbed spear heads and a socketed sickle with a central circular perforation which is very fine and reminiscent of a bird's head. Near where the hoard was found there is a cremation burial with a bronze bucket-shaped vessel of a type originating in the Alps and also known in Brittany, dated around 500 BC.

In Guernsey there is very little late metalwork known from this period, although one palstave axe was found near Jerbourg (Burns 1988). In Sark a deposit of three broken socketed axes were found in ploughsoil in the centre of the island. This metalwork is the subject of current research. Little has been found on Guernsey suggesting that the island was not as involved in the network of exchange at this period to the same extent as Jersey or Alderney.

There is not space here to go into the detail of the hoards but they indicate that the islands were part of a trade exchange route along the Atlantic seaboard during the Late Bronze Age. The burial of the hoards of metalwork poses many questions. Who buried them and why? Were they ceremonial deposits, the prerogative of some rich chieftain or a ritual deposit of propitiation to unknown gods or deities? Whatever the answers, the practice came to a fairly abrupt end with the phase of Armorican axe hoards and as the use and knowledge of ironworking was spreading across Europe, the islands maintained their importance as links between France and England, culminating in a sophisticated trading network in the late Iron Age.

So few objects survive from the earliest Iron Age that we cannot exactly date the first use of iron in the Channel Islands. Bronze axes, most of them nonfunctional because of their high lead content, were probably deposited until around 600 BC, but iron was probably in use before that. Knowledge of the trade in metalwork throughout the Bronze Age period has been increased by the excavation of a sewn-plank boat with moss caulking found at Dover and dated to *c*.1500 BC (Owen & Frost 2000). Debate as to whether this vessel was suitable for crossing the channel is ongoing but an offshore underwater find containing palstaves from Brittany in Langdon Bay near Dover harbour, and a smaller find off Salcombe in south Devon, would suggest that maritime exchange was thriving around 1200 BC.

DEFENCES OF THE FIRST MILLENNIUM BC

Throughout the years of the millennium before the birth of Christ, defensive earthworks were built in the islands, which may have been a response to some outside threat or an indication of pressure on land within the islands themselves. The largest earthwork of its kind in the Channel Islands is at Jerbourg, Guernsey, and was assumed before excavation to be Iron Age in date. Three banks run across the narrowest part of an isthmus from Petit Port in the west to Divette in the east (Burns 1988). Although the centre of the site has been transformed by medieval and later works, the banks on either flank are well preserved. Above Petit Port there are no ditches, as the cliff itself serves the purpose of defence equally well. On the opposite flank above Divette the banks and associated ditches are most impressive, although this area is heavily wooded. On both sides of the innermost bank are massive platforms erected in the fourteenth century to command the seaward approaches (a contemporary MS mentions mangonels, ballistae and other engines at the site). The Doyle Monument stands on a mound which is probably part of these late medieval defensive works.

The inner rampart was excavated in the early 1980s (37). Lying immediately upon the granite bedrock is a buried soil containing pottery and flint in the form of petit-tranchet and barbed and tanged arrowheads of Late Neolithic/ Early Bronze Age date. On this soil the first stone-faced bank was constructed. This bank was improved at a slightly later date in the form of another stone-faced component placed in front of the original work; the finds from these two phases are similar in nature. During the Bronze Age a massive stone wall, backed by earth, was constructed. Pottery in the fill behind this wall indicates a date of *c*.1200/1000 BC. After a period of neglect during which the Bronze Age work fell into disrepair, the rampart was improved by the addition of a finely constructed stone wall which survived to a height of some 1.5m. The finds from this phase (v) indicate a date range of 600/400 BC. At approximately the same time, a further wall was constructed some 3m down the face of the rampart. Finds from this area are identical to those from phase (v) and it is possible that the two structures were in use at the same time.

During the late third/early second century BC the whole succession of defences was incorporated into a massive glacis-style turf rampart. This was built using material stripped from a nearby occupation site and the turf contained large quantities of pottery dating to the period. Also discovered were many carbonised examples of the Celtic Bean. This turf addition was sparsely reinforced on its outer face by a thin layer of small stones including several broken querns and rubbing stones.

Also in Guernsey, pottery which dates from around the fifth-sixth centuries BC was found during excavations at the Vale Castle 1980s indicating that it was a defended hill fort. Many other defended sites have now been identified along Guernsey's south coast (Burns et al. 1996).

In Jersey, at Le Câtel De Rozel, a large scale promontory fort, also known as La Petite Césaree, is another defensive system which appears to have begun around the same time as Jerbourg. The earliest phase was an early bank consisting of a linear pile of stone slabs and turf just over 2m wide and 0.8m high which was built in the Late Neolithic or Early Bronze Age (Cunliffe 1992). The earthwork may have stayed in use throughout the Bronze Age as the main rampart was

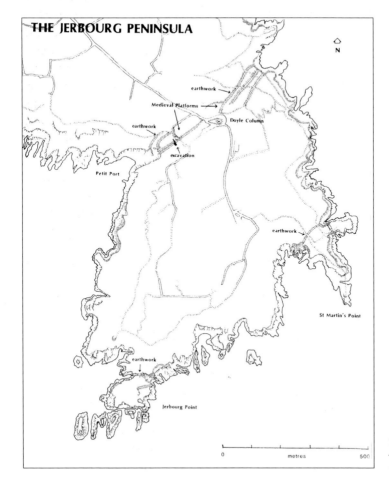

37 Earthworks at Jerbourg, Guernsey. *After Burns* (1988)

constructed in the Middle Iron Age c.400 BC. This was massive a bank c.10m wide and 6m high and Barry Cunliffe suggests that to build it might have been an act of the entire island population. Building terraces between the bank and the next headland gave evidence of settlement into the Late Iron Age. Other defended sites in Jersey included Frémont Point which was excavated in the 1950s (Cotton 1958) but little was found; the earthworks consist of a single bank and ditch. At Câtel de Lecq, two concentric banks and ditches make a larger site. In Alderney, Essex Hill has similar defences. Evidence of a bank and ditch suggest a small defended hill fort existed in the period c.850 BC.

THE EARLY IRON AGE 700–400 BC

Evidence for Early Iron Age settlement in the islands is not plentiful but in Alderney at Les Huguettes a site from this period was excavated in the 1970s. It is situated on the golf course, just inland from Longis Bay, which has a good natural harbour, on the east coast of Alderney. An enclosed platform was revealed within an area of 120m² which was interpreted as a pottery working site (*colour plate 18*). The whole was surrounded by a drystone wall. The pottery found included large jars with neck cordons, decorated with finger impressions, shouldered bowls, some with domed (omphalos) bases, shouldered jars and hemispherical bowls (*38*). A razor was also recovered, of a type most common in Britain and contemporary with Armorican socketed axes, all pointing to a date of the eighth or seventh centuries BC. Spindle-whorls were also recovered and animal bones included red and roe deer, sheep and oxen. The material from Les Huguettes is

38 Pottery from Les Huguettes, Alderney. *Alderney Museum drawn by Barbara McNee*

similar to pottery from British sites of a similar period (Cunliffe 1986). Some of the pots were carefully restored by Peggy Wilson and are on view at Alderney Museum. The proximity of the site to Longis Bay on the east coast of the island might be indicative of early trading between the Islands, France and Britain.

In Guernsey, during the Kings Road excavation (Site 2, see below), an Early Iron Age ditch was excavated with pottery of fifth- or sixth-century date, including a large cylinder-necked jar. Another sherd was coated with haematite, similar to one in the Lukis collection from Herm. A group of sherds from Jerbourg Point have also been recovered which are similar to pots from Brittany dated to the fifth century BC. These finds, while not of any great importance in themselves, give evidence of contact with Brittany, Normandy and Southern Britain. Kimmeridge shale bracelet rough-outs, which have been found on Herm and underwater in St Peter Port harbour, provide further evidence of early trade links, indicating trade with the south coast of Britain in the Early Iron Age.

In 1994, during deep trenching for drainage works on L'Ancresse Common, a small group of bronze items was discovered, including four copper alloy bracelets with knobbed terminals and a twisted copper alloy neck ring. There was also a human tooth, discoloured by proximity to metal, which suggests that this may have been an Early Iron Age burial.

SALT WORKING

The Middle Iron Age period, from around 400-120 BC has less tangible evidence, however, but it is likely that maritime links continued in the search for tin and other commodities. At St Helier, Jersey, a site with pottery similar to Breton material was excavated in Broad Street by Margaret Finlaison in the 1970s. Amongst the material is a fine shallow bowl with incised half palmette decoration on the exterior which has been dated to c.400-300 BC (Finlaison 1977). There was a stone-built structure with a hearth from which carbonised grain of five-row barley was recovered.

Salt working or briquetage sites have been recently examined in Guernsey and Herm and were previously known from Jersey at Bulwarks Bay, St Aubins (Godfray 1931). Salt was an important commodity in the Iron Age and islanders seem to have exploited the low-lying areas where access to the sea was relatively simple and wood for burning was in sufficient supply. Many of the sites have been identified because of modern day coastal erosion and the characteristic finds include firebars, hand bricks and cylindrical vessels in a bright red earthenware. The sites are difficult to date but Iron Age coins from Armorica and north-west France were found in the vicinity of the site at Richmond, Guernsey. The sites in Guernsey appeared to have a distribution along the low-lying west coast but recent excavations in St Peter Port on the east coast have also produced hand bricks and sherds in early Roman contexts. Professor Cunliffe remarks that it is difficult to tell from current evidence if the salt was produced on an industrial scale or whether it was for domestic use (Cunliffe & de Jersey 2000). Similar sites are found on the north Breton coast and were most productive from 100 BC-AD 100.

LATE IRON AGE 120-50 BC

During the hundred years or so before the birth of Christ the situation in the individual islands seems to have differed substantially. This may be partly explained by geography, in that at this time Guernsey was more approachable in larger boats than Jersey. Currents, tidal ranges and the reefs and rocks around the islands make the approaches difficult even today. Sea levels which, as we have seen, are so crucial to the accessibility and very size and shape of the islands and islets, fluctuated at the end of the first millennium BC and rose in the Roman period. During the lowered sea level Jersey would have been very unapproachable because of the extensive rocks and reefs which surround the main island. Iron Age pottery has been found on both reefs of Les Écréhous and Les Minquiers, which would have been substantially larger than today. Evidence of increasingly important settlements and trade routes between the Islands, northern Brittany and Normandy exists from the Late Iron Age. By this time exotic goods from the Mediterranean were making their way across France into the Atlantic exchange networks. The most distinctive were wine amphorae of the type known as Dressel 1a (see Chapter 6), which have been found at both Kings Road in Guernsey and, more recently, at the Bonded Store, St Peter Port. At this period, Guernsey seems to have been the principal port used by those involved in the systems of exchange linking Armorica with central southern Britain.

WARRIOR GRAVES

In Guernsey a warrior class of chieftains, who were presumably tribal leaders, have been found buried in graves with a full range of their highly prized material possessions. No such graves have been found to date in Jersey or Alderney, although there are some spectacular examples of depositions of coins and metalwork in Sark and Jersey in the Late Iron Age (see below), including a possible part of a shield boss from Jersey (Fitzpatrick & Megaw 1987). The chance discovery of two glass beads typical of the period at St Aubins and St Helier in Jersey may be indicative of further settlements in that island but to date they are undiscovered.

Several warrior burials were recorded in Guernsey by Lukis in the nineteenth century, including those at Les Issues, Les Adams and La Hougue Au Comte, which were single cists. Others were found at Le Catioroc, Richmond and

St Saviours Church, and, more recently, at Kings Road, where there were larger groups of burials associated with a late La Tène settlement. Kings Road, Guernsey was excavated in the early 1980s and a new part of the site is being excavated in 2005.

The excavations revealed a settlement surrounded by a palisaded ditch. The post-holes from a single round house were on a high part of the site. Other features included a blacksmith's forge and weaving equipment. Wine was imported in Dressel 1a amphorae. This type is well documented from wreck sites and came by sea from Italy to southern France, then overland to the east coast probably to Bordeaux and from there up the western coast of France to Armorica and beyond. Fine pottery was imported from France including rilled wares, black cordoned wares and graphite-coated wares. Fragments of shale bracelets were found as well as part of a turned shale vessel, which must have come from Dorset and possibly through Hengistbury Head (Burns et al. 1996).

A small cemetery was excavated in 1982 as part of a rescue operation prior to the building of a small housing estate. The cemetery was situated approximately 50m away from the settlement site, which was excavated in 1980 and 1983. Graves were found over quite a large area. At Site 3 two graves were found surrounded with angular, unworked granite stones and contained no finds. They were aligned almost east–west. At the adjoining Site 2 two further graves were found. The smaller of these had no contents, the larger contained a variety of grave goods. These graves were aligned north-south. The largest grave had originally been outlined by a four post structure which was presumably visible above ground. Traces of timber planking were visible on the eastern side of the burial. The contents of the grave included an iron sword in its scabbard, an iron knife and pair of shears, a shield boss, spear head, iron fibula, an iron and a bronze ring, amber bead and various sheet-iron fittings. During conservation a great deal of information was able to be extracted from the objects. The leather thongs used to suspend the sword were preserved as mineralised products and the knots and suspension methods survived, the amber bead was attached to the sword, a habit still prevalent during the Anglo-Saxon (Merovingian) period. The knife and shears were kept in a sheepskin sheath with fleece on the inside; the outside was decorated with tooling. The shield appears to have been laminated with layers of wood, leather and horn. Two types of cloth were also mineralised into the corrosion products, a finer weave worn close to the body and a coarser variety worn as outer clothing. A reconstruction of the warrior is displayed at Guernsey Museum (*colour plate 17*).

Another Late Iron Age settlement site at the Tranquesous, Guernsey, was discovered by aerial photography in 1976. Post-holes from up to 15 circular huts were found, each surrounded by a penannular ditch. A double-ditched trackway and a series of ditched enclosures, possibly for livestock containment, were also found. There was evidence of metalworking. The settlement is dated from the finds to c.50 BC to AD 150 (Burns 1977).

COIN HOARDS

The situation on Jersey is completely different. No warrior burials have been discovered but substantial hoards of Armorican coinage have been found at Le Câtel de Rozel and at other Jersey sites. At Rozel the discoveries have been made on several occasions mostly in the nineteenth century by chance finds and from landslips and exposure after storms (39). The coins, about a thousand in number, are mainly Staters of the Coriosolites tribe who were centered on Alet in northern France. In the parish of Grouville, a hoard of some 3000 Coriosolites coins was found, along with some other precious objects, including three bronze fibulae, two small rings and a small amount of metal braid (McCammon 1984). These hoards are small, however, compared to that found at La Marquanderie, St Brelade's, Jersey, which contained almost 12,000 coins and still forms one of the largest single deposits in the western Celtic world (de Jersey 1998). These hoards have been interpreted as the result of unrest on the French mainland because of Caesar's expansion northwards in 56 BC. The Marquanderie hoard fits this pattern but the others are later. The Le Catillon hoard contains coins of other Gaulish tribes including the Redones, Aulerci Cenomani, Osismii, Baiocasses and Abrincatui and although the hoard does not contain any Roman coins it has been dated to between 40-20 BC (ibid.).

There is little known from Alderney in the Late Iron Age, although the island was important in the Roman period (see Chapter 6). On Sark, however, a spectacular hoard was found in the eighteenth century which has since been lost. It did contain some coins, apparently in an earthenware pot, which were

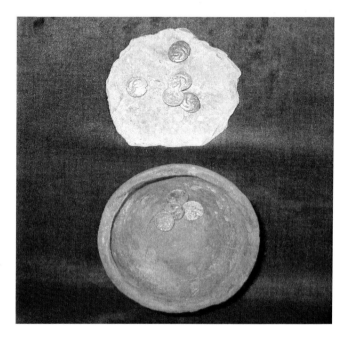

39 A small hoard of coins from Rozel, Jersey found in a pot with a stone lid in 1883. *Courtesy of the Jersey Heritage Trust / Société Jersiaise Collections*

mainly Gaulish with three Roman, but there was also a deposit of elaborately decorated metalwork (Allen 1971). These were silver-gilded phalerae or discs in a Thracian style (*40*). An unidentified lump of material may have been amber or horn. Fortunately excellent engravings were made at the time so the find is not entirely lost. One possibility is that this was booty hidden by a Roman soldier on the move from mainland France (de Jersey 1998).

The explanation for the differing archaeological record of the main islands may be one of geography or, as Dr de Jersey suggests, the islands may have had differing political control by this time. The more northerly geographical position of Guernsey may also have been a factor. Any shipping sailing on the hazardous route across the Channel from, for example, Alet to Hengistbury Head, would be far more likely to call in at Guernsey for water, supplies or shelter from inclement weather, than at Jersey, situated just a few hours from the Gaulish mainland. It must be said, of course, that the opposite case would prevail in the event of a north–south voyage.

It seems then, that Guernsey's geographical position on the busy trade route between Gaul and Britain was occupied and exploited by a warrior caste which no doubt played a part in the trade and took its dues. Similar warrior burials are found in Normandy, the richest of which was excavated at La Maille-raye-sur-Seine (Seine-Maritime), (Verron 2000). In Jersey the inhabitants may have been more affiliated to the Coriosolites tribe but, as is suggested by Caesar himself, the Veneti may have controlled the trading routes. The subject of who controlled the seas at this time is a complex one, but it is interesting that so few coins have been found on Guernsey.

For a long time it had been assumed that the islands were bypassed in the Roman period but new discoveries both on land and under the sea have changed the picture considerably as shown in the next chapter.

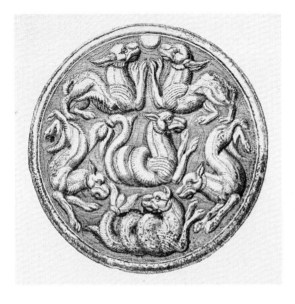

40 The six beast phalera from the Sark Hoard, drawn by George Vertue in 1725. *By kind permission of the Society of Antiquaries of London*

6

ON THE EDGE OF EMPIRE: THE ROMANS IN THE CHANNEL ISLANDS

Now of all the peoples of the coastal part of that area, the Veneti are by far the strongest. They have a great many ships and regularly sail to and from Britain. When it comes to knowledge and experience of navigation they leave all the other tribes standing. (Caesar *De Bello Gallico* iii 8. Trans. Wiseman 1980)

In the year before his first expedition Caesar had fought and destroyed at sea the fleet of the Veneti of Brittany, whose ships had controlled the carrying trade between Armorica and south-west Britain. (Salway 2000)

The Romans probably never conquered the islands...(Bender 1986)

INTRODUCTION

Until relatively recently the latter of the quotes by Barbara Bender summed up what Channel Island schoolchildren were taught about the Roman period. This was due to the fact that 20 years or so ago the only Roman discoveries in the islands were chance finds of coins, including small hoards from Jerbourg and St Sampsons in Guernsey, and Les Quennevais in Jersey, and a few sherds of Samian pottery from the earlier megaliths. The story has now changed dramatically as many rescue excavations and underwater discoveries have provided enough evidence to show that the islands must have been 'Romanised' and in fact played a vital role in the transportation of goods from various parts of the Roman world to northern Gaul and Britain (*41*).

By the beginning of the Late Iron Age period, *c.*150 BC, the islands were already part of an intricate trading network. Later, this involved both regional and long distance interaction, although as we have seen in Chapter 5 the two larger islands appear to have had different settlement patterns.

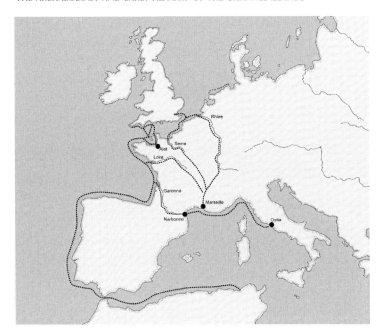

41 Roman trading routes at the end of the first millennium BC

Developments in the wider Roman world began to impinge on the Channel Islands around 120 BC, when the Romans occupied southern Gaul. The province of Gallia Transalpina was established and soon after new trade routes came into use, bringing Roman goods to North Gaul and the coast of Britain. The shipment of cargos of wine was the main concern but other merchandise was also transported to ports such as Narbonne in southern Gaul from where it was distributed to various parts of the country, overland and by river, e.g. down the Gironde to Bordeaux and up the Atlantic coast by ship and onwards to Poole or Southampton (Clausentum). Goods destined for Britain may have taken this route and the Channel Islands, and in particular Guernsey, offered an ideal stop-off point between the ports of northern Gaul and southern Britain.

Wine, which was carried in amphorae or large storage jars, was exchanged for slaves and raw materials such as tin and hides. The most common amphora at this time was a type known as Dressel 1a which dates from the first half of the first century BC. They have been found in Nacqueville and Coutances in western Normandy (Cunliffe 1986a) and Brittany, particularly from shipwrecks off Les Sables d'Olonne and Île d'Yeu (Galliou 1986). They are found at Hengistbury Head and other sites in central southern Britain which suggests that the wine trade was well established before Caesar's abortive campaigns to the British mainland (Cunliffe 2001). Sherds of Dressel 1a amphora have been found in Guernsey at Les Tranquesous, St Saviours, Kings Road, St Peter Port and at the Bonded Stores (see below). At Kings Road four of the sherds were in a distinctive 'black-sand' fabric. This has been shown to originate in the Pompeii-Herculaneum area of Italy (Williams 1996). In Jersey a sherd of Dressel 1a was found during excavations at Old Street in St Helier, on the south coast (Wood 1989). These trade routes are likely to have been disrupted during Caesar's Gallic campaigns, but after the defeat of the Veneti at sea in 56 BC, northern Gaul was also taken into the Empire. Britain, of course, remained outside full Roman control until the Claudian invasion of AD 43.

The Romans are often considered to have been reluctant sailors and so would have hugged the coast of western France and Brittany before venturing out into the open sea. The tidal movements of the Atlantic coast and the Channel would have been completely alien to those used to the Mediterranean (Salway 2000). Seán McGrail has studied shipping and seamanship in the first millennium BC (1983) and suggested that the route between the north coast of France, the Channel Islands and onward to Britain is not without its problems. These routes would also have required goods to be brought via the Gironde or Loire Rivers and overland to the River Rance. Despite any difficulties, however, it is now well proven that this route was used for a long period of time, as the Dressel 1a amphorae were only the first indicators of Roman presence in the islands.

The Late Iron Age inhabitants of the islands were still very much in occupation when the first Roman traders or soldiers arrived. At the Tranquesous, St Saviour's, in Guernsey, a Late Iron Age ditched village with round post-built houses was excavated in 1976 (see Chapter 5). It was in use from c.80 BC–AD 50 and alongside the later Iron Age material were finds from the early Roman period including two sherds of Samian pottery, terra nigra wares and other locally made, but Roman inspired, pottery. Amphora sherds of Dressel 1a were found alongside a sherd from an amphora from southern Spain which dates to c.AD 75. These goods were initially thought to represent material traded from north-western Gaul and used by the native population, but more recent discoveries would suggest that the islands in fact became part of the Empire at the same time as the rest of Gaul (officially this was not until 12 BC when an altar to Augustus was dedicated in Lugdunum – modern day Lyons).

Early pottery of the same types as that found at Le Tranquesous has been excavated at the Bonded Stores, St Peter Port, where there is also an Iron Age horizon sealed below a layer of silt.

In the latter half of the first century BC the wine trade continued from Italy in a type of amphora known as Dressel 1b, suggesting that the trade routes went further east overland via the Rhone valley and the Seine to eastern England, although some Dressel 1b sherds were also found at Kings Road. Professor Cunliffe remarks on the later first century BC that, 'overland routes through Gaul to the southern North Sea ports now took the bulk of the trade leaving the Atlantic sea lanes to shrink back to local cabotage' (Cunliffe 2001, 399).

However, some trade continued around the Channel Islands, but the amphorae sherds found suggest that it was Spain rather than Italy that the ships set out from at that time with their cargos of wine. Spanish amphorae known as Pascual 1 were found at the Bonded Stores in Guernsey (see below).

It would be possible to follow the Romanisation of the islands and the trading patterns that ensued just by examining the amphorae that have been recovered both from land sites and under the sea around the islands, but a much fuller picture emerges when the rich array of finds, and in particular pottery, from recent excavations is considered.

GUERNSEY

At Kings Road, St Peter Port, there was a reoccupation of the first century BC settlement (see Chapter 5) by the Romans during the late second century AD. The sherds of a complete Samian bowl were among the finds (*42*), surviving miraculously between two builders' trenches and carefully restored by Bob Burns (former Archaeology Officer at Guernsey Museum). The bowl was made in Trier in eastern Gaul *c*.AD 160 and had the makers stamp 'HONORATI' on the interior (*43*). Although there was no evidence for structures in the area that was examined in this later phase at Kings Road, a range of domestic ware was recovered, including North Gaulish grey wares, terra nigras, Romano-British wares and coarse grey wares (Hartley, Williams and Wood in Burns et al. 1996). By the time this activity was going on at Kings Road, which is set in a wooded plateau some distance from the sea at St Peter Port, the site of La Plaiderie would have also been in use. At the time of writing further excavation is going on in a new area of the Kings Road settlement now being redeveloped, so further Roman finds may be uncovered.

La Plaiderie is at the north end of the town and during excavations between 1983 and 1985 it provided the first evidence of Roman life in the islands as well as evidence of Guernsey's role as an entrepôt or stopover for the entrepreneurs making their way on the trade routes north or south between northern Gaul and southern Britain.

The site takes its name from the medieval courthouse or 'pleading place' of the town, but had served as a waterfront trading station during the Roman period between *c*.AD 100-400. There were two large stone buildings found, interpreted as warehouses, which had replaced earlier wooden structures. The buildings originally had thick low granite walls about 3-4ft high with wooden studwork or plaster and wattle partitions above. Their roofs were tiled and the outside yards had well-made stone drains. Various pits and gullies were also found associated with the buildings (*44*).

The buildings stood close to the high water mark (slightly inland today). As such they were ideally situated to take advantage of the gently sloping beach where vessels could be unloaded with little difficulty (Burns 1985). Special features on the site included a small smelting complex possibly used for coin counterfeiting; many broken coin moulds were discovered. Two of the complete examples were used to copy coins of Severus Alexander AD 222-235, and Philip I AD 224-249.

42 Sherds of a complete Samian bowl in situ at Kings Road, St Peter Port Guernsey. *Photograph: Guernsey Museums and Galleries*

43 The Kings Road Samian bowl from Trier in eastern France, after restoration. *Photograph: Guernsey Museums and Galleries*

44 The waterfront site at La Plaiderie, St Peter Port, under excavation. *Photograph Guernsey Museums and Galleries*

Dating for the site is provided by this coin evidence and points to a life-span from the early second century AD until the late fourth century AD. Mark Wood, who is examining the pottery, has suggested that this might imply a military or naval presence at the site, when considered alongside pottery types from northern France and the Picardy region (see below), and also from further east in Germany (Wood 2000). Was the Classis Britannica (the Roman fleet) calling into the islands in search of shelter or raw materials?

A human cremation burial in an earthenware urn was also excavated and to the south of one of the buildings the complete skeleton of a pig was found. An indication of what might have brought the use of the site to a close was found in the form of large areas of burning and apparent rapid demolition of the buildings, although the burning could also have occurred as a result of purely domestic fires.

Over 6000 sherds of pottery were recovered, of which nearly 400 were Samian ware. The pottery was from Gaul, particularly Le Pas-de-Calais and Picardy, but also from Spain, the Rhineland and Britain, strongly suggesting that there was movement of goods both north and south and their import and export may have been controlled on the site. The Samian pottery from La Plaiderie ranges from the Tibero-Claudian period to the third century. The material is divided into South Gaulish, Central Gaulish (mostly Lezoux) and East Gaulish (information, Brenda Dickinson).

Metal finds included bronze and silver coins, a stylus for writing, intaglio finger-rings, one with a cupid, another inscribed 'VALE' (farewell) and portions of bronze vessels. Evidence was found of Roman religious practice in the form of a pipe-clay figure of Venus and a mortarium with an inscription which reads 'DIV.I.S.' (INVICTUS SYLVANUS). The inscription refers to Silvanus the god of orchards, groves and of kitchens! Amongst the objects made of glass were beads, finger-rings and bottle and window glass. One of the glass vessels was from Cologne reflecting the provenance of some of the pottery.

It seems likely then that the Plaiderie served as a stopping-off place for ships engaged in the cross-Channel trade, perhaps needing to shelter from bad weather but also taking on water and supplies (Burns 1985).

THE BONDED STORES, GUERNSEY

The excavation of the Bonded Stores site in St Peter Port has increased our knowledge about the Roman period in the islands considerably. Excavations began in January 1996 in advance of the Victorian Market Buildings being redeveloped. The massive foundations of this part of the market were built in 1872 before mechanical excavators were used on building sites, so the archaeological layers survived intact in between the piers. Digging conditions were difficult, however, as the excavation work was inside the vaulted basement of the market buildings and had to be carried out under electric arc lights. Although it was not physically possible to sieve the contents of every feature, this was done where possible to retrieve the maximum amount of material.

The site is situated in the heart of modern St Peter Port very close to the parish church of St Peter (built by 1052). It is at the bottom of one of the two valleys that border the town and in the Roman period would have been a hundred metres or so from the waterfront. The main finds from the excavation were from the Roman period around the second century AD, although there were several earlier phases. Structural remains of buildings were sometimes located under later medieval walls. There was evidence of metalworking in the higher part of the site. Part of a small iron smelting furnace was excavated. It had been vertically truncated by the foundations of the Bonded Store but it was possible to reconstruct the furnace from what was left. It was built with a dome of clay over a clay floor from which a flue directed the molten metal to a sump area. Quantities of slag were recovered which suggested that the material had been reused and heated to a high temperature (Salter pers. comm.). Vitrified furnace lining fragments were also found in some quantity (45). In another area of the site a building appeared to have burnt down in situ leaving traces of burnt timbers and quantities of floor and roof tile. Inside the buildings many types of cooking pots and jars were found. In all, over 5000 sherds of pottery were

45 A reconstruction of metal working at the Bonded Stores, Guernsey. Artist's impression. *Guernsey Museums and Galleries*

recovered of which approximately 450 were Samian ware. There are many other types of pot present including flagons and bowl and cup forms from a wide variety of sources in southern, central and eastern Gaul. A considerable number of tripod bowls were found with blackened surfaces which may suggest their use as portable cooking pots or holders of oil for lamps (M. Wood, pers. comm.). No clay lamps, so common elsewhere, have been found in the islands. The pottery dated from the later first century through to the third century AD. The Bonded Stores assemblage indicates that Guernsey was receiving high percentages of products from East Gaul, which Wood considers is unusual as this is not the case on sites west of the Seine in France or south-western Britain. The coarse wares also show strong links with the areas of the Rhine, the Argonne and northern France (Wood 2002). Amongst the Samian ware were two pots with the makers stamp on them, COBNERTIANUS, and another, MAGIO. (50) Cobnertianus was a potter who worked at Lezoux, in Central Gaul, around AD 160-190 and Magio also worked at Lezoux in the same period (information Brenda Dickinson).

Along with the sherds of Dressel 1a amphora mentioned above, Dressel 20 amphora sherds from Spain were also present. These would have held wine, fish sauce or olive oil from the Mediterranean. Mortaria for preparing food were also found. Glass fragments were retrieved including several pieces of vessel handles and a tiny fragment of a polychrome pillar-moulded bowl (V. Ferneyhough pers. comm.). A lump of raw glass was also found, which might imply that glass working was going on in the area (Price 2002). Although Roman coin evidence from the Bonded Stores was lacking, a single Iron Age coin from the Baiocasses tribe was recovered from one of the earlier phases (de Jersey pers. comm.). Of the more exotic finds, there were two intaglios or engraved gemstones, one was of cornelian, showing a three-headed figure (Gryllus). The three heads were a bald and bearded head of Silenus, a second head possibly of Dionysus and a boar's head (46). The second intaglio was of glass, showing Prometheus creating man. Both dated from the second century AD (Henig 1999). As with La Plaiderie religious observance is suggested by parts of two Venus figurines. The site is in an area of known fresh water and, indeed, one of the neighbouring streets is now called Fountain Street. A stream runs through the site and the parish church of St Peter Port is also very close by and it is not unreasonable to assume that an earlier temple structure might have been in the area (McCormack 1986). Many of the finds are undergoing specialist examination, but results so far indicate that the Roman presence was quite substantial and long lasting and that Roman St Peter Port was not just a trading outpost but a lively bustling town (47).

OTHER ROMAN MATERIAL FROM GUERNSEY

Many rescue sites that have been excavated in Guernsey have produced Roman finds. Also, beach walking during very low tides along the foreshore around St

46 An intaglio on carnelian with a three headed figure (Gryllus). The three heads were a bald and bearded head of Silenus, a second head possibly of Dionysus and a boar's head (Henig,1999). *Photograph: Institute of Archaeology, Oxford*

47 An artist's impression of the harbourside of St Peter Port around AD 160. *Photograph: Guernsey Museums and Galleries*

Peter Port and in particular in the area below Castle Cornet, known as Cow Bay, has produced considerable quantities of pottery. One sherd of Samian ware was recently recovered with the maker's stamp 'AKPERRI' on it. This was a potter working at Lezoux about AD 150. From recent fieldwalking in the Bailiff's Cross area of Guernsey a lead curse tablet was found amongst roof and floor tiles. The tablet was unrolled but did not have writing on it. We are left to imagine the curse that whoever discarded it might have inscribed on it!

In the 1980s a small excavation at 18/20 the Pollet revealed a small quantity of Gallo-Roman finds beneath the medieval levels. More recently Roman material has been recovered from the Royal Hotel site on the waterfront of St Peter Port. Slightly further inland at Les Canichers, briquetage or salt working material was found in association with early Roman pottery, some of which was from the Durotriges tribe from southern Britain (Wood pers. comm.). Perhaps of more interest, as the site is in the centre of Guernsey, is material recovered from excavations in 1998 at the Castel church, during renovations. In 1878 Sir Edgar MacCulloch had described what he thought to be part of a Roman hypocaust (or underfloor heating) system which had been uncovered by workmen during refurbishment of the church. A considerable amount of Roman building material had also been identified in the fabric of the church and it has long been considered a prime location for a Roman camp (as the name Castel would indicate – from castellum or castrum). This building material included floor tile, roof tile, bipedalis tile from a hypocaust and opus signinum or Roman plaster, all suggesting a Roman building in the vicinity. In addition, built into the south-west wall of the porch is part of an inscription on two squared blocks of Caen stone (limestone) both showing capital 'N's (McCormack 1986). No sign of the Roman feature described by MacCulloch was found during the excavations in 1998; however, an undisturbed Roman layer was located next to the ossuary which MacCulloch described and the cut made by the Victorian workmen was located. A small area of this Roman feature yielded a large quantity of roof tile and at least one sherd of pottery. It was also thought that a wall running parallel with the north wall of the present church was from a Roman building. However, recent trenching for electrical cables around the church did not reveal any structure, although quantities of mortar and tile were retrieved indicating Roman occupation in the vicinity.

JERSEY AND THE OFFSHORE ISLANDS

Although Jersey has not yet produced the same amount of excavated Roman material as Guernsey, the accumulated evidence from antiquarian records and recent finds suggest the island was also Romanised. Because of its geographical position and its reefs, currents and the tidal conditions, it did not have the same number of good natural landing places as Guernsey, although some areas of the south-east coast were approachable and the east coast by the present Gorey harbour is very close to France. The earliest ceramic evidence of Roman contact is the Dressel 1a amphora from Old Street in St Helier mentioned above. However, during 1930-1936 excavations at the multi-phase site at Le Pinacle, sherds of two bowls were uncovered which were burnished on the insides and had rims that were later recognised as typical of black burnished ware (Finlaison 1978). These were indeed from the Dorset black burnished ware industry. One sherd was from a cooking pot and one from a shallower 'dog dish' (Wood 1989). The sherds were examined for heavy mineral analysis by David Williams of Southampton University, who confirmed that they were similar to those from Poole or Wareham in Dorset. They were typical of pots made between AD 250-400 which coincides with a period of increased activity at Alet, the capital of the Coriosolites from AD 275-320 (Langouët 1973). During work at St Ouen's Bay, on the west coast of Jersey, Roman pottery was recovered particularly at the prisoner-of-war camp. These are mostly wheel-made grey wares.

Another find now in the Jersey Museum collections is a small Roman brooch described as 'from a Druids temple near St Aubin, Jersey'. The brooch was classified as a 'Colchester derivative' type after the distribution of similar types in the centre and south-east of Britain. It is likely to date to the late first or early second century AD. On the Écréhous reef other finds of pottery include the rim and neck of single-handled ring-neck flagon found during excavations. This was a large vessel, wheel-made with a smooth, slightly micaeous grog-tempered fabric. It is known as the 'pulley-wheel' form which is characteristic of mid-second century AD. Other sherds included the base of a flagon, mortaria sherds, grey wares and a sherd of a Gauloise amphora (Wood 1996). The most substantial evidence to date of a Roman site in Jersey is at St Clements churchyard. In 1987, the Jersey Museum Service was alerted to the fact that Gallo-Roman pottery was being found during digging in the area of the new graveyard to the west of St Clement's church, which is situated in the south-west of Jersey. A rescue excavation directed by Hilary Stuart-Williams revealed a pit and drainage gullies containing the majority of the Gallo-Roman pottery sherds from the site, which have been examined by Mark Wood. The sherds represent about 25 vessels, over half of which are internally grooved rim jars and everted rim cooking-pots produced in a coarse, mainly reduced fabric. There is also a cup, sherds of Beakers and jars in a variety of 'fumed' and black-slipped terra nigra and imitation terra nigra-type fabrics, of Central and West Gaulish origin, many of which are identical in both fabric and form to those found at the Tranquesous in Guernsey, described by Burns (1977, 207-208). There is also a body sherd of South Gaulish Samian ware, 15 sherds of fine Gallo-Roman grey wares, 30 flagon sherds (representing at least three vessels), and a single body sherd of a Dressel 20 Spanish amphora (Henig and Wood 1990).

This pottery from St Clement's ranges in date from the first to the late second century AD. Early in 1989, fieldwalking in the area and grave-digging near to where the rescue excavation took place produced further pottery. A rim sherd of a Samian ware mortarium, probably made at Lezoux and dating to the second century AD, was among the finds as was the only stamped sherd of Samian ware from Jersey. This basal sherd (examined by Brenda Dickinson) bears the name stamp of the potter (S)COTNVS who worked at La Graufesenque in southern Gaul during the Claudio-Neronian period (AD 41-68).

The evidence produced by the pottery from St Clement's demonstrates that the site was occupied from the Bronze Age until the end of the second century AD, although the major presence is undoubtedly of Roman date (ibid.). In the same area of St Clements a bronze figure was found which was examined by Martin Henig and Mark Wood (1990). The figure was the upper part of a cast bronze of a nude male figure. It is broken at the waist, immediately below the navel, which may have provided a point of weakness and in relation to the body the pear-shaped head is large. These naturalistic bronzes were imported across the Alps and up the Rhone valley and copied in Gaul. Early bronzes are also known from Britain. The bronze figure could indicate that the area fulfilled some sort of religious function during the Late Iron Age or Early Roman period, and it may be significant that there is a long tradition of buildings with a religious function in the immediate vicinity. These include a priory, and the church of St Clements itself, dedicated to St Clement who was Bishop of Rome in the second century AD (Messervy 1913, 345).

A more substantial structure survives at Le Pinacle, St Ouen's, on Jersey's west coast. The foundations of walls of a rectangular stone-built construction were excavated in the 1930s. The structure has been interpreted as a Gallo-Roman *fanum*, or temple, dating from about AD 200 onwards (48). There is an outer wall with an entrance to the east with surviving door jambs. This surrounds a second inner wall, again with entrance to the east. This was a rudimentary Celtic type similar to the *fana* of Armorica (Langouët 1986). The layout has been interpreted as a central *cella* with a surrounding *ambulatory* of north-west Gaulish type. The excavator Burdo's original notes suggest that there were pits under the walls which may have had a ritual nature (Finlaison pers. comm.). There was also evidence that small altars were present. Coin finds and the imported Roman pottery suggest a period of use in the third century AD. This is the only surviving Roman building in Jersey that is known at present although there is great potential at the St Clement's site for further discoveries.

Not only is Jersey prolific in Iron Age coins (see Chapter 5) but this practice of burying hoards of coins continued into the Roman period. These were studied by R.W. Higginbottom in 1979, who remarked that the coins with secure provenances were mostly from around the coast. Unfortunately many of the coins are now missing but some records survive. The first recorded hoard was from Le Quennevais, St Brelade, in 1848. The coins were in a pot, now lost, and consisted of around 400 *folles* of the Constantinian period *c*.AD 290-354; 337 of these coins are in the collections of Jersey Museum. A smaller hoard of 18 *antoniniani* was found during excavations at the Île Agois, St Mary, on

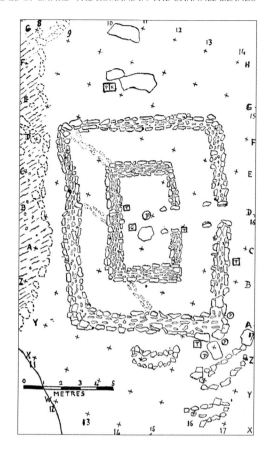

48 Plan of the Roman *fanum* at Le Pinacle, Jersey. *After Godfray & Burdo, 1949*

Jersey's north coast (see Chapter 7). These date to *c.*253–268 and are similar to those found on the Roman ship found in St Peter Port harbour (see below). A further 17 or so have been recorded by the numismatic section of La Société Jersiaise since the 1970s, including two of Trajan (in 1988) and two of the fourth century (in 1997), indicating a considerable time span. Most of these are metal detectorists finds. In considering the two hoards Langouët (1986) considered that they represented fear of sea-borne incursions after AD 354 (Le Quennevais) and similarly after AD 268 at Île Agois, which has parallels with Corseul, the capital of the Coriosolites civitas, up to the middle of the fourth century. However, with the recent finds and the material from St Clement's, it is reasonable to assume a Roman presence in Jersey that at least reflected that of Guernsey and Alderney, if not to the same extent.

ALDERNEY

At Longis Common in Alderney (also spelt Longy) many finds from the Roman period were found in the nineteenth century. The Lukis family recorded various burials and other Roman finds in the late 1880s. In 1889, Baron Anatole von Hügel, who was the first Curator of the Archaeology and Anthropology Museum at Cambridge University, along with a Dr F.P. Nichols, excavated a site they called the 'Longy Refuse pit', which was a little distance to the north-east of the Nunnery (see below). Considerable quantities of pottery were recovered, representing up to 100 pots, brick and tile, two bronze finger-rings, a bronze thimble, a piece of bone comb and three bone pins. Some large fragments of glass were found which Dr Jennifer Price considered were from high prestige vessels and dated from the first to the fourth century (Price 2002). A coin of Commodus was also found. The next year these finds were supplemented by a bronze bowl and a glass vessel inscribed with FRODS (a Frontinus bottle) and a coin of Gordianus III (AD 238-244). A piece of ostrich shell in association with 13 burials in the area was also recovered (Winder 1995); this is likely to have originated in North Africa. The material suggests a thriving Roman community in the second century AD using a wide range of goods from Gaul and Britain. One other item of interest was a Late Roman military buckle.

The most intriguing Roman structure on Alderney, however, is a small fort to the south of Longis Bay. Lukis gives a useful description from long before it was converted into a German stronghold in World War II.

> The Nunnery is constructed of old masonry and deserves some notice. Its form is square, having at each corner a circular Tower of solid masonry about 6 feet diameter: a bent line of wall unites the Towers of 60 feet length, the height is 17 and terminates in a herringbone work, as often seen in Norman Buildings. The last four courses are herringbone work, and contain portions of Roman pantiles and bricks intermixed with stone work. These bricks appear to have been found among the roman remains formerly strewed about the plain. (Lukis 1850, Coll. Ant. Vol V)

The fort is on a map by Bastide in 1759 as 'Le Forts des Murs'. It is now known as 'the Nunnery' so nicknamed by soldiers billeted there in the eighteenth century. It had a very similar plan to signal stations found on the Yorkshire coast such as Scarborough, Goldsborough and Huntcliff, which are dated to c.AD 367 and so may also have started life as a late Roman shore fort (49). A similar 'castellum' at Cherbourg dates to the same period. A small trial excavation in 2002 produced a few sherds of Roman pottery and a careful examination of the walls suggest that the present fort is medieval or later in date but that an earlier Roman building may well lie underneath. This exercise was greatly aided by considerable documentary research by Felicity Crump of the Alderney Society. If a Roman building does lie beneath, this structure can been linked to late Roman defences known as the Saxon Shore forts (Wood & Sebire 2003). The area of Longis is very likely to have been used as a harbour in Roman times (as it was until the eighteenth century) and may have been a base for the Classis Britannica, patrolling the channel.

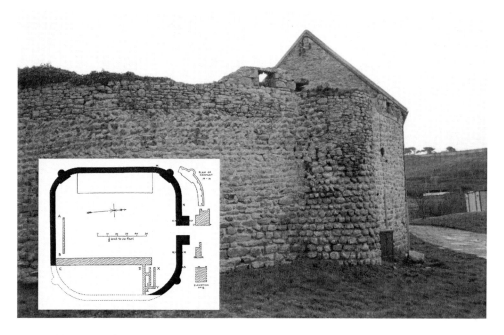

49 Possible Roman fort at Longis Bay, Alderney, showing the ground plan. *Photograph: Guernsey Museums and Galleries*

Possible evidence of the use of Longis as a harbour is found at Fishbourne Roman villa near Chichester harbour on the south coast of England. In levels dating to the first century AD, water-worn boulders were found including hornblende diorite from Jersey, hornblende quartz diorite from Guernsey and a coarse arkosic sandstone, possibly from Alderney, alongside stones from Brittany and Cornwall (Cunliffe 1986). The stones may well have been ballast but they give direct evidence of trade with Britain shortly after the conquest.

HERM

During rescue excavations in Herm in 1999 in an area where briquetage was eroding out of a bank below Fisherman's Cottage, Roman pottery was retrieved. This was considered in light of antiquarian discoveries and spanned the period from the first century BC to the second century AD. There were light grey wares similar to early Roman pots from Armorica and sherds of flagons, amphorae and terra sigillata which represent imports from further afield (Cunliffe & de Jersey 2000). One find of note from the Fowler collection, now in the Ashmolean Museum in Oxford, is a small fragment of tessellated pavement of seven black stone tesserae, set in a pinkish mortar labelled Herm. If this is from a Roman building with a tessellated floor on Herm it has yet to be located, but it is not unreasonable to surmise that a high class building was home to an exiled Roman officer and his family.

50 Sherd of samian bowl
showing the maker's name
(MAGIO) from Lezoux in
eastern France. *Photograph:
Guernsey Museum and Galleries*

A ROMAN SHIP

If conclusive proof were needed about the importance of the Channel Islands as part of a trading network in the Roman period, it was provided by underwater discoveries in the late 1970s and 1980s. The first significant underwater find was a group of Spanish amphorae discovered by Richard Keen, just off the harbour mouth of St Peter Port in 1977. Later Keen, a local diver, was scalloping on Christmas morning in 1982 (a regular seasonal jaunt for local divers as it is the only day there is no commercial traffic in the harbour). He came across massive waterlogged timbers which he thought were unusual, but it was not until a year later that he recognised that the timbers might belong to a Roman ship. The wreck contained pottery, and other objects which were obviously of late Roman date, and the structure seemed reasonably intact. The vessel was in fact a Romano-Celtic trading vessel with its associated cargo and the personal possessions of its small crew (*colour plate 19*). The boat, which became popularly known as 'Asterix' to the islanders, is one of the few vessels of its kind known in the maritime world and is comparable to a similar boat found at Blackfriars (Marsden 1994) and more recently at Barlands Farm (McGrail & Roberts 1999; McGrail 2001). It is of the type used by the Veneti tribe described by Caesar himself. The Guernsey Maritime Trust was formed to rescue the wreck from destruction and excavation work began in 1984, under the direction of Dr Margaret Rule. The final timbers were raised in 1985 and together comprise a substantial part of the aft bottom of a Roman cargo ship (see Chapter 9). The cargo consisted of blocks of resin or pitch from south western France.

Several hundred sherds of pottery were also found both in and around the wreck. These included Gallic flagons, Nene Valley beakers, flanged bowls and black burnished cooking pots which all date to the later third and early fourth centuries (Rule and Monaghan 1993). Sherds of up to five amphorae were recovered. These are thought to have come from Algeria and Spain and originally held olive oil.

Eighty bronze coins were retrieved; eight were official Roman *antoniniani* of the third century, all minted before AD 275, 66 were local copies of *antoniniani*, late third century, known as barbarous radiates. These were all minted after AD 275 but before AD 286. Five worn *sestertii* and one *as* of the second century were also present. These had all fallen out of circulation by AD 300. Taken together, the dating evidence suggests that the ship sank between AD 280 and AD 286. Dendrochronology (dating by tree rings) was not possible at the time of recovery so it is planned to be done when the timbers are fully conserved. It will be a useful indication of the date of the ship and may provide a provenance for the timbers.

Bronze finds from the ship included four fish-hooks, belt buckles, brooches and ship fittings. A pair of bearings from the ships man-powered bilge pump survived. Many small wooden artefacts also survived the fire and 1700 years at the bottom of the harbour. There were a great many parts of barrels found; staves, hoops and string to bind them. There was also a very fragile, finely turned lantern base and a turned maple wood bowl was also found. The hearth from the ship's galley was found broken into dozens of fragments. It is thought that it was covered with a small roof, constructed of standard Roman roofing tiles. However, box-flue tiles were also found. Among the food remains were a few animal bones and edible shellfish such as oysters, ormers, scallops, crabs, winkles, cockles and limpets. Fruit skins and stones, walnut shells and a large quantity of grain survived. A portion of a quernstone was also found.

Although there were amphorae on the ship, barrels were the common container. One of two North African 'Dressel 30' amphorae from the wreck has a graffito on the shoulder which reads 'PP CXV'. It is dated to the late third century AD and is thought to have carried olive oil. There are other finds of amphora located from around Guernsey's waters, particularly from sites in the Little Russel, the channel that runs between Guernsey and Herm. These include sherds of types from south-west Spain, thought to have been carrying fruit extract; the neck of an amphora which had a flat base and was made in Normandy and may have carried wine; the neck of the most common amphorae found in Britain, also made in south-west Spain, which usually carried olive oil; and six amphorae just east of St Peter Port harbour, from south-west Spain, which were likely to have been carrying 'garum' or fish sauce.

PLACE NAMES OF THE ISLANDS IN THE ROMAN PERIOD

So if the islands were part of the Roman Empire as now seems very likely what were they called? This topic has been the subject of scholarly research for many years and most recently by Coates (1991). There are two main sources for possible names, the Antonine Itinerary (Itinerarium Antoninum) and the Peutinger table (Tabula Peutingerana). The Antonine Itinerary, which is a notebook of Roman routes covering the whole Empire, has an annex listing islands which are grouped together:

> … in mari oceano quod Gallias et Britannias interluit, insulae orcades mum iii, insula clota
>
> in Hiverione, vecta, riduna, sarnia, caesarea, barsa, lisia, andium, sicdelis, vxantis, sina, vindilis,
>
> siata, arica. (Maritime section, 508–509)

This has been interpreted as *Riduna*, Alderney, *Sarnia*, Sark, *Caesarea*, The Minquiers, *Barsa*, Herm or Jethou, *Lisia*, Guernsey, and *Andium,* Jersey. The more common names of Sarnia and Caesarea for Guernsey and Jersey respectively had been assigned by William Camden in the sixteenth century. The Peutinger table is based on a map thought to relate back to Agrippa's map of the world *c*.AD 350. The Lenur isles, 'i lenur' are in a likely position to be the Channel Islands although Coates is not convinced that this evidence is reliable. Until an inscription is found this subject remains one of scholarly debate.

THE CHANNEL ISLANDS IN THE ROMAN PERIOD

The evidence gathered above shows that the Channel Islands were under the influence of Rome for at least 400 years. It is likely that the initial contacts were made through trade and then after the conquest of northern Gaul, the islands would have been 'Romanised' with all the trappings of both military and civilian life. Local native settlements such as Kings Road most likely carried on alongside the more elaborate Roman 'towns'. Although there are no inscriptions as such, just potters' names and numbering on amphorae, it is surely just a matter of time before one is found to enlighten us further about the nature of the Roman settlement in the islands. Part of a Roman column from a building is to be found at St Lawrence church on Jersey. Made of granite in Doric style it was later inscribed in the early medieval period and in the later medieval period was adorned with a strap work design (see Chapter 7) (Davies et al. 2000). Whether this was from a Roman building on Jersey is a matter for debate. The settlement at the Bonded Stores in Guernsey continued throughout the four centuries of the Roman period as Wood points through his work on the pottery (Wood 2002). Early terra nigras and Italian and Spanish amphorae are followed by imports from France and later Germany. Samian ware is supplied initially from south and central Gaul followed by a high percentage from eastern Gaul.

The third century was a period of great upheaval in the Roman Empire. This is also reflected at the Bonded Stores through contact with Germany in the form of Eifelkeramik jars from the Urmitz region, which are found in Guernsey, Alderney and Alet, and Avranches in northern France (Wood 2002). The Guernsey Romano-Celtic ship from St Peter Port gives evidence for continuing trade, with barrels taking the place of vast numbers of amphorae in association with ceramique à l'eponge bowls. Late British pots from Alice Holt, the New Forest and Oxfordshire were found along with black burnished ware pots from Dorset.

The collapse of the Roman Empire in the western world began in the early fifth century. A recent find of two Bronze Nummus coins, in St Peter Port, of Honorius or Arcadius (AD 395-403) from the mint of Rome is interesting as these were last coins that were reaching Roman Britain in any quantity. What happened in the islands after the hand of Rome was withdrawn is problematic as the archaeological record becomes sparse. However, what evidence there is will be examined in Chapter 7.

7

HOLY ISLANDS: THE EARLY MEDIEVAL PERIOD

Civilisation is a movement and not a condition, a voyage and not a harbour. (Arthur Toynbee 1958)

You [monks] should live as islands, unto yourselves, being your own refuge. (Buddhist text *c.*second century BC)

The transition from Armorica to Celtic Brittany was a gradual process which took place between the late fourth and early seventh centuries AD, largely because of an important influx of population from Late and post-Roman Britain. (Galliou & Jones 1991)

INTRODUCTION

The post-Roman period in the Channel Islands, as with many areas, is less tangible than other periods in the archaeological record. This was traditionally known as the 'Dark Ages', after the heyday of the Roman Empire, although as a recent exhibition at the British Museum on the Transformation of the Roman World from AD 400-900 suggests, dynamic and influential, cultural and intellectual shifts were going on during the period (Anderson 1997). As always with Channel Island archaeology the influence on the islands is from the mainland of Europe. The rule of the Anglo-Saxon kings of England did not affect the islands as far as we can tell, other than to cause migrations of people. The Frankish King Clovis founded a dynasty in France and Germany known now as the Merovingian period which lasted from AD 500-750. This was followed in the ninth century by the Carolingan period named after Charlemagne. In the years after the late Roman Empire early references to the travel of bishops and saints who founded the early churches exist. While these records are helpful they can also be misleading and modified by oral tradition. It is likely that the situation in the Channel Islands was similar to Brittany. People, driven to leave Cornwall, Devon and southern England because of pressures from the Anglo-Saxon invasions and Irish attack, migrated from Britain and merged with the indigenous population changing Gallo-Roman Armorica to Celtic Brittany (Galliou & Jones 1991).

SAINTS IN THE CHANNEL ISLANDS

The life of St Sampson was well documented in a work commissioned by the abbot-bishop Tigernomalus and written c.AD 610 (McCormack 1986, 37). Sampson was born in Wales c.AD 485 and studied at Llantwit in Glamorgan, where a monastery had been founded by St Illtud, where many of the Saints associated with the Channel Islands were trained. Having worked in Ireland, Sampson, like many of the Celtic Saints, then began his peregrinations or wanderings which involved a high level of self discipline and solitude. It is likely that this was how the tradition of establishing hermitages and monasteries in remote locations began. Late in his life, c.AD 560, Sampson is thought to have stopped off in Guernsey with his company of followers on his way to St Malo and later Dol-de-Bretagne in northern France. The parish church of St Sampson, which dates from the twelfth century, stands near the smaller natural harbour on the east coast of Guernsey (51). An earlier church founded by Sampson is likely to have stood on the spot. Sampson's successor at Dol was his cousin, St Magloire, who founded a monastery on Sark in the sixth century. This is thought to be located near the present Seigneurie based on the place-name evidence of La Moinerie, La Moinerie de Haut and L'Écluse which may have been the mill of the monastery. Magloire is said to have died in Sark c.AD 565 (ibid. 39). On the smaller island of Herm, remains of a chapel thought to have been founded by St Tugual, a nephew of St Brioc from Cornwall, are incorporated into a later twelfth-century building.

Saint Marculf (or Marcoul) is alleged to have visited Jersey in the fifth century and was the first holy man to teach Christianity in the island. His disciple Helier was from Tongres in Belgium. Helier lived as a hermit on Jersey, on a rock just by Elizabeth Castle, now known as the Hermitage Rock (52). His home was a single austere cell and was open to the elements. Helier is alleged to have been murdered by pirates c.AD 555. The study of medieval coins from the Channel Islands draws attention to the fact that many of the earliest records are of the church authorities listing dues (money) payable by dative priories, such as that at Lihou (see below), back to the mother houses in Normandy (McCammon 1984,77). This may have been part of a situation which began with the early saints who very likely received title to lands in the islands for their services. However, there is little tangible archaeological evidence or coins in either Guernsey or Jersey or the smaller islands for the Merovingian period, but an early eremitic site was excavated on Jersey at the Île Agois in 1974-5 (see below). Here traces of a ninth-century monastic site were found within

51 St Sampson's Church crest showing Sampson travelling to France with his followers, based on a stained glass window from Dol-de-Bretagne. *Photograph: author*

52 Chapel of St Helier on the Hermitage Rock, Jersey. *Photograph: author*

an earlier Iron Age settlement. Previously, in 1925, the broken fragments of five coins had been discovered alongside an early medieval decorated jar, but the provenance was merely described as 'from the summit of the Île Agois' (Finlaison & Holdsworth 1979). The coins were examined by Dr M. Metcalf who recorded that there were two complete examples of 'Gratia di Rex' series which was brought in by the Edict of Pîtres in AD 864. The other fragments have enough of their inscription surviving to suggest that they are deniers of the period minted at Rennes. During later excavations a small hoard of third-century Roman coins was found suggesting the site had been occupied over a long period (see chapter 6).

By the time of the Carolingians the centres of Rouen, Le Mans, Angers and Tours had assumed importance and in c.AD 754 Pepin the Short set limits on the currency which became the libra, solidi and denarii that coins circulating in the Channel Islands were based on (and of course in Britain and the Empire until decimalisation). At the Edict of Pîtres the new deniers were to have the name of the king in legend around the edge of the monogram and on the other side the name of the city where the coin was struck.

ARCHAEOLOGICAL EVIDENCE

Despite extensive rescue and some research excavations on medieval sites in both Jersey and Guernsey only a few sites have produced archaeological material from the early medieval period. The Île Agois mentioned above is a tidal stack that lies off the north coast of Jersey rising c.76m above sea level. Access is difficult but may be gained at low tide from the mainland by a steep descent, a crossing of the rocky beach and a climb up to the summit of the islet. Remains of hut structures were found, 25 of which are visible today, on the sloping surface of the island. On the north-western side, a number have slipped into the sea.

Among the finds was a socketed axe, typical of the seventh and eighth centuries, associated with glass beads in the foundations of Hut 1. There was also early medieval pottery (53). This, along with the discovery from excavations of the 1920s of coins of Charles the Bald, strongly suggests an early medieval date for their construction. The huts may have been connected with seasonal fishing activity. The island cannot have had a defensive role as it faces more or less seawards and is overlooked by the coastal cliff. No economic advantage over the mainland is likely, and to live on the Île Agois, even for a short period of time, would mean a harsh life. A number of sites with a similar geographical position to the Île Agois are known around the coastlines of the British Isles and Brittany. They possess buildings which, though varying in size and number, have a similarity in shape and layout. These settlements have been compared to the Skellig Michael, an eremitic monastery in the Atlantic Ocean off the Kerry coast of Ireland (Finlaison & Holdsworth 1979).

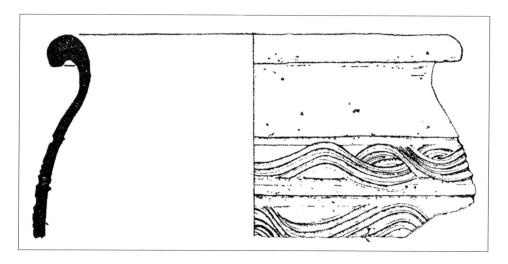

53 Early medieval pot from Île Agois, Jersey. *After Finlaison & Holdsworth, 1979*

On Guernsey a small eremitic site at Grandes Rocques was excavated by Bob Burns in the 1980s. The community here may have been a religious one favouring a remote spot to eke out their existence. Two apsidal-ended buildings, one complete and one almost destroyed, were uncovered (*54*). They were simple oval long houses similar to buildings at Pen-er-Malo in Brittany. Building 1 had a central hearth and Building 2 had an internal wall separating the living area from the possible byre end (Batt 1998). As at Pen-er-Malo, the site is situated by the sea and so the economy may have been mixed, based on land and sea resources. Although architecturally the site is similar to the Breton example, the pottery is from Normandy. Gritty wares from large pots with applied strip decoration were found. There is also a group of early glazed wares in the pottery which would suggest a date of the early ninth century (Barton 1998).

Other early ceramics which have been found in the islands include Merovingian pottery from Old Street, St Helier, which was found in association with a possible defended settlement (Finlaison 1976a) under a later aisled hall (see below). In Guernsey two jugs which date to the Merovingian period were found in St Peter Port harbour (Monaghan 1988). They are coated with a tar-like residue and may have been used to hold tar for caulking ship timbers. It is now known that many ships from the twelfth century, if not earlier, foundered in St Peter Port harbour (see Chapter 9). One of the jugs is complete (*55*). It was handmade in a grey sandy fabric with a faint banding around the pot. The other is in a distinctive micaceous fabric typical of Brittany. Dark Age pottery was also found at Les Écréhous the reef to the north-east of Jersey (see below) (Wood 1996). Three sherds from a jar in a coarse sandy fabric, which had roller-stamped decoration on the shoulder, were found during excavations on the island in the 1980s. Similar sherds are in the assemblages from La Plaiderie and the Bonded

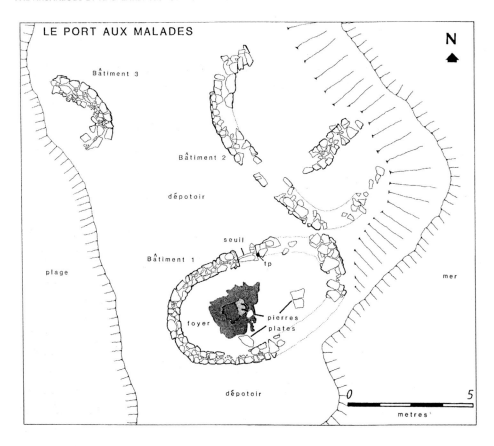

54 *Above* Plan of early medieval buildings at Grandes Rocques. *After Burns & Batt, 1990*

55 *Left* Merovingian pot from St Peter Port harbour. *Photograph: Guernsey Museums and Galleries*

Stores (Wood forthcoming). These were dated to the late seventh or early eighth century.

In Alderney during excavations in 1930 by Durtnell, a sherd of bar-lip pot pottery was recovered in white sand on Longis Common. These pots have a distinctive ear-like spout and bar for hanging and this example may have been made on Alderney itself or more likely Cornwall. The sherd dates to the ninth century AD (Johnston 1981).

INSCRIBED STONES

Other evidence of Breton influence exists in the form of inscribed stones which have recently been examined by Dr Wendy Davies and team from the Institute of Archaeology in London. In Jersey the St Lawrence pillar (see Chapter 6) has an inscription which is thought to date from the sixth century. It may have been reused as a piece of church furniture intended to be seen from the ornamented side. The pillar may not be local to Jersey but may have been brought in from Normandy or Brittany (Davies et al. 2000). At the Vale church in Guernsey, to the south of the west door of the church, a christianised menhir has an inscription that may be eighth to tenth century in date (56). Another stone, currently a gatepost in a house in St Saviours, Guernsey, has an early medieval inscription (Bernier 1982). On Maître Île on the Écréhous reef, there was evidence of early Christian activity. A burial was found which may have been a foundation burial or a saintly burial. Associated with it were a timber structure and also a recumbent menhir (Rodwell 1996).

HOUSE STRUCTURES

In Jersey the remains of an aisled hall were excavated on the site of 13 and 13a Old Street (57). The building lay near the surface and apart from robbing for stone, the foundations had remained undisturbed under blown sand until about 1700, when building began in that area of St Helier. Nineteenth-century foundations and cesspits had caused disturbance. The one remaining wall, an average of 2ft wide, was built of locally gathered granite from the Fort Regent area. Most of the stones were sea worn and none appeared to have been quarried. Inside, the single clay floor contained a sunken hearth lined with stones. This had been patched at least once and in the surrounds were the sooty bases of several cooking pots and food rubbish, particularly limpet shells. The roof was almost certainly thatched and a wide gully caused by drips from the eaves ran outside the walls. At one end of the house was a byre. The presence of two large post holes in the floor at this point were almost certainly for roof support or screening to divide animals from the family area (Finlaison 1986).

THE ARCHAEOLOGY AND EARLY HISTORY OF THE CHANNEL ISLANDS

56 *Left* Christianised menhir at the
Vale church with early medieval
inscription. *Photograph: author*

57 *Below* Reconstruction of medieval
building at Old Street, St Helier. *After
Finlaison, 1986*

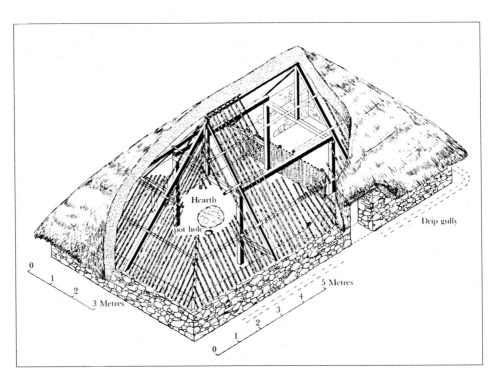

The finds included coins, a key, nails, blades and possible door hinges. A coin embedded in the floor of the house was identified as an English Short-cross halfpenny of Henry II, minted at York between AD 1180-1189. A second coin found in a rubbish tip in the yard is a French Regal denier tournois of Louis VIII or IX, probably minted between AD 1226-1270. The pottery, scattered on the yard and in two rubbish tips, contained fine glazed wares from Beauvais and Rouen. The cooking pots, jugs and storage jars have a wide variety of forms and designs. During the final stages of the excavation a level of earlier occupation was found dating to between the eleventh and thirteenth century (dated by the collared rim pottery collected). This occupation layer was found beneath the house under a metre of wind-borne sand which separated the two.

In Guernsey at Le Feugré, near Cobo, pottery was found during excavations for the foundations of a house in 1967. Emergency excavations by Jean Le Patourel uncovered the remains of a long house. The walls were of rough masonry and had been bonded in various ways, with a reddish clay on the east wall and a shelly mortar on the west side. A large hearth or oven was found in the south-west corner and a drain ran diagonally across the floor and under the hearth (Jee 1968). Post-holes were located in the floor indicating an internal partition. A midden area was excavated to the east which contained a considerable amount of pottery. The structure was interpreted as a long house in which people lived at one end with their animals at the other. There was evidence that it had been rebuilt at least five times. Pottery included large Normandy gritty ware pots with applied strip decoration and some cooking pots with rouletted decoration on the shoulder. One unusual find was a gaming piece which may be Viking in origin (58). It is of bone and is carved to represent a creature with a long snout, two small ears or horns and an eye with a snake-like body (Girard 1981). During the excavation in 1967 an iron dagger was also found wedged into one of the walls, suggesting that a Viking attack may have been made on the community who occupied the building.

The question is often asked whether or not the Vikings ever came to the islands. The answer is undoubtedly yes, although tangible evidence is very limited. Place names and comparable information from neighbouring France enables us to say that the 'men from the north' must have landed on Channel Island shores. It is likely that the Celtic monasteries in Sark, Jersey and Guernsey were attacked by Viking raiders in AD 841 when Normandy suffered similar attacks.

The Normans had expanded from Scandinavia in three great waves during the ninth to the eleventh centuries. They sailed north to Iceland, south to the eastern shores of Britain and also to the northern coast of France (Bertaux & Marin 1987, 16). They colonised areas along the mouths of many great rivers such as the Humber, the Rhine, the Seine and the Loire. In 911, Rollo and his followers were granted land in the area now called Normandy and by the eleventh century his descendants were well established in France. The Normans had great administrative skills and established a legal system. The *Coutume de*

58 Gaming piece from Cobo long house. *Photograph: Guernsey Museums and Galleries*

Normandie linked the Frankish law of the continent with the Common Law of England and established trial by jury (Evans 1969, 7).

The Normans brought a new distinctive style of architecture both in the castles they built and in church architecture. Monasteries and cathedrals were built in neo-classical Roman style and castles developed from simple wooden motte and bailey enclosures as at Grimbosq in Normandy to the great ducal castle of William at Caen (Bertaux & Marin 1987, 58). Also at Caen a great Exchequer building was erected where dues were paid and accounts tallied. This monetary system was established throughout Norman England where calculations were made over a chequered cloth.

THE CHANNEL ISLANDS IN THE NORMAN EMPIRE

The Channel Islands had come within control of the Dukes of Normandy at the treaty of St-Clair-sur-Epte, *c.*911 (Le Patourel 1958). William Longsword, son of Rollo, acquired lands previously held by the Bretons which included the Channel Islands and the Cotentin peninsula. By 1020 Guernsey had been divided into two large fiefs held by Norman Seigneurs. The invasion of England by Duke William of Normandy in 1066 brought Guernsey and the other Channel Islands closer to England, though their laws and language continued to follow that of the Normans. The islands became part of a realm that eventually stretched from the North of England to south-western France.

By the early twelfth century Benedictine monks from Mont St Michel in Normandy had set up priories in the Vale, Guernsey, and on Lihou Island (see below), a small islet off the west coast (Ogier 1998). In 1204 Philippe Auguste of France won the Duchy of Normandy from his cousin King John of England, who failed to hold together the dominions over which he had control. Guernsey and Jersey had been under the control of Pierre de Preaux, the Lord of the Isles, who surrendered his Norman holdings to Philippe Auguste at Rouen. However he managed to omit the Channel Islands from the terms of the submission. This was possibly a deliberate attempt to please King John, as de Preaux had land holdings in England as well as in France. The Channel Islands thereafter remained with the English Crown (Powicke 1960).

THE HOLY ISLES

So the 'peregrini' or wandering saints of the early medieval period, who sought out lonely isolation, and the priests who led their flocks to new shores, brought the early Christian Church to the Channel Islands (Chadwick 1965). Later in the eleventh and twelfth centuries the great parish churches were built, often on sites that had been occupied previously. In Jersey at St Lawrence church, two long cist burials from the Norman period were excavated in 1980. The body of a woman of about 60 years old was found lying with her head to the west. A pottery vessel had been placed by the head and analysis showed that it had contained olive oil. The burial, when considered alongside the early medieval inscription on the Roman column in the church (see above), suggests that an earlier church must have been on the site (Finlaison 1998).

In Guernsey by the twelfth century the abbey of Mont St Michel in Normandy had control of one half of the island (St Pierre de Bois, St Saviours, Castel and the Vale) and Marmoutiers the other (Town Church, St Sampsons, St Andrews, St Martins, Forest and Torteval) (McCormack 1986), although the situation in Jersey was much more complicated. Recent excavations at two sites have helped to illuminate early Christianity on the islands, Lihou Priory, on an islet off Guernsey and Maitre Île on the Écréhous reef off Jersey.

The great abbey of Mont St Michel founded a priory at the Vale in Guernsey some time in the tenth century and later in the twelfth century a priory was founded and consecrated on Lihou Island. The island lies off the west coast of Guernsey. It is accessible by foot only during low spring tides and is otherwise cut off for days at a time, twice a month. The remains of a Benedictine priory and its associated domestic buildings survive on the island. It is likely that the priory was built as a challenge to pagan worship. In the seventeenth century it was reported that it was a source of great irritation and dread to witches who

met at the Catioroc, a headland on Guernsey opposite Lihou. Their chant
'Que! Hou! Hou! Marie Li Hou!' demonstrated the defiance of the pagans
towards the new Christian faith and the Virgin Mary (Marie). Ste Marie de
Lihou is mentioned in documentary sources as having been consecrated in AD
1114 and was definitely standing in AD 1156. The priory was a dependency of
Mont St Michel and as a dative establishment it had to pay dues back to the
mother house in France. The priory seems to have continued after the Alien
Priories Act of 1414 when it fell under the supervision of the English crown.
A reference of 1444 suggests that Henry IV gave the priory to Eton College.
In 1519 a documentary reference mentions a house in Fountain Street 'where
the Prior of Lihou lives'. However, by 1629 Heylyn describes the priory as
being 'ruinous' and, in fact, it appears that it was deliberately partly destroyed
in the late eighteenth century to prevent it serving as a marker for French
invaders.

Guernsey Museum Service carried out archaeological excavations at Lihou
Priory over a 10-year period (*colour plate 20*). The excavations examined the
domestic building range and what remained of the priory itself. Several phases
of occupation were found. The plan of the church is rectangular with chancel
and nave joined in the fourteenth century by a glazed tiled floor. Below this
there was evidence of a cross wall and a suggestion of up to three earlier phases.
Evidence from the domestic buildings gives a date of the early twelfth century for
the first phase, which consisted of a small rectangular cell with a lancet window.
The buildings were later extended in the fourteenth and fifteenth centuries. A
large dwelling house was built with a fine fireplace, an evier and indications of a
second storey. A dovecote stood just north of these buildings and fishponds were
located on the intertidal rocks below the priory.

FINDS FROM LIHOU PRIORY AND LES ÉCRÉHOUS

Finds from the excavations have produced considerable evidence that the
Benedictine priory on Lihou was a thriving community sending dues back to
the mother house of Mont St Michel in northern France.

The priory itself was a small, beautifully decorated church, with stained
glass windows, and highly carved limestone internal vaulting. The church was
decorated with carved Caen stone in Romanesque style including beak head
decoration. There appears to have been at least two phases of construction. This
view has been reinforced by stylistic analysis of over 500 pieces of the carved
stone which have been recovered, which included voussoirs (for arches), pillars,
ribs and chevron-moulded pieces. A small, carved face was found under the
tiled floor of the church which was very likely part of a standing structure or
part of a feature such as the font. Two sundials were also found. The first was
found near the south door of the priory. This was a vertical direct south-facing

dial – measurements of the hour lines (from the vertical) indicate it was most likely made specifically for this location (59). The second is a less ornate scratch dial.

A very extensive range of mostly French pottery has been recovered, with some almost complete vessels found in the garderobe. Rare medieval painted glass has also been recovered from the church, and almost a complete window was excavated from the earliest domestic building. Another special find was a Roman intaglio carved on a cornelian. This may have been kept as a special item by a monk and does not necessarily mean that the Romans visited Lihou; however, some Roman tile was also recovered. Along with an ivory piece, perhaps from a musical instrument, amber beads and book binding metal strips, two items of slate are perhaps the most evocative and personal. One has a name and tallies scratched on it, and the other has part of a game – probably nine men's morris.

In the graveyard to the south of the church several burials were excavated. One body lay in a well-constructed stone-lined grave; the skeleton belonged to a tall man who was 25-40 years old when he died. The burials were dated to c.AD 1250. The bones were not in very good condition but Charlotte Roberts of Bradford University examined them and suggested that the man had had leprosy when he died (though this was not necessarily the cause of death). A maladerie which may have been for lepers is known at Richmond headland, not far away on Guernsey itself.

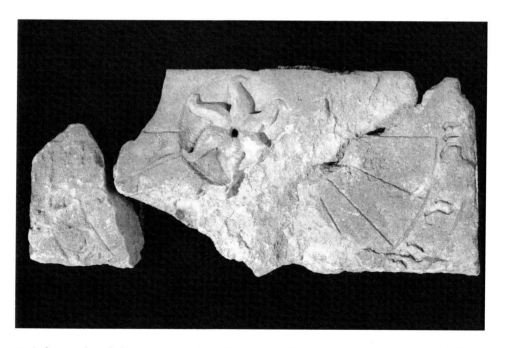

59 A decorated sundial in Caen stone from Lihou Priory. *Photograph: Guernsey Museums and Galleries*

On Les Écréhous, the reef off the north-east coast of Jersey, excavations directed by Dr Warwick Rodwell took place in 1987-88. On Maître Île, the largest of the islands, a priory dedicated to Saint Mary the Virgin was founded in 1203. This was also a dative priory (Rodwell 1996). It belonged to Le Val-Richer in Normandy and was the only Cistercian establishment in the Channel Islands. It was built on the remains of an earlier establishment (see above) showing that the reef had been the focus of religious activity for many generations. It was a small self-supporting community similar to that on Lihou Island. At the beginning of the thirteenth century it consisted of a communal hall and the priory itself, which was a rectangular cell, and the two were connected by a door. The chapel was then rebuilt, with a west door and openings in the north and south wall. Later, a new stone-built chancel was typical of the work of Jersey masons with stone barrel vaulting. The closest comparison is the chapel of Notre Dame de Pas which was destroyed in 1814 (60). It was completely plastered and limewashed inside and out, and there was painted glass in the windows. The roof is likely to have been Normandy slate and the floor a mixture of cobbles and earth (Rodwell 1996, 366).

Finds include pottery from France with fine decorated jugs from Rouen alongside Normandy gritty wares which can be paralleled on Jersey at Old Street and on Guernsey at Le Château des Marais. Among the metalwork were coins, bronze buckles and lead window came. An exceptional find was a silver-gilt ring-brooch which was found on the floor of the hall. One half has a plain squarish section and the other has a spiral twist. Three lobed rosettes of silver, each with eight petals, are attached to the plain section of the ring (*colour plate 21*). Dr Rodwell considers that the complex is similar to that on Lihou and also points out that in the thirteenth century the islands of Les Écréhous would have both been larger and environmental evidence suggests that there was shrub and tree cover which would have provided material for the monks to keep a light burning on the reef. This was included in their charter although no trace of a medieval beacon survives today.

THE DEVELOPMENT OF TOWNS IN THE ISLANDS

As the medieval period progressed the towns of St Helier and St Peter Port grew up around the parish churches and the harbours (see Chapter 8.) In Jersey rescue excavations by Margaret Finlaison in the 1970s and 1980s have shown evidence of settlement from the thirteenth century (Old Street) and it is generally accepted that the square, now known as the Royal Square, formed the centre of activity for the people of St Helier (61). Traditionally the site of the market is thought to have been established by the Priory of St Helier which is under the Barrack Square (Finlaison 1974).

In Guernsey the medieval town hugged the shoreline along the strand and eventually a 'new town' was built higher up away from the squalor of the medieval

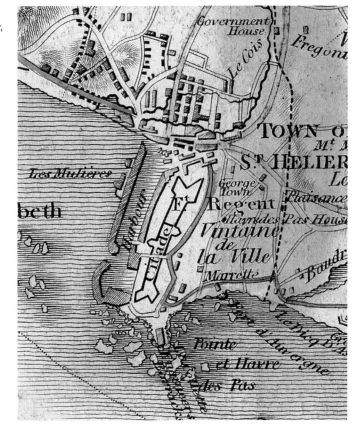

60 *Above* Chapel of Notre Dame de Pas, Jersey, which was destroyed in 1814. By Francis Grose 1776. *By kind permission of the Society of Antiquaries of London*

61 *Right* St Helier in 1840. *Anon. 1840*

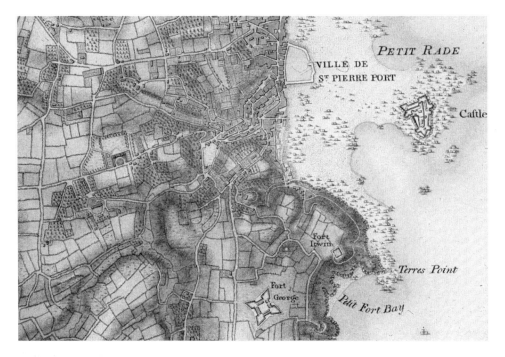

62 St Peter Port in 1787 from the Duke of Richmond map. *Photograph: Guernsey Museum and Galleries*

town as the inhabitants became more prosperous through trade and sea faring. Excavations have not yet given evidence of a town wall which is mentioned in documentary sources but a ditch thought to border the south of the town was excavated in Cliff Street in the 1980s (*62*). Out of town a medieval settlement of small square houses was excavated at Albecq on the west coast in the 1990s. This was a small farmstead around a courtyard with evidence of field systems over the adjoining area. Geophysics has shown that there are several other dwellings yet to be investigated. A small hoard of silver coins, sterlings of Edward the Black Prince (1362-72), was found in a leather pouch in a pine box which had been buried by one of the houses (information Marion Archibald). This may have been buried because of fear of a French raid documented in 1372.

The town of St Anne in Alderney grew up later in the late fourteenth century when the Crown leased the island and settlers from Guernsey arrived there. Most of what can be seen today are houses built in the eighteenth and nineteenth centuries when the town expanded around the open air court at Rue de Grosnez which was renamed Victoria Road. All three of the main towns were ably surveyed in the mid-1970s by Charles Brett who was commissioned by the National Trust to report on the architecture of the towns (Brett 1975, 1976, 1977).

8

FORTRESS ISLANDS: CASTLES AND FORTIFICATIONS

The castles were constructed as fortifications, for defence against invasion from France. (Everard & Holt 2004)

The sudden need to hold the islands in support of the English claim to parts of France, as in the case of Calais, prompted a rapid flurry of fortification around 1204. (Barton 1980)

Mont Orgueil Castle is a lofty pile,
Within the Easterne parts of Jersey Isle,
Seated upon a Rocke, full large and high,
Close by the Sea-shore, next to Normandie.
(William Prynne, Late Exile, and Close Prisoner in the sayd Castle: Mount Orgueil 1641 [Cited in Dixon & Kennedy, 2002])

INTRODUCTION

In 2004, the Îles Anglo-Normandes, or Channel Islands, celebrated 800 years of allegiance to the English crown. In 1204, after the loss of English-controlled lands in Normandy to Philippe Auguste of France, the islands retained allegiance to England rather than to France, the land that was in sight of their shores. The strategic importance of the Channel Islands was a determining factor in their economic and political role throughout the medieval period and indeed from later prehistory (Burns et al. 1996). After 1204, King John recognised the strategic importance of Guernsey and Jersey and the fortifications on the islands were reviewed. In Guernsey a new fortification at the entrance to the good natural harbour of St Peter Port, 'the king's castle', was built some time later, which was known as Castle Cornet. In Jersey, Mont Orgueil or Gorey Castle was, by tradition, started in the latter decades of the twelfth century although archaeological excavation suggests that it, too, was begun in response to the events of 1204 (Barton 1984). The political separation of the islands from Normandy meant in effect that an enemy was always close at hand. A series of continuous raids from the French ensued and in fact Castle Cornet was held by the French from 1338–45 (Le Patourel 1958). Because of the closeness of France the islands' defences were constantly being reviewed from that time.

CHÂTEAU DES MARAIS

It is possible that at least one fortified castle was standing in Guernsey before 1204, at the Château des Marais, a short distance north of the town of St Peter Port. This fortification was built on a natural hougue or mound surrounded by marsh land and a short distance from the sea. In the first phase of building, the mound was scarped and a ditch and bank fortified the inner bailey. Later, the mound area was raised with rubble from the ditch and an outer bailey was created. The dating evidence from the coins (see below) and pottery suggests the castle was built around the beginning of the thirteenth century.

Barton (1980), in his discussion following his excavations in 1975–7, suggested that despite the problems of dating some of the French medieval pottery (Thomson 1980) and the problems of dating French coins outside France (Archibald 1980), the first phase of the castle was built in the early years of the thirteenth century, perhaps in response to the events of 1204. A second phase began in the late thirteenth and early fourteenth centuries when the outer ditch silted up and further buildings were added. The excavations at the Château des Marais provided the earliest stratified medieval coins in the Channel Islands, which help to illustrate the fact that at this critical period in the history of the islands the coinage of medieval France was in use alongside that of England. Undoubtedly, however, the most significant castles in the Islands are those of Mont Orgueil at Gorey in Jersey and Castle Cornet in St. Peter Port in Guernsey.

CASTLE CORNET

Castle Cornet, Guernsey's ancient Royal Fortress, has stood guard over the town and harbour of St Peter Port for nearly 800 years (*colour plate 22*). It is built on a rocky islet just off St Peter Port.

The medieval castle
The castle, which was first called Cornet Castle in the early fourteenth century, was accessible on foot only at low tide and used the highest outcrop on the islet for its first development. It was situated out of range of the weapons of the day

and so was easily defended, as long as supplies came in by sea. At least twice in its history the castle held out against those who controlled Guernsey. The entrance to the earliest castle was reached along a low, rocky path, and through a gatehouse on its north-eastern side. The outer walls, which occupied the upper levels of the rock, enclosed several buildings. These included a chapel, a half round tower or bastion to the west, and a square tower, and the Tour Carré to the south (Le Patourel 1958).

The early history of the castle is dominated by the continuing threat from France and in 1338 the Channel Islands were invaded twice. The French held the castle for a total of seven years from 1338-45 despite several attempts to oust them. For most of the time, however, the medieval castle served the island well in a defensive role, and also provided a residence for the Warden of the Isles. This was the monarch's representative in the islands replaced later by governors. By the end of the medieval period new developments in weaponry necessitated many changes.

The Tudor castle

With English involvement in Europe throughout the sixteenth century, invasion of the Channel Islands continued to be a threat. A Commission of Enquiry in 1567 resulted in the modification and extension of the defences according to the most up-to-date 'science of fortification'. The castle owes much of its present appearance to this period when the outer works were built. The Crown ordered Sir Thomas Leighton to strengthen the castle against cannon fire. Many of the changes to Castle Cornet under the governorship of Leighton were the responsibility of Paul Ivy, the foremost military engineer of his day who also worked at Elizabeth Castle in Jersey (see below) (Le Patourel 1958).

At the outbreak of the English Civil War in 1642, Guernsey declared its support for the cause of Parliament. Castle Cornet, under its Governor Sir Peter Osborne, remained stubbornly Royalist. Again the castle was under siege for eight years but managed to last out as supplies were brought in by sea. Eventually in 1651, the Parliamentarian fleet obtained command of the seas and was able to force its surrender.

A traumatic event in 1672 caused great damage to the castle. A powder magazine in the old keep exploded during a thunderstorm. The explosion killed seven people including the wife and mother of the Governor, Lord Hatton, and completely altered the appearance of the upper part of the castle. The keep was blown away along with the chapel and the Governor's residence. After the explosion the Governors of the island when resident lived on Guernsey and not in Castle Cornet.

The American and Napoleonic Wars

After the 1672 explosion Castle Cornet was eventually repaired, although the keep was not rebuilt. It is due to this that the castle today has a slightly truncated look as if its top tier is missing. During the mid-eighteenth century, at a time of increased international tension, accommodation for the garrison was increased by the construction of new barrack blocks. The last Garrison Regiment was stationed in Guernsey in 1939. With the fall of France in 1940 the Channel Islands were occupied by the German forces. In Castle Cornet concrete emplacements for guns and equipment were built on top of earlier works. Two years after the Liberation, in 1947, King George VI presented Castle Cornet to the Islanders of Guernsey as a gift in token of their loyalty during the two World Wars.

Archaeological excavations at Castle Cornet

John Le Patourel, a Guernseyman who became Professor of History at Leeds University, excavated at the castle in 1953, particularly in the conjectured site of the donjon or keep (Le Patourel 1954). He concluded that the area may have been lowered to the ground after the explosion in 1672 as no trace of the tower survived. Later, in 1981, Ken Barton began a series of excavations which ran until 1988 and were followed in 1989-92 by shorter investigations directed by Bob Burns (63). In his report Barton (2003) provides archaeological evidence to suggest that the castle was constructed towards the end of the thirteenth century (between 1270 and 1290), although this does not tally with the many early thirteenth century references to the 'king's castle'.

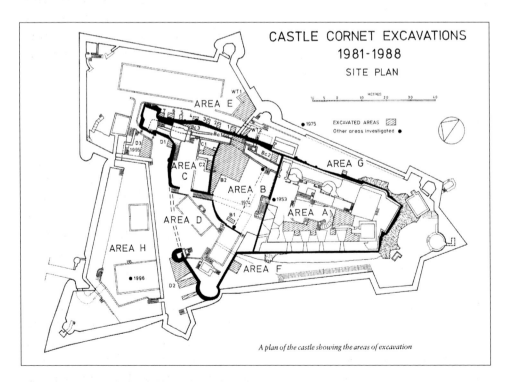

A plan of the castle showing the areas of excavation

63 Plan of Castle Cornet, Guernsey showing the extensive areas excavated by Ken Barton in the 1980s. *After Barton, 2003*

The excavations revealed a series of structures initially built for the most part on steeply sloping bare rock. Barton considered that this posed a problem for the builders, who had resorted to filling the lower parts of the structures as they were raised with thick layers of imported material from the town of St. Peter Port. Within this rubble was contained a significant amount of one form of pottery jug amongst many others, namely Saintonge polychrome pottery. This is a very distinctive ware, fine in quality and decoration, instantly recognisable, and firmly datable to the late thirteenth century. In Barton's view the dating of the pottery gives a firm indication that the foundation date of the castle is close to 1275.

Barton's excavations were followed by two investigations prior to installation of new services (Sebire 2002 and Wessex 2004). In 2001 the areas examined included the basement of the lower guard (now housing the Story of Castle Cornet exhibition), the inner ward and that directly in front of the former armoury building (which includes the western sally port). The lowest levels of part of the medieval curtain wall that was believed to run between the gunner's tower and the barbican, were located. This wall is missing from the plan by Romer of 1694 and must have fallen into disrepair by the fifteenth century. In the area just outside the armoury building (whose footprint is on the plan of 1694 by the engineer Romer) the footings of another substantial stone wall were revealed. In 2003 an excavation was undertaken by Wessex Archaeology as part of the replacement of paving next to the barbican. No medieval deposits were recovered and the finds from this exercise were mainly eighteenth century in date. The amazing array of finds from the excavations generally, showing contacts from all over Europe, and the story of the castle's development, are on display in the castle (see Chapter 10).

MONT ORGUEIL CASTLE, JERSEY

The great castle of Mont Orgueil in Jersey was also founded early in the thirteenth century after the events of 1204 and, in fact, the history of Mont Orgueil closely reflects that of Castle Cornet (*colour plate 23*). Many of the early documentary references refer to the 'king's castles' in both islands and then of 'Cornet and Gurrey' together. In 1206 there is a record of bretaches or wooden stakes being brought from Sussex to Guernsey which may have been used as scaffolding for the castle building. In 1225 quantities of timber and of lead were being sent to Jersey and Guernsey from Southampton.

Mont Orgueil sits on a rugged promontory overlooking Grouville Bay and the Normandy coast and cuts a dramatic figure on the skyline. The castle, according to tradition, received its name from Thomas, Duke of Clarence, the brother of Henry V, who, whilst engaged in the protracted war with Normandy, visited the Channel Islands. He was so impressed with the castle's unique position and great strength that he called it Mount Pride – a name it has borne ever since. The castle, as with Castle

Cornet, was not just for defence but housed the administrative centre of the islands, first the Wardens of the Isles and then Governor for the crown.

The medieval castle

The earliest part of the castle was constructed around the summit of the rock in the early thirteenth century. A large rectangular hall was raised above an undercroft, lit by four regularly placed windows, and entered on each floor level by a door on the north-western side. As with Castle Cornet it is difficult to visualise the appearance of the castle at this early stage as the building operations of the sixteenth century have substantially altered the layout and levels of the whole of the upper ward. The highest part of the rock was long and very narrow, no more than was covered by the raised hall and the adjacent two storey tower, the keep tower. The ground falls away sharply on all sides but particularly to the north and east. A curtain wall enclosed an area lower down, that of the middle ward.

During the latter half of the thirteenth century the castle had been left in an inadequate state, as shown by the surveys made after Warden Otto de Grandison's death in 1328. Documentary records show something of the cost of restoration, but provide only a little detail of the actual construction. However, there are records of the bridge in the thirteenth century, and in the fourteenth century of the hall, the pantry, the kitchen, the cellar, the larder and the bakehouse; the chamber and the chapel; the court room, the prison and the forge; the granary and the stables; and the bridges, the garden and the garden tower, all or some built around 1348-9 (Dixon et al.1998). As with the records for Castle Cornet it is difficult to pinpoint all of these structures precisely. In the fourteenth century, too, there was development under warden John de Roches in the area of the north-east bastion and sally port.

The Tudor and later castle

The castle was approached through the King's warren to an early gate where a new gate tower was built by Sir Richard Harliston in 1470 after regaining the castle from the French, so with this major rebuilding in the fifteenth century, the castle became a complex military site. However, the conversion of the old medieval castle, when defence was by bow and arrow, into a fortress strong enough to respond to the new forms of warfare, mainly cannon, was a slow and complex process which lasted for nearly two centuries (Dixon et al. 1998).

The bastion towers spaced along the outer wall of Mont Orgueil were part of the medieval defensive system. The wall of the lower ward originally ran in a straight line between two towers. This ward is dominated by the machicolated bastion, known as La Tour du Mont, an important feature of the medieval castle. Dating from the fourteenth century, it underwent extensive modifications later, during the time that Henry Cornish was Governor under the Duke of Somerset in the sixteenth century, and his coat of arms, sculpted in Caen stone, was inserted into the bastion at the time that the modifications were made.

In the late sixteenth century the Royal Commissioners examined Mont Orgueil alongside Castle Cornet and the castle was seen to be considerably lacking. Remodelling for cannon was undertaken. The second gateway gave entrance to the lower ward and was a square gatehouse with portcullis and drawbridge over a dry ditch. There was a long ascent through the middle ward to the keep. The third gateway was originally built by Sir George Carteret in 1648 and cut through the wall which cuts across the lower ward. It was renamed 'the Queen's gate' in 1846 when Queen Victoria visited the island and was presented with the keys of the castle.

Towards the end of the sixteenth century and after the close of Mont Orgueil's active medieval career, Sir Amias Paulet rebuilt the iron gateway, naming it after Queen Elizabeth I in an effort to please her. In the middle of the gate is the Royal Coat of Arms with the initials E.R. and the date 1593. He is recorded as spending over £3000 on building works. Paul Ivy (see above) was brought to Jersey to examine the island's defences. He recognised the vulnerability of Mont Orgueil castle in the age of cannon and recommended that the main effort be put to Elizabeth Castle. Mont Orgueil continued in use but in a much reduced capacity and was no longer the front line of defence of the island.

At the time of the Civil War the castle housed many famous political prisoners within its walls. Perhaps Puritan William Prynne who was imprisoned in what became known as Prynne's Tower from 1637 to 1640, for seditious libel, is the best known. He is also known for the poem cited above which he wrote during his confinement. The castle was besieged by the Parliamentarians but not taken until 1651.

The revival of English concerns about French intentions in the 1770s saw some modifications in which new barrack rooms were formed and repairs done to the collapsing walls. Further work was carried out c.1800, when the old castle served as a base for Philippe d'Auvergne, who acted as a spymaster for the British from here and his tower at La Hougue Bie (see Chapter 4), and whose changes involved principally the restoration of the castle as a residence. By c.1840 the central area of the upper fortress is thought to have been unroofed and empty.

During the nineteenth century a military presence was maintained, at a diminishing level, and little effective repair was carried out. It appears that most work during this period was confined to the domestic buildings of the lower ward. In 1907 the castle was finally demilitarised and was placed in the hands of the Office of Public Works, for preservation as a historic monument.

Excavations at Mont Orgueil

Archaeological excavations have taken place at Mont Orgueil on several occasions. A substantial record was created by E.T. Nicolle (1921) in which he drew together all the documentary evidence and then provided a description of the main features. Rybot (1930) gave an account of his excavations in the late 1920s in the middle ward and the grand battery and included a section through the main ditch. Some 20 years later, after the German Occupation, Rybot sectioned the outworks below the north-eastern walls of the castle (1950). In the early 1970s Ken Barton, then Director of Hampshire County Museum Service, directed training excavations in the middle ward. Alongside the examination of the medieval aspects of the castle important Neolithic and Iron Age material was uncovered (Barton 1984). This was followed by his publication of pottery that had been found previously at the castle (Barton 1977). La Société Jersiaise excavated in Prynne's Tower in 1982 and concluded from early pottery that it was built in the thirteenth century (Finlaison 1997, 2001). Seven floor levels were excavated which produced pottery and animal bone. Fragments of high quality painted medieval glass were also found. The finds included crossbow bolts (documented as being brought in between 1224-35). Mont Orgueil had not received a sustained programme of archaeological and historical research since the early 1980s, so the Jersey Heritage Trust, prompted by the 800th anniversary of King John's loss of France in 1204, began a programme of research and restoration in 1997. Dr Warwick Rodwell has been carrying out excavations in tandem with the production of a conservation plan since that time. The Jersey Heritage Trust's proposals caused considerable debate as they involve re-roofing the area thought by Dr Rodwell to be the Tudor Great Hall and major refurbishment of the monument.

Many scholars including Dr Philip Dixon, who compiled a list of the archives of the castle (Dixon et al. 1998) and Professor Colin Platt who produced a volume on the 'Defence of Jersey 1540-1630' and a dossier on the Tudor documents (Platt 2001, 2003) have been involved in a debate about the architectural developments in the castle. Dr Neil Rushton also published a consideration of the early documents that survive of the castle (2003). Dr Rodwell is due to publish a new guide book based on his work in 2006, in tandem with refurbishment of parts of the medieval castle and new interpretation for visitors (Rodwell forthcoming, 2006).

ELIZABETH CASTLE, JERSEY

As Mont Orgueil came to the end of its useful life as a military fortress new defences were built to defend St Helier and St Aubins Bay. Elizabeth Castle stands on a tidal islet where there was an earlier religious site associated with Saint Helier. The Chapel of St Helier dates to c.1150. It is shown on a map of Jersey of 1545 and again on Popinjay's 'platte' of 1563 (BL Cott. Aug. l ii 62) but was in a ruined state when the castle building began sometime after 1550 during the reign of King Edward VI. A gun platform was built on the highest point of the islet and called the mount or upper ward. The lower ward beneath was the site of much building in the eighteenth century. In the 1590s Edward's sister, Queen Elizabeth I, sent her military engineer, Paul Ivy, to organise the construction of a new castle. A platte of Ivy's also survives which shows the castle as 'Fort Isabella Bellissima' (Rybot 1947). Sir Walter Raleigh, who was governor in Jersey between 1600 and 1603, named the Castle after his Queen, Elizabeth.

By the 1640s, when Jersey was drawn into the English Civil War, the castle had been extended twice and included the lower ward. Fort Charles was built to defend the causeway approach to the castle in 1646-7. The castle was captured by the Parliamentarian forces in December 1651. Although today Elizabeth Castle appears to be built on one islet it is actually built on two. The outer ward was joined in 1668 to the lower and upper wards, when the walls were extended and the gap between them was turned into a ditch.

As at Mont Orgueil and Castle Cornet during the first half of the eighteenth century the lower ward was extensively remodelled with new barracks being built for both officers and men. Elizabeth Castle was built as an artillery fortress. During the siege of 1651 there was a report of over 15 cannon in the castle: a report in 1783 gives the number as 84, the largest being 24-pounders, while in 1804 there was a reported 62 guns which included five massive 68-pounders.

Elizabeth Castle is surrounded by the sea except for a short period at low tide which changes daily. This proved to be a weakness, highlighted in 1781, when the French landed at La Rocque, marched to St. Helier and captured the town. As a result of this, a new fortification was later built above St. Helier, on Mont de la Ville, called Fort Regent.

Elizabeth Castle continued as an army garrison until 1923 when it was sold to the States of Jersey to be used as an historic monument. During the German Occupation the castle was used as one of the strongpoints in St Aubin's Bay commanding the sea approaches to St. Helier. There have been no major archaeological excavations at the castle since Rybot wrote his detailed account in 1934 other than in 1986 when spoil heaps from various areas were examined but produced only nineteenth century finds (Tanguy 1987). An excellent view of the castle was drawn up by an engineer John Henry Bastide in 1730.

It is outside the scope of this book to detail all the fortifications of the Channel Islands due to lack of space but some others are worthy of mention. At Grosnez Castle on the north-west coast of Jersey there was an ordered, military-based fortification, probably built about 1330 on the orders of Sir John de Roches, who was Warden of the Isles. On three sides it is protected by natural features and on the fourth by a ditch. The walls are built from locally quarried granite and are thickest on the landward side. It probably only ever served as a refuge. The gatehouse is protected by a drawbridge and portcullis, and is flanked by two strong towers. However, it had a number of weaknesses. There were no sally ports for counter-attacks, accommodation was limited and, most seriously, there was no water supply inside the walls. The castle was taken by the French in 1373 and 1381 and was probably demolished either during or after the French Occupation of 1461-68. In 1806 a naval signal station was set up here to allow messages to be passed over to Guernsey which is visible to the north-west.

The Vale Castle in Guernsey is situated on a hill overlooking St Sampson's harbour (*colour plate 24*). It thus defended the northern part of Guernsey when it was separated from the rest of the island by the Braye du Valle. The north islet was not joined to the main part of Guernsey until the early nineteenth century when General Doyle drained the Braye and built a bridge. The castle itself was probably built around 1370-1400. In 1616 the gateway and walls had to be repaired at the expense of five parishes, and further extensive repairs were recommended in 1680 after the Civil War. Nearly a century later it was reported to be in a state of disrepair. The increased threat of invasion during the American War of Independence from 1778-83 prompted the castle's complete repair and the building of barracks.

Two divisions of Russian troops were stationed in Guernsey, at the Vale Castle in 1799. Several hundreds contracted disease and the dead were buried close to the castle. By the end of the nineteenth century the barracks were once more abandoned and left in a neglected state. During World War I the local militia had a small garrison in the castle and between the wars the barracks were used by the States of Guernsey as homes. German forces demolished the barracks during the Occupation from 1940-45 and built concrete fortifications in and around the castle. Thus the site has been used for military purposes for over 2000 years.

Ken Barton excavated the Vale Castle in 1980 but found that little of the medieval deposits survived due to later damage. Barton identified three main periods of occupation: an Early Iron Age hillfort, a fifteenth-century walled and defended enclosure and an eighteenth-century conversion of the fortification to an artillery fort in AD 1776 (Barton 1984a). It was subsequently abandoned and refortified in 1942.

The castle appears in the Legge report (1680) as 'an old Round piece of Fortification, of no strength at present' and in earlier documents referring to Owen of Wales in 1372. However, Barton does not consider that a castle occupied the site until the fifteenth century, based on surviving archaeological evidence. It is possible that the early references refer to the prehistoric earthworks as at Jerbourg, in the south of the island.

ALDERNEY AND SARK

The smaller islands have little to indicate military constructions as early as 1204, but these islands remain to be more fully investigated. In Alderney, Essex Hill overlooking Longis Bay was fortified in Tudor times and later the fort became a Victorian garrison hospital. Sir John Doyle fortified the early coastal batteries in the early 1800s. However, it was in response to the threat from France in the early nineteenth century that saw a massive construction in the island of 18 forts and batteries (Partridge 1991). The finest was at Fort Albert which was of polygonal construction. As with all the islands the vantage points were refortified by the occupying German forces from 1940-45 and many large bunkers and batteries were built.

Sark, with its steep cliffs and narrow harbours, is naturally defensible but a star fort is visible at La Vermondaye. There are two other forts at Chateau des Quenevets and Le Grand Fort, which possibly date to the French occupation between AD 1549-1553. The island was then colonised from Jersey by Helier de Carteret the Seigneur of St Ouen in 1565.

NAPOLEONIC DEFENCES

On the two larger islands coastal batteries were built as a response to the Napoleonic wars, many reusing sites which had been fortified earlier. A survey of the islands' defences was carried out in 1680 by a Colonel Legge and some time later in 1787 a map was drawn up for the Duke of Richmond which plots coastal batteries and fortifications. Both these documents are useful for the study of the islands' defences. Towers were also built in Guernsey and Jersey. In Guernsey 15 loopholed towers were built between AD 1778-9 partly because of the threat from the new alliance between the French and the newly independent American colonies. They are technically pre-martello towers (*64*). They comprise a lower floor for storage with the entrance at first floor level. Above this there are two floors with loophole slits for musketry defence.

64 Guernsey pre-martello Tower at L'Ancresse Common, Guernsey. *Photograph: Guernsey Museums and Galleries*

65 Jersey martello tower no. 3.
Photograph: author

66 A German observation tower
at Pleinmont, Guernsey. *Photograph:*
Guernsey Museums and Galleries

The open roofs were later adapted to mount 12-pounder guns on specially constructed traversing carriages. The towers batter out at the base with vertical faces above differing distinctly from the slightly later Jersey towers (Grimsley 1988).

In Jersey, General Conway, the Governor, ordered a series of round towers to be built around the coast to defend the island (65). The first four were completed by 1779. After the French invasion of 1781 the building programme took on a new urgency.

The towers were entered by a door on the first floor which was reached by a ladder which could be drawn inside if there was any danger. They tapered slightly from about 10.5m in diameter at the base to about 8.7m at the top. Inside the tower was divided so that the magazine and storeroom were on the ground floor and the upper two floors served as accommodation for the militia – one officer and eight or 10 men. The main armament was a heavy cannon set on a traversing platform on the roof. Typical of the Jersey towers are four machicolations which project from the top to allow marksmen on the roof to fire downwards (Davies 1991).

The story of the fortifications of the Channel Islands continues into the twentieth century to 1940, when the islands were occupied by German forces and became part of Hitler's Atlantic wall (66). This changed the landscape of the islands radically, despite only achieving a fraction of their building programme (Partridge pers. comm.). In spite of 60 years of peace in Europe, at the end of the twentieth century a fortified private house has recently been built on the island of Brecqhou, complete with 28 replica cannon!

9

SEA-GIRT ISLANDS:
MARITIME ARCHAEOLOGY

On the one hand islanders can have a passive relationship with the sea, using it only for the most local purposes ready to take the alarm at each strange sail on the horizon, and open to be plundered or exploited by the next raider or trader to reach their shores. On the other hand, islanders can be active users of the sea, taking control of their own trade, building up their own fleets and projecting both economic and military power to the furthest reaches of the wider world. (Jamieson 1986, xxix)

Ironically it is the ships that daily pass in and out of St Peter Port that have revealed the remains of some of their historical predecessors....(Adams and Black, 2004)

As previous chapters have illustrated the Channel Islands have been visited and settled by people arriving by sea for thousands of years. As the islands lie strategically placed between Britain and France, they provided a convenient stopping-off place in antiquity on long sea journeys. St Peter Port harbour was a natural haven for shipping and more approachable than St Helier or other harbours in Jersey due to the currents and tidal conditions. For thousands of years, however, the rocky approaches and the often severe weather have taken a toll on vessels and throughout the ages many were wrecked in Channel Island waters. So, as we have seen in previous chapters the sea continues to play an important role in the lives of islanders today.

The discovery of a Gallo-Roman ship in St Peter Port harbour (see below and Chapter 6) and much more recently the discovery of several land sites have given evidence of a substantial Roman presence in the islands, and Guernsey in particular, over many hundreds of years. After the Roman period the travels of visiting clerics and saints are documented throughout the early medieval period and by the time of the great castle building in the thirteenth century documentary records exist of materials and people arriving by sea. In the post-medieval period, islanders took a very active role in the Newfoundland fishing trade followed by the development of privateering, i.e. using their private ships in the service of the British government to attack enemy ships. This arrangement enabled the islands to flourish until it was brought to an end by the British government in 1807. A new demand grew for shipping to service the stone industry after this time but the inability of the shipbuilders to change from sail to steam effectively brought the island's active commercial role with the sea to an end. At the end of the second millennium the main experience of the sea that the majority of Channel Islanders will have had is a voyage on the ferry to England or France or a trip in a pleasure craft plying between the islands.

Alongside actual shipwrecks, harbour installations have been observed. Just south of St Peter Port harbour at Fermain Bay, in Guernsey, wooden structures have been visible on occasions after storms shifted sand from the seabed. These are assumed to be from the Roman period. Although remains of Roman shipping have been found no structural remains of a harbour have been located to date, at St Peter Port or in Jersey at St Helier or anywhere else, but one can assume that a lighthouse or beacon may have guided ships into harbour and a stone pier or jetty would have been in place. Documentary sources in the medieval period suggest that the first harbour installations at St Peter Port in stone were from the thirteenth century. In 1275 the Patent Rolls record that on 2 March a custom of 12 tournois and 6 tournois from every boat touching at the port of St Peter Port would be raised and applied to the construction of a wall or 'causey' between the King's castle and the town of St Peter Port to try to prevent the many wrecks that are found there. An assemblage of medieval ships lies wrecked in the harbour of St Peter Port as testament to this statement. In Jersey the population has been estimated at about 11,000 at the beginning of the thirteenth century, of whom some 3000 were involved in the fish trade, as witnessed by the quantities exported annually (Podger 2003). It is likely, however, that medieval ships were small enough to come close inshore and be beached when the tide receded. However, there is no direct evidence of a harbour in Jersey before the platte of c.1545 mentioned in Chapter 8 which portrays the haven of Jersey, showing a pier at St Helier.

In 1680 a review of the Islands' defences was carried out by Colonel Legge on the command of Charles II as a result of an appeal made by the local governor Lord Hatton. This was after considerable damage to Castle Cornet had been caused some eight years previously by an explosion after a lightning strike (see Chapter 8). The report includes detailed sketches of St Peter Port harbour and the roadsteads. In Jersey the accompanying text suggests that the people of St Helier had been trying for some years to get a proper harbour without success. In Guernsey the later harbour has been recorded by Sharp (1959), and David (1961) produced a comprehensive list of all known shipwrecks, the earliest then being the *Valentine* wrecked in 1780 off Sark. This list included 392 wrecks around the Bailiwick of Guernsey alone. If known wrecks off Jersey were included the number would almost double (Ovenden and Shayer 2003).

Two projects in particular however have put Guernsey on the maritime archaeological map; the discovery and subsequent excavation of a third century AD Romano-Celtic trading vessel and the current medieval wrecks project.

ST PETER PORT I

Richard Keen, a local commercial diver, discovered the substantial remains of a Romano-Celtic trading vessel on the floor of St Peter Port harbour while looking for scallops on Christmas morning in 1982. The vessel was located between the pierheads, suffering badly from the scouring action caused by the overhead passage of harbour traffic. Shortly after this the Guernsey Maritime Trust was formed to plan how to rescue the wreck from destruction. Excavation began in 1984, under the direction of Dr Margaret Rule of the Mary Rose Trust (67). The final timbers were raised in 1985 and together comprise a substantial part of the aft bottom of a Roman cargo ship (see Chapter 6). The surviving length amounts to about 18m with at least 4m of the bow missing.

The ship was a merchant vessel, originally some 25m in length. It was built of oak and held together by iron nails which are up to 60cm long (McGrail 2001). There is evidence that 1500 nails were used in the floor timbers alone. It is carvel-built which means all the timbers were butted against each other without using carpentered joints. The seams between them were plugged with

67 The Roman ship being excavated in St Peter Port harbour in 1985. *Photograph: Guernsey Maritime Trust*

caulking made from oak shavings and the nail holes were made watertight with moss grommets. Nailed across the keel was a series of 38 huge floor timbers. These form the shape of the ship's bottom which survives to a width of 4.5m at its centre. Between some of these were found futtocks; elements of the frames which form the shape of the sides. Nailed onto the outside of the floors and the futtocks were the strakes. These are relatively thin and delicate and the only ones which survived came from the stern, which was the most heavily buried.

The ship's timbers are very impressive, in both size and state of preservation. Marks of carpenters' tools are still visible on the surfaces. The divers found the aft half of the ship in position on the seabed. They also managed to collect additional pieces of wreckage which lay loose on the seabed so that about three-quarters of the length of the ship below the waterline was saved. The ship had a flat bottom suitable for grounding on the beach. The stern post was a curving timber which formed the shape. Although the other side is missing it is likely that the ship was double-ended. Two thirds of the way forward is the mast step, the square hole cut into the top of a large floor timber, where the mast is fitted. The ship had one mast, probably carrying a single square sail (68).

The wreck timbers themselves are now undergoing conservation at The Mary Rose Trust in Portsmouth. The programme will take approximately four to five years and includes immersion in PEG (polyethyleneglycol) and freeze drying.

68 A reconstruction of St Peter Port 1 based on information from the wreck. Model by R. Farrow. *Photograph: Guernsey Museums and Galleries*

However, many of the small finds have already been conserved and some are on display in the Maritime Museum at Castle Cornet, which is located only 100m from the wreck site. The Guernsey Museum Service is hoping to display the wreck when it is conserved in a new museum telling the story of St Peter Port harbour.

The next phase of research on the wreck is underway as the conservation programme moves into its final stages. This will consist of: dendrochronology, which will help with the dating of the ship and its provenance; re-examination of the conserved timbers; reassembly of the conserved timbers; scale models of the timbers; comparison with other vessels; and research on a possible reconstruction model which would help to estimate the performance of the ship. The pitch which formed part of the cargo has been the subject of recent research by Connan et al. (2001) and is currently part of a research programme at Bradford University.

NAVIS PROJECT

In 1996 Guernsey Museum was invited to join the Navis programme which was being funded by the European Commission. The project was designed to bring together maritime archaeologists from all over Europe to make a database of ancient wrecks up to AD 1000. The main partners were the Museum Für Antike Schiffahrt in Mainz, Germany, and the Centre for Maritime Archaeology at Roskilde, Denmark. Although Guernsey has only one excavated Roman ship it was considered important enough to be included in the database. Plans, drawings and photographs of the ship are now accessible on the internet along with other ancient ships from all over Europe. Navis II is now also accessible. This includes a database of iconography, including ship depictions on coins, monuments, pottery, mosaics and other media. It also includes web pages on harbours and installations and which includes St Peter Port, Guernsey, in the Roman period. The website can be accessed on www2.rgzm.de/navis/home/frames.htm

GUERNSEY MEDIEVAL WRECKS PROJECT

During the excavation of the Gallo-Roman boat it became clear that there was other wreck material in the harbour mouth which was of equal interest. Dr Jonathan Adams, Director of the Centre for Maritime Archaeology at Southampton University, dived on the Gallo-Roman ship and at the time, while carrying out a seabed survey, noticed some other timbers lying some way off, of a type that he was particularly interested in. These were parts of ships and were clinker-built and on the basis of their construction should have been late medieval in date, but recent artefactual evidence suggests that at least one is thirteenth century. At the time of the excavation of the Roman ship Dr Jon Adams surveyed the sea bed in detail and recorded what he could see at the time. At the end of the Roman project it was decided that the Guernsey Nautical Archaeology Group would take responsibility for monitoring these timbers.

However, as erosion was progressing at an alarming rate, in 1997 Dr Adams was invited to re-examine the site and following his report on the erosion of the silts protecting the timbers, the Guernsey Medieval Wrecks Project was initiated. In collaboration with the Centre for Maritime Archaeology at the University of Southampton an ongoing programme of survey and recording began in the hope that it would keep pace with erosion.

Many of the sections of timbers discovered in St Peter Port Harbour come from a fairly large clinker-built ships; one at least was probably in excess of 25m in length and perhaps nearer 30m. Most sections of timbers show heavy, well-squared framing, tree-nailed to solid planks whose overlap is a good third of their breadth. They are clenched at intervals between 90mm and 200mm. The plank widths obviously vary within any one vessel, depending on their position in the hull but these are typically between 250mm and 280mm wide and around 45mm thick (Adams 2002).

A large quantity of pottery is associated with the medieval wrecks, from the 'Saintonge' region of south-west France. Here, a particularly fine, elegant, green glazed pot was produced between AD 1260-1310. Of the Saintonge ware from St Peter Port harbour the quantity of sgraffito is greater than the total of that found on all other finds from land sites in England to where it was being exported (Duncan Brown pers. comm.). There is also a great quantity of other Saintonge types. The quantity of Saintonge pottery found in the harbour makes it likely that one of the wrecks was carrying it as a cargo. During excavation in 2002 parts of a leather shoe and lengths of rope were recovered and in the maststep of the largest vessel the remains of a silver coin of Alphonso III of Portugal (1248-79) was retrieved. Incredibly Dr Barrie Cook of the British Museum was able to read the legend from the concretion around the coin. It was a tradition of ship builders to step the mast with a coin so one can assume they would not use a coin that was worn. This would indicate that at least one of the vessels might have belonged to a Portuguese merchant working out of Bordeaux. There are many records of vessels going in and out of Guernsey and Jersey in the early medieval period carrying large cargos of wine (Childs 1986). In Southampton the custom records of AD 1397-8 record ships from Jersey bringing cargoes of weight between 3 and 56.5 tons (*colour plate 25*).

The association of the Saintonge pottery (*69*) makes these wrecks, or one of them at least, early examples of the sort of heavily framed Nordic ship that was not eclipsed as a premier carrier until the adoption of carvel-built (edge to edge timbers) vessels in the second half of the fifteenth century (Adams 2002).

69 A jug of Saintonge type found lying next to one of the wrecks. It had been very recently exposed. *Photograph: Guernsey Museums and Galleries*

THE OTHER ISLANDS OF THE BAILIWICK OF GUERNSEY

The islands of Alderney, Herm and Sark are home to many known wreck sites and no doubt many unidentified wrecks also. One vessel, the 'Valentine', lies off Sark and has been subject to research over many years by the Guernsey Nautical Archaeology Group among others. The vessel, which was a three-masted sailing ship, made her first voyage in 1768 and was damaged on her return from India with a cargo of saltpetre, raw silk and red wood. The East Indiaman was repaired and was then part of a convoy which sailed to Ireland in 1779. On their return bad weather struck and she was forced onto a reef between Sark and Brecqhou. The crew survived but the ship was looted as some of the cannon on Sark today bear witness.

In Alderney an Elizabethan wreck was discovered in 1970 and relocated in 1990 by members of the Alderney sub-aqua club. It lies some 400m off the north coast of Alderney in an area known as 'The Ledge' in about 30m of water, exposed to currents. Over the next two years over 1000 objects were brought to the surface despite the difficult conditions, including cannon, armour, pot sherds and whole pots (Bowyer 1998). The pottery was examined by Bob Burns, then Archaeology Officer at Guernsey Museum, and the wreck was subsequently dated to the sixteenth century. Two pan weights of Elizabeth I also supported this date (*70*). The wreck was then scheduled under the Guernsey Wreck and Salvage (Vessels and Aircraft) (Bailiwick of Guernsey), Law 1986 and in 1993 Mike Bowyer was appointed Project Director by the States of Alderney with advice from Guernsey. Later the Alderney Maritime Trust was formed to oversee the work on the wreck. Three years of survey work followed. In 1999 the Trust appointed Dr Jason Monaghan to bring together the results of the research to date (Monaghan & Bound 2001) and also to seek sponsorship for further work. Further excavation is hampered by deep water, currents and, more importantly, a lack of funding. However, valuable conservation work has been carried out on many of the artefacts raised, some of which, including one of the cannon and its splendid gun carriage, are now on display in Alderney Museum. Prince Andrew has recently become patron of the Alderney Maritime Trust and a new phase of work has just begun under Dr Mensun Bound.

RICHARD KEEN

One local diver merits special mention when discussing the maritime heritage of the Channel Islands. Richard Keen began diving as a schoolboy and went on to form his own salvage company and become a professional diver. His interest in history and archaeology combined with his skill as a diver has meant a steady stream of discoveries and information about historic wrecks around the islands. The most important find, arguably, was the timber from the Roman vessel described above which he famously discovered in St Peter Port harbour on Christmas morning in 1982. It is a tradition in Guernsey to go diving on Christmas morning as it is the one day that there is no commercial traffic. While attending maritime archaeology conferences in the UK, Richard met Margaret Rule and consulted her about the Roman wreck; she subsequently organised the excavations. More recently he has been assisting with the medieval wrecks project and continues to add to the corpus of information on wrecks around the shores of Guernsey and the other islands, both historic and recent (*71*). One of his particular skills is giving information to other divers and persuading the local groups to report their finds.

Jersey boasts no early wrecks to date, although many sport divers are active in local waters. It seems inconceivable that Jersey waters will not eventually yield historic wrecks similar to those in Guernsey waters. Channel Island wrecks have recently been surveyed by John Ovenden and David Shayer (2003). In their interesting volume they clearly illustrate that since the nineteenth century equal numbers of vessels have come to grief around the larger islands in the treacherous Channel Island waters.

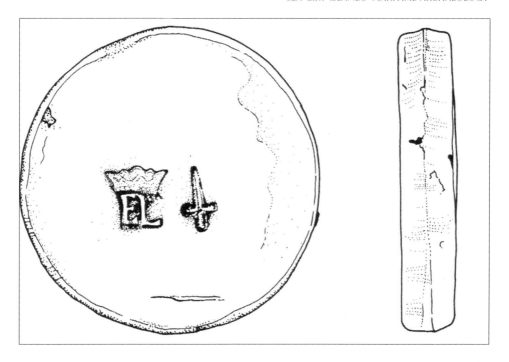

70 *Above* Pan weights of Elizabeth
I from a wreck off Alderney. *By kind
permission of the illustrator Helen Ford
and the Alderney Maritime Trust*

71 *Right* Richard Keen and Heather
Sebire examining a timber from
a medieval wreck in St Peter Port
harbour. *Photograph: Guernsey Museums
and Galleries*

10

MUSEUMS AND MONUMENTS: THE LEGACY

Historically, the Channel Islands stand at the crossroads of Europe, where movements and influences from the mainland and the Atlantic coasts meet, and where they become complicated and embellished with the particular effects of the islands' character. (Kinnes & Grant 1983)

The richness of the Atlantic region has been a leitmotif running through this story. (Cunliffe 2001)

THE ARCHAEOLOGY OF THE CHANNEL ISLANDS

The quotation from Barry Cunliffe's *Facing the Ocean* is particularly appropriate to the story of Channel Islands archaeology. So much of it is due to the geographical position of the islands and the all–encompassing role of the sea in the lives of Channel Islanders in the past and today.

As we have seen, in the Lower Palaeolithic period the islands were still part of mainland France and a few bands of people found shelter and eked out their existence in cave dwellings. In the Mesolithic there is evidence of coastal communities, as on Lihou Island, and habitation sites slightly further inland, such as Canal du Squez on Jersey and L'Emauve on Alderney. In the Early Neolithic the first farmers worked the fertile soils on the islands, much of which is now lost beneath the waves, but traces remain at The Royal Hotel site in St Peter Port and at Le Pinacle and Mont Orgueil on Jersey. In the later Neolithic, megalithic, ceremonial burial tombs were built, some of which survive today. The Bronze Age is characterised by the construction of fortifications and later depositions of hoards of metalwork. By the Iron Age the defensive earthworks are considerable and farmsteads of circular houses are found. In the later Iron Age members of an élite warrior class were buried in Guernsey with impressive grave goods and large quantities of coins are buried on Jersey, possibly by people fearing the advance of Rome. As the Romans move north through Gaul we see the Channel Islands brought into the Empire as their strategic maritime position is recognised and trade routes become firmly established.

After the Roman period the islands are visited by 'peregrini' or wandering saints, many of whom built chapels and cells for Christian worship in remote locations. St Helier, St Sampson and St Magloire are among those who are thought to have brought Christianity to the islands in the sixth and seventh centuries. At the end of the ninth century the islands very likely suffered Viking raids and then eventually became part of the Norman Empire. This changed in 1204, when John, King of England, lost his interests in France. After this the islands took on another strategic role, that of defence for the English crown and the great period of castle building took place, resulting in Mont Orgueil in Jersey and Castle Cornet in Guernsey. The islands then grew in importance and the towns of St Peter Port and St Helier developed to service their wealthy merchants and townsfolk. The archaeology of the Channel Islands is a rich story of the interplay between people and their environment, small areas of land surrounded by a dangerous and powerful sea which through time has acted as both a barrier and a highway.

MUSEUMS AND MONUMENTS TO VISIT

As we have seen in the previous chapters, people have been coming and going to and from the Channel Islands for thousands of years, leaving behind their remains for those of us who come after to see. Although many sites mentioned in the chapters above do not now exist because of destruction due to development or coastal erosion, or in some cases total excavation, there are still wonderful museums and monuments in all the islands for the visitor to experience.

A NOTE ON MAPS OF THE CHANNEL ISLANDS

Ordnance survey maps exist for all the islands but in 1998 a new digital map was created for the Bailiwick of Guernsey with a new grid. This is available to researchers through Digimap, see the website www.digimap.gg (for the Bailiwick of Guernsey including Alderney, Sark and Herm). Jersey is currently creating a similar map, see the website www.digimap.je. For ease of reference the relevant Ordnance Survey co-ordinates have been given by the name of the site, from the Jersey Official Leisure map 1:25000 and Guernsey, the M824 series Guernsey sheet WV 1:25000. The sites can also be found by reference to local street guides known as 'Perry's'. The Perry's guides are recommended to visitors and the references are given where appropriate from the 2001 small format edition for Jersey and 2005 small format edition for Guernsey.

JERSEY

All the Museums run by the Jersey Heritage Trust are featured on their website. Visit www.jerseyheritagetrust.org for up-to-date opening times and visiting information.

La Hougue Bie, parish of Grouville
OS 682 504 Perry's 42 D3
At the site of the Neolithic burial mound dating back 6000 years, not only can the visitor see the tomb itself but there is an excellent museum of the island's prehistory and its natural environment with geology and archaeology galleries (*72*). Among the Museum exhibits there are stone tools from the Palaeolithic cave at La Cotte de St Brelade, stunning reconstructed Neolithic pots from Le Pinacle and other sites, and displays of the magnificent coin hoards which have been found in the island. Since the recent excavations the entrance to the tomb itself has been restored and it is possible to imagine what part of the burial rite might have been when one enters the passage and moves into the chamber. Two small chapels on top of the mound can be visited, and there is a World War II German bunker open to the public.

72 Prehistoric objects on display at La Hougue Bie Museum, Jersey. *Courtesy of the Jersey Heritage Trust / Société Jersiaise Collections*

Jersey Museum, the Weighbridge, St Helier
Perry's Town map D9

The Jersey Museum is in St Helier (73) and starts the story of Jersey with a diorama of the site at La Cotte de St Brelade. In the archaeology gallery the display starts with Palaeolithic material from La Cotte and then finds from every period including Neolithic pots, bronze axes from the Mainlands hoard and the spectacular gold torc from St Helier. Part of the coin hoard from La Marquanderie is dramatically displayed, giving the visitor an idea of what these large hoards looked like. There are also interesting exhibits on the medieval period, and of note is material from Les Écréhous, including the beautiful silver brooch that was found during the excavations.

Jersey Maritime Museum, New North Pier, St Helier
Perry's Town Map C9

Jersey does not boast any known shipwrecks before the seventeenth century but the Maritime Museum is well worth a visit for the later maritime history of the island. There is also an interesting exhibit on conservation of objects which has active work going on in the gallery. The museum is set in the historic harbour of St Helier and has as its theme the islanders' relationship with the sea through the elements, the boats and the people who became the key players in Jersey's maritime history.

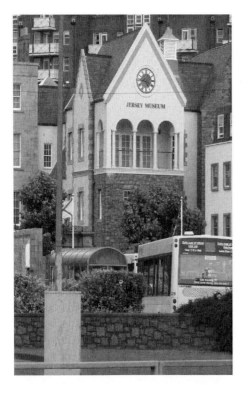

73 The Jersey Museum, Weighbridge, St Helier.
Photograph: author

Mont Orgueil Castle
Perry's 44 D3
The castle towers over the harbour at Gorey on Jersey's east coast and is well worth a visit both for the castle itself, in its stunning position, and also for its history and prehistory. The exhibitions within the castle will be redisplayed in 2006 including material from previous excavations and more recent work by Dr Warwick Rodwell and La Société Jersiaise. The results of research on the fabric of the buildings within the castle and the fortification itself alongside the historical documents which relate to the castle will also be part of the exhibit.

Elizabeth Castle
Perry's Town map D6 for West Park access point
This fortress, built on an islet in St. Aubins Bay during the reign of Elizabeth I, is worth a visit to fully appreciate the topography and the views of St Helier and St Aubins Bay. The earliest parts of the castle, built by the great engineer Paul Ivy, are particularly interesting. Within the castle there are exhibits about its construction and history and there is a museum dedicated to the Jersey Militia. Access is either by a causeway at low tide or by a DUKW (ex-army amphibious vehicle) from West Park beach. The hermitage of St Helier, which is very atmospheric, situated on a rocky outcrop to the east of the castle, can also be visited.

MONUMENTS TO VISIT IN JERSEY

Jersey Museum provides a very useful guide to the major prehistoric monuments in a leaflet which can be obtained from any of their sites or the local tourist office. Most of the surviving megaliths can be visited but if the visitor is limited for time the best place to start is at La Hougue Bie, which is one of the finest passage graves in Europe. The site of La Cotte de Saint Brelade is not open to the public as access is very difficult and the site is somewhat unsafe. Others that can be visited include:

Le Pinacle, in St Ouen's parish (OS 544 555, Perry's 6 A4), is an important multi-period site comprising a Neolithic activity centre where axes were produced *c.*4800-4000 BC, an Early Bronze age ceremonial site *c.*2850-2000 BC and a Gallo-Roman temple *c.*AD 200.
Les Monts Grantez, also in St Ouen's parish (OS 567 537, Perry's 15 F4), which is a passage grave with an asymmetrical chamber and external side chamber dating to *c.*4000-3250 BC.
La Pouquelaye de Faldouet, in the parish of St Martin (OS 710 507, Perry's 44 C2), a passage grave with an unusual double chamber, the main chamber is open and surrounded by cists, the second is covered by a single massive capstone *c.*4000-3250 BC.

Ville-ès-Nouaux, in the parish of St Helier (OS 635 499, Perry's 39 G4), is a remarkable complex with a gallery grave *c.*3250-2250 BC, a cist-in-circle *c.*2850 BC and evidence of Late Bronze Age urn burials *c.*800 BC.

La Sergenté, in St Brelades parish (OS 561 486, Perry's 46 D3), is the only corbelled passage grave known from the Channel Islands and possibly the earliest megalith in Jersey, dating to *c.*4500-4000 BC.

The Ossuary, in St Ouen's parish (OS 571 500, Perry's 25 G4), is a rectangular megalithic cist which contained the disarticulated remains of 20 individuals and dates to *c.*2850-2250 BC. The Broken, Little and Great Menhirs nearby are part of the same prehistoric landscape.

Le Couperon in the parish of St Martin (OS 703 542, Perry's 24 B3), is a gallery grave with a rectangular enclosure of upright stones and a porthole slab. The geology of the stones is particularly interesting *c.*3250-2250 BC.

Mont Ubé, in the parish of St Clement (OS 677 475, Perry's 56 C1), is a large passage grave, originally with four internal cells, which was badly destroyed by quarrying sometime before 1850, *c.*4000-3250 BC.

Dolmen de Géonnais, in St Ouen's parish (OS 573 558, Perry's 7 G3), is a passage grave with an unusual rectangular chamber, which was almost certainly open, *c.*4000-3250 BC.

La Motte, in the parish of St Clement (OS 675 457, Perry's 56 B5), is also known as Green Island where excavations revealed a Cairn of unknown date, Neolithic midden material *c.*4000 BC and a series of 18 cist burials possibly Bronze Age *c.*2000-1200 BC or medieval.

The earthworks at Câtel de Rozel (OS 692 547, Perry's 23 F2), can be seen on the north-east coast and are marked on the Ordnance Survey map. The Roman *fanum* can be seen at Le Pinacle (see above). Many of the parish churches stand on ancient sites and those of St Lawrence, where part of a Roman pillar can be seen, and St Clement's, where Roman material has been found, are of particular interest. For the later fortifications, the Jersey Heritage Trust provides a leaflet on the Jersey Coastal Towers and there are many publications on the WWII fortifications.

GUERNSEY

In Guernsey all the museums run by the States of Guernsey are featured on the museum website. Visit www.museums.gov.gg to see up-to-date opening times and visiting information.

Guernsey Museum and Art Gallery, St Peter Port, Guernsey
Perry's Town Map H5
Guernsey Museum (74) tells the story of Guernsey from prehistoric times to the present day. There is a gallery dedicated to Frederick Corbin Lukis, Guernsey's

74 Guernsey Museum and Art Gallery, St Peter Port. *Photograph: Guernsey Museums and Galleries*

great Victorian antiquarian, with his cabinet of curiosities. In the remaining galleries the story starts with the island's early prehistory and displays artefacts from, among others, the megaliths of Le Déhus and La Varde. Archaeological material from Alderney was brought to Guernsey at the beginning of the twentieth century and so Guernsey Museum has the Alderney hoard of bronzes on display also. A reconstruction of the warrior who was buried at Kings Road St Peter Port around 50 BC sits on a rock of Guernsey granite in the main prehistory gallery. All the information for this reconstruction, the weapons, the shield and the cloth, was gained from the early 1980s excavations. There are also exhibits showing trade connections from prehistoric times including items of shale and pottery. Medieval exhibits include the Cobo long house gaming piece and material from Lihou Priory including a column capital with beakhead decoration.

Castle Cornet and Maritime Museum, Castle Pier, St Peter Port
Perry's Town Map, O9
Castle Cornet, built sometime at the beginning of the thirteenth century, guards the entrance to St Peter Port harbour. A museum telling the story of the castle and its development is housed at the entrance in the restored eighteenth century lower barracks. In this exhibit, which opened in 1996, material from the many excavations that have taken place is displayed including French medieval pottery, medieval coins, metalwork and an impressive display of clay smoking pipes.

The Maritime Museum at Castle Cornet was opened in 1990 by Lord Lewin, then Admiral of the Fleet, and has displays on the excavation and subsequent raising of the St Peter Port Roman ship alongside evidence of a Roman waterfront site in St Peter Port at La Plaiderie. The museum is located in the eighteenth-century barracks known as the 'married quarters' and goes on to trace Guernsey's nautical history from prehistory to the present day. Island ship building and fishing, the nineteenth-century redevelopment of St Peter Port harbour and Royal Navy connections are portrayed.

Fort Grey, St Pierre-du-Bois, Guernsey
Perry's 20 A5

Fort Grey was erected in 1804 as part of coastal defences to defend Guernsey against the French. It is situated on a tidal islet on the southern west coast in Rocquaine Bay, on the site of an earlier fort. In 1970 it was restored by the States of Guernsey and opened as a maritime museum in 1976. It is now approached across a stone-built causeway and commands a strong position in the approaches to Rocquaine and Portelet Bays. The fort is painted white as a mark to shipping. This area of the west coast has always been and continues to be a hazard to shipping and as recently as January 2003 a large container vessel the Vermontborg was grounded in high seas nearby. The earliest recorded wreck is in an assize roll of 1309 and over a hundred other shipwrecks have been located by local researchers between 1734 and the 1970s. Artefacts from several of these form the basis of the museum alongside information about navigation and the Hanois lighthouse which was one of the last manned lights in the British Isles. Exhibits about shipwrecks include HMS Sprightly, HMS Boreas, SS Yarouba and SS Breseis to name but a few. Maritime archaeologist Robert Stenuit located, identified and excavated HMS Sprightly in 1973 and HMS Boreas was located by local divers Richard Keen and David Archer in 1970.

75 Fort Grey, Shipwreck Museum, Guernsey. *Photograph: Guernsey Museums and Galleries*

MONUMENTS TO VISIT IN GUERNSEY

In Guernsey the tourist office has leaflets to help the visitor to find the sites and for the main prehistoric monuments there is a detailed guide available in *Les Fouaillages and the Megalithic Monuments of Guernsey* by Ian Kinnes and Jenny Grant (Ampersand Press 1983) which is available from Guernsey Museum and all good book shops.

There are no Palaeolithic sites that are easily visited in the Bailiwick of Guernsey but the Mesolithic site on Lihou can be found at the north-east tip of the islet (see below). Many fine Neolithic monuments can be seen, however, and the visitor may like to start with a visit to Les Fouaillages, in the Vale parish (OS 335 82, Perry's 6 B3), a long mound which covered a complex burial monument with adjacent settlement site *c.*5000-1800 BC. This is the earliest prehistoric monument in the island. Other sites that can be visited include:

The Castel statue-menhir, in the Castel parish (OS 311 788 Perry's16 A4), outside the Castel parish church *c.*2500-1800 BC. This decorated menhir is a unique monument and not to be missed. There is also an exhibition in the church about the 1998 excavations which uncovered the bell pit and Roman features.

La Gran'mère du Chimquière, in St Martins (OS 324 765, Perry's 24 D5), is a statue-menhir, *c.*2500-1800 BC, situated at the parish church, which was carved in prehistoric times and then remodelled in the Roman period.

Le Creux ès Faïes, in the parish of St Pierre-du-Bois (OS 251 784, Perry's 12 A5), is a bottle-shaped passage grave, excavated by Lukis in 1840, latest phase *c.*2000-1800 BC.

La Longue Rocque, in the parish of St Pierre-du-Bois (OS 265 772, Perry's 20 D3/4), is a menhir, *c.*2500-1500 BC, on private land but can be seen from the road, Les Paysans.

L'Islet cist-in-circle, in the parish of St Sampson's (OS 331 822, Perry's 10 A1), can be difficult to find in the Sandy Hook housing estate; walk to the interior of the estate on Sandy Hook Road *c.*2500-1800 BC.

Le Trépied Passage Grave, in the parish of St Saviour's (OS 260 789, Perry's 12 D4), is a megalith dramatically positioned overlooking the west coast of Guernsey, *c.*4000-2000 BC.

La Longue Pierre and Le Crocq (OS 271 797, Perry's 13 F3) in St Saviour's parish are menhirs, *c.*2500-1500 BC, on private land but can be seen from the road, Route de La Marette.

Le Déhus Passage Grave, in the parish of the Vale (OS 358 831, Perry's 7 H4), is one of the most complex of the megalithic tombs in Guernsey, with a chamber and passage and several side chambers. Do not miss the carving on the capstone in the interior, *c.*4000-2000 BC.

La Varde Passage Grave, in the Vale parish (OS 337 836, Perry's 6 C2), is the largest of Guernsey's passage graves, with a bottle-shaped chamber and a possible side chamber, *c.*4000-2000 BC.

La Platte Mare, cist-in-circle in the Vale parish (OS 336 831, Perry's 6 C3). Look for the cup marks on the upright facing north, c.2500–1800 BC.
La Mare és Mauves, cist-in-circle in the Vale parish (OS 339 834, Perry's 6 C3); the remains of a cist-in-circle in a low-lying area of L'Ancresse Common, c.2500–1800 BC.

Neolithic settlement sites are generally not accessible but the former Royal Hotel site which had Early Neolithic remains is now the site of the Royal Bank of Scotland (Perry's Town map L5) on the sea front. The earthworks at Jerbourg which were started in the Bronze Age can be seen on the walk down to Marble Bay over National Trust land commencing at the Doyle Monument (OS 338 752, Perry's 31 G3). There are no Iron Age or Roman sites in Guernsey which can be visited but substantial Roman settlement was uncovered beneath the Market Buildings in St Peter Port (Perry's Town Map K8) and opposite Moore's Hotel in Le Pollet (Perry's Town Map L8).

The Vale Castle
OS 355 818 Perry's 11 G2
Little of the original castle can be seen today but one of the oldest parts is the gate which is fourteenth century in date. The standing walls are all much later mostly eighteenth century when barrack blocks were built inside. The castle affords magnificent views of the Roadsteads however with the islands of Herm, Jethou and Sark nearby, Alderney and the French coast in view to the north and Jersey to the south. It is worth a visit for the view alone.

Château des Marais
OS 336 802 Perry's 17 G1
The original clay bank and mound, very likely erected after the events of 1204 is now disguised by stone walls which date to the eighteenth century, reinforced as a defence against the threat from France. The mound was raised up above the Marais or marsh which surrounded it and may have been navigable. It is just about still visible as low-lying land now bordered by housing estates.

As in Jersey the parish churches are all on sites of great antiquity and the Parish Church of St Sampson has the oldest surviving features. The Vale Church has an early medieval inscription, the Castel Church has Roman material in the fabric and the menhirs at St Martins and the Castel have been described above. For details of the churches on all the islands see *Channel Island Churches* by John McCormack (1986). There are many excellent publications on the later fortifications (Grimsley 1988) and World War II sites (Gavey 1997) available from local book shops.

Lihou Priory
The island of Lihou lies off the west coast of Guernsey and is approached by a tidal causeway from the car park on L'Eree headland (Perry's 12 A5). Care

must be taken when visiting the island which is only possible at certain times of the month - see the local Press for details or the tide times that are posted at the Guernsey end of the causeway. The ruins of the twelfth century Priory can be visited OS 241 789 (Perry's 12 B2) and the Mesolithic site GU582 is to the north-east OS 244 791. The island is a nature reserve. The dovecote makes one of the best picnic spots in the islands!

ALDERNEY

Alderney Museum
Guernsey Perry's 36 F3 and OS M824 Alderney 1:10560
The excellent award-winning Alderney Museum is well worth a visit, not least to see the magnificent Iron Age pots from Les Huguettes which were restored by Peggy Wilson soon after the excavation. Peter Arnold has also organised displays of flint work from Alderney and the neighbouring islets with the help of Dr Mark Patton. Roman material including the high-status glass from the Longis area is also displayed. A maritime gallery was added in 1989 which is currently home to an exhibit on the Alderney Elizabethan wreck, showing many of the artefacts including a cannon in its original gun carriage from the ship. This is a rare and important find.

The Museum is run by the Alderney Society, see their website www.alderneymuseum.org for details of opening times and visitor information.

MONUMENTS TO VISIT IN ALDERNEY

Perry's references are from the Guernsey edition, OS Series M824 Alderney 1:10560
The prehistoric monuments on Alderney are not very accessible. However, a small megalith at Tourgis (OS 564 077 Perry's 36 D1/2) can be seen from the road. The whole area of Longis Common is interesting archaeologically, as the megaliths of Les Porciaux are on high ground to the north-east and the Early Iron Age site at Les Huguettes lies to the south of the area. It can be visited on the edge of the golf course at OS 593 081, Perry's 38 D4. Many of the Roman finds on display at the museum were found during excavations on Longis Common. The small fort known as the Nunnery (OS 595 081, Perry's 38 D4), is not open to the public but the exterior can be viewed from the road. Essex Castle (OS 595 078, Perry's 38 C5), dominates the hill to the south which was fortified in the Iron Age period. Enquire at the museum for further details if you wish to visit Les Porciaux (OS 603 086, Perry's 39 F4).

There are excellent books available on the Later Fortifications by Trevor Davenport available from the Alderney Museum and local bookshops.

THE SMALLER ISLANDS

Herm

Perry's Guernsey edition 34 and OS M824 Herm & Jethou 1: 10,000
Prehistoric burial monuments are visible on the Sandy Common along the path
from the harbour and on the Petit and Grand Monceau. A ruined passage grave
at Robert's Cross (OS 398 808) is signposted. The sites are marked on the Tourist
Map available from the shop. Please enquire for further details at Guernsey
Museum if you require them. Prehistoric material from sites on Herm is on
display at Guernsey museum. The Chapel of St Tugual possibly stands on the site
of an earlier one established in the sixth century.

Sark

Perry's Guernsey edition and OS Series M824 Sark 1:10000
A small exhibit is currently being put together by La Société Serquiaise on
various aspects of research on the island in a new room alongside the Visitors
Centre where enquiries can be made. There are no monuments that are easily
accessible but the area near the mill is where the Sark hoard was found in the
eighteenth century. The area of l'Eperquerie (OS 463 776, Perry's 41) may have
been an ancient landing spot and there is evidence of banks and ditches which
run down the cliff. There are also earthworks at Le Fort (OS 466 770, Perry's
41), which may be prehistoric in origin with later reuse in the medieval period.
St Magloire's monastery is by tradition at La Moinerie (now a restaurant)
(OS 463 766, Perry's 41), and there are remains in the gardens of La
Seigneurie (OS 464 766, Perry's 41), which are thought to be remnants of the
monastery but this is unproven by excavation. On Little Sark overlooking Clouet
Bay (OS 456 734, Perry's 40) there are the remains of a stone cist recorded by
Lukis in the nineteenth century. Also on Little Sark at Le Vermondaye (OS 468
742, Perry's 40), are the remains of a star fort thought to have been erected by
the French during their occupation in 1549.

Les Écréhous and Les Minquiers

There is no regular boat service to the islands but enquire at the Jersey Tourist
Office for details of possible visits to the Priory of St Mary on Les Écréhous or
Les Minquiers where there is a little remaining of the prehistoric occupation.

ARCHAEOLOGY IN THE ISLANDS TODAY

As the Channel Islands have their own legislation in which, at present, archaeology
is not a major condition in the planning laws, there has been very little developer-
funded archaeology carried out in the islands. As a result most of the recent work
has been carried out by local volunteer groups and visiting researchers.

In Jersey, La Société Jersiaise (www.societe-jersiaise.org) has an archaeological section which meets regularly at La Hougue Bie, and carries out small research excavations. Currently a review of Sites of Special Interest is taking place and many areas of St Helier, in particular, have been given special protection within the planning law meaning that developers will have to take account of archaeology. In practical terms this means that outside archaeological contractors are starting to be used and this will very likely become the norm for major developments. There is currently no full-time Field Officer, however. The Jersey Heritage Trust has a part-time Curator of Archaeology who is based at La Hougue Bie where most of the archaeology collections are housed.

In Guernsey, the Guernsey Museum Service has supported an Archaeological Research and Rescue Group since 1985, run by the Archaeology Officer (the author) which was established to carry out limited rescue excavations with a small working budget allocated. The Archaeology Officer also acts as Curator of Archaeology in the Museum Service and is based at the Museum Service's Store in St John Street, St Peter Port, where the majority of the archaeology collections are housed.

La Société Guernesiaise (www.societe.org.gg) also has an archaeological section which organises activities such as fieldwalking, lectures and meetings. New planning law currently on the statute books will address the problem of the lack of developer funding so that adequate recording can take place on development sites.

In Alderney there is an archaeology section of the Alderney Society whose members carry out small research excavations, monitor planning applications and encourage research by visiting academics and locals alike.

SITES AND MONUMENTS RECORDS

Jersey Heritage Trust is currently compiling a Sites and Monuments Record for Jersey which is based at the Archive Service of the Jersey Heritage Trust, to whom enquiries should be made (see website above).

Guernsey Museum has developed a Sites and Monuments Record for the Bailiwick of Guernsey which currently has over 5000 records and covers all the islands in the Bailiwick. Although this is not accessible to the public at present, requests from anyone involved in local research will be addressed (see website above).

BIBLIOGRAPHY

ABBREVIATIONS

ASB   Alderney Society Bulletin
Arch. J.   Archaeological Journal
Antiq. J.   Antiquaries Journal
BSJ   Bulletin of La Société Jersiaise
B. Gsy. Soc.   Bulletin of the Guernsey Society
BSPF   Bulletin de la Société Préhistoire de la Française
IJNA   International Journal of Nautical Archaeology
PPS   Proceedings of the Prehistoric Society
TSG   Transactions of La Société Guernesiaise

Adams, J. 2002. *Guernsey Medieval Wrecks*. Guernsey Museum. Privately Circulated Paper
Adams J, & Black, J. 2004. From rescue to research: medieval ship finds in St Peter Port Guernsey. *INJA* **33**, **2**, 250-2
ADAS 1989. *Report on the soil and land evaluation on Guernsey*. ADAS
Anon. 1908. Report on the monthly meeting. *TSG* **5**, 424
Anon. 1840. *Caesarea, The Island of Jersey*. London: Baker
Allen, D.F. 1971. The Sark Hoard. *Archaeologia or Miscellaneous Tracts relating to Antiquity* **53**, 1-31
Anderson, R. 1997. Foreword in L. Webster and M. Brown (eds.) *The Transformation of the Roman World. AD 400-900*. London: British Museum Press
Archibald, M.A. 1980. The Coins in K.J.Barton, Excavations at the Château des Marais. *TSG* **20**, V, 673-677
Baal, H.J. & Sinel, J. 1915. Exploration of 'La Hougue Mauger' October, 1914. *BSJ* **8**, 58-61
Baal, H.J., Godfray, A.D.B., Nicolle, E.T. & Rybot, N.V.L. 1925. Report on the Discovery of a Pre-Historic Burial Chamber at La Hougue Bie *BSJ* **10:3**, 205-17
Bahn, P. (ed.) 1996. *The Cambridge Illustrated History of Archaeology*. Cambridge University Press: Cambridge
Barton K.J. 1977. Medieval pottery from Gorey Castle, Jersey. *BSJ* **22:1**, 69-82
Barton, K. J. 1980. Fortifications of the Channel Islands. *Review of the Guernsey Society*. **36:1**, 5-8
Barton, K.J. 1980a. Excavations at the Château des Marais. *TSG* **20**, V, 657-702
Barton, K.J. 1984. Excavations in the Middle Ward Mont Orgueil, Gorey, Jersey. Arch. J. **141**, 216-242
Barton, K.J. 1984a. Excavations at the Vale Castle *TSG* **21:4**, 485-538
Barton, K.J. 1998. Towards a Ceramic Sequence in Guernsey. In H. Sebire (ed.) *Guernsey Connections. Historical and Archaeological Papers in Honour of Bob Burns*. Guernsey: La Société Guernesiaise, 21-25

Barton, K.J. 2003. *The Archaeology of Castle Cornet, Guernsey*. Guernsey Museum Monograph No. 7

Batt, M. 1998 in *Medieval Peasant Buildings In Brittany*. In H. Sebire (ed.) *Guernsey Connections. Historical and Archaeological Papers in Honour of Bob Burns*. Guernsey: La Société Guernesiaise, 80-95

Bellis, R. & Cable, E.K. 1884. Mont Cochon Cromlech. *BSJ* 1, 422-435

Bender, B. 1975. *Farming in Prehistory. From hunter-gatherer to food-producer*. London: John Baker

Bender, B. 1986. *The Archaeology of Brittany, Normandy and the Channel Islands*. London: Faber and Faber

Bernier, G. 1982. *Les Chretientes Bretonnes Continentals depuis les origins jusqu'au IXéme Siecle*. Dossiers du Ce. R.A.A.

Bertaux, J-J. & Marin, J-Y. 1987. *Les Chateaux Normands de Guillaume Le Conquerant à Richard Coeur de Lion*. Caen:Musée de Normandie

Bishop, A.C. & Woolley, A.R. 1978. A note on some jade implements from Jersey. *BSJ* 22, 160-162

Bonamy, S. 1749. A Short Account of the Island of Guernsey. Unpub Add. Mss 6523 British Library

Bordes, F. 1968. *The Old Stone Age*. London: Weidenfeld and Nicolson

Bowyer, M. 1998. A Late sixteenth century shipwreck off Alderney. In H.Sebire (ed.) *Guernsey Connections. Archaeological and Historical Papers in Honour of Bob Burns*. Guernsey: La Société Guernesiaise, 123-130

Bradley, R. 1998. *The Significance of Monuments*. London: Routledge

Brett, C.E.B. 1975. *Buildings in the Town and Parish of St Peter Port*. Guernsey: The National Trust

Brett, C.E.B. 1976. *Buildings of the Island of Alderney*. Alderney : The Alderney Society

Brett, C.E.B. 1977. *Buildings in the Town and Parish of St Helier*. Jersey : The National Trust for Jersey

Briard, J. 1986. Les Relations entre Les Îles Anglo-Normandes et L'Armorique en Chalcolithic et L'Age du Bronze. In P. Johnston (ed.) *The Archaeology of the Channel Islands*. Chichester: Phillimore, 34-55

Bukach, D. 2002. A Petrological study of Prehistoric Pottery from Guernsey, Channel Islands. *TSG* **25:2**, 326-340

Burdo, C. 1960. *La Cotte de Saint Brelade, Jersey, British Channel Islands: Excavation of a pre-Mousterian Horizon 1950-58*. St Helier: Société Jersiaise

Burgess, C. & O'Connor, B. 2004. Bronze Age rotary spits: Finds old and new, some false, some true. In H. Roche, E. Grogan, J. Bradley, J. Coles, & B. Rafferty (eds.) *From megaliths to metal. Essays in honour of George Eogan*. Oxford: Oxbow, 184-199

Burns, R.B. 1977. The Late Iron Age site at the Tranquesous, St Saviour's, Guernsey. *TSG* **20** II: 191-218

Burns, R.B. 1985. *Archaeological Excavations at La Plaiderie, St Peter Port*. Guernsey Maritime Trust, privately circulated paper

Burns, R.B. 1988. *Excavations at Jerbourg, Guernsey*. Guernsey: Guernsey Museum Monograph No. 3

Burns, R., Cunliffe, B. and Sebire, H. 1996. *Guernsey. An Island Community of the Atlantic Iron Age*. Guernsey Museum Monograph No 7: Oxford Monograph No 47

Burns, R.B. & Batt, M. 1990. *Un habitat Cotier du XIIe Siecle le port aux malades, Guernsey, Iles Anglo-Normandes*. Revue Archéol Ouest, 7, 111–114

Cable, E.K. 1877. Report of the excavation of 'Beauport cromlech', Jersey, under the direction of the archaeological committee of La Société Jersiaise. *BSJ* 1, 89-95

Callow, P. 1983. *Palaeolithic deposits at the caves of La Cotte à La Chèvre and La Cotte de St Brelade. Field Excursion to the Channel Islands March 1983*. The Prehistoric Society:Privately circulated paper

Callow, P. 1986a. The stratigraphic sequence: description and problems. In P. Callow & J.M. Cornford (eds.). *La Cotte de St Brelade 1961-78. Excavations by C.B.M. McBurney*. Geo Books: Cambridge

Callow, P. 1986. Discussion in P. Callow & J.M. Cornford (eds.) *La Cotte de St Brelade 1961-78. Excavations by C.B.M. McBurney*. Geo Books: Cambridge

Callow, P. & Cornford J.M. (eds.) 1986. *La Cotte de St Brelade 1961-78. Excavations by C M McBurney*. Geo Books: Cambridge

Campbell, J. 2000. *Holocene Paleoenvironments of Guernsey and Alderney, Channel Islands*. University of Coventry: Unpublished PhD thesis

Carey Curtis, S. 1912 An account of the discovery and examination of a cist or dolmen of a type novel to Guernsey in October and November 1912. *TSG* **6**, 400-414

Cassen, S., Audren, C., Hinguant, S., Lannuzel, G. & Marchand, G., 1998. L'habitat Villeneuve-Saint-Germain du haut Mée (Saint-Etienne-en-Coglès, Ille-et-Villaine). *B.S.P.F.* **95:1**, 41-75

Cassen, S. 2000. *Éléments d'architecture*. Conseil Général du Morbihan

Chadwick, N. 1965. The Colonisation of Brittany from Celtic Britain. *Proc. Brit Acad.* **51** London: University Press

Childe, G.D.V. 1925. *The Dawn of European Prehistory*. London: Routledge Kegan and Paul

Childs W. 1986. Channel Island Ships as Recorded in the English Custom Accounts 1300-1500. In A.G. Jamieson (ed.) *A People of the Sea*. London : Methuen, 44-58

Chippendale, C. 1985. Foreword in R. Jossaume. *Dolmens for the Dead. Megalith-building throughout the world*. London: Batsford

Coates, D. 1991. *The ancient and modern names of the Channel Islands: a linguistic history*. Stamford: Paul Watkins

Cole, S. 1970. *The Neolithic Revolution*. London: The British Museum

Coombs, D. 1981. The Late Bronze Age hoard from Clos de La Blanche Pierre, Jersey, Channel Isles. An interim report *BSJ* **23: 1**, 129-142

Connan, J., Maurin, B., Long, L., Sebire, H., 2001. Identification of pitch and conifer resin in archaeological samples from the Sanguinet lake (Landes, France): export of pitch on the Atlantic ocean during the Gallo-Roman period. *Revue d'archéometrie* **16**, 177-96

Conneller, C., Connelly, J., Renouf, J.T., Schadla-Hall, R.T. & Sebire, H.R. (forthcoming) Recent finds from a submerged Upper Palaeolithic site at Crevichon

Constantin, C. 1985. Fin du Rubané, ceramique du Limbourg et post-Ruban: le Néolithique le plus ancien en Bassin Parisien et en Hainaut. *BAR* (International series) 273

Cotton, M.A. 1958. Early Iron Age earthworks in Jersey. *BSJ* **17:2**, 171-80

Coysh, V. (ed.) 1959. *The Channel Islands a New Study*. Newton Abbott: David and Charles

Cunliffe, B.W. 1984. The Prehistoric Pottery. In K.J. Barton Excavations at Mont Orgueil *Arch. J.*, **141**, 78-80

Cunliffe, B.W. 1986. The First Eight Thousand Years, 700BC-AD1000. In A.G. Jamieson (ed.) *A People of the Sea*. London: Methuen, 3-18

Cunliffe, B.W. 1986a. The Iron Age of the Channel Islands, a review. In Johnston, P. (ed.) (1986) *The Archaeology of the Channel Islands*. Chichester: Phillimore, 56-67

Cunliffe, B.W. 1992. Le Câtel de Rozel, Jersey: The Excavations of 1988-90. *Antiq. J.* **72**, 18-53

Cunliffe, B.W. 2001. *Facing the Ocean*. Oxford: Oxford University Press

Cunliffe, B. & de Jersey, P. 2000. Rescue excavations on Guernsey and Herm, 1998, 1999 *TSG* **24** V, 867-944

Davies, W. 1991. *The Coastal Towers of Jersey*. Jersey: La Société Jersiaise

Davies W., Graham-Campbell, J., Handley, M., Kershaw, P., Koch, J.T., Le Duc, G. & Lockyear, K. 2000. *The Inscriptions of Early Medieval Brittany*. Oakville: Celtic Studies Publications

David, J. 1961. Wrecks in the Bailiwick of Guernsey. *TSG* **27**, 224-45

De Guérin, T.W.M. 1921. List of Dolmens, Menhirs and Sacred Rocks. Compiled from Guernsey Place-names, with Legends, &c. *TSG* **21** 30-64

de Jersey, P. 1998. Celtic Coins in Guernsey. In H. Sebire (ed.) *Guernsey Connections. Archaeological and Historical Papers in Honour of Bob Burns*. Guernsey: La Société Guernesiaise, 43-52

Derrick, G.T. 1904. Jerbourg and its Fortifications. *TSG* **5**, 248-265

Derrick, G.T. 1907. Archaeological Remains in Guernsey *TSG* **5**, 229-30

Deyrolle E. & Mauger, P. 1912. Note sur le dolmen sous tumulus de la test-du-Fief de la Hougue-Boëte (Jersey) *Bull. Soc. Anth. Paris* **65.3**, 165-72

Dixon P., Jones M. & Phillpotts C., 1998. *Mont Orgueil Castle: A Report on the Archives*. Heritage Projects: University of Nottingham

Dixon, P. & Kennedy, J. 2002 *Mont Orgeuil Castle Conservation Plan*. Jersey Heritage Trust

Edwards, G.B. 1981. *The Book of Ebenezer le Page*. Harmondsworth: Penguin

Evans, J. 1969. *Life in Medieval France*. London : Phaidon

Everard, J. & Holt, J. 2004. *Jersey 1204. The forging of an island community*. London: Thames and Hudson

Falle, P. 1694. *Caesarea, or, An account of Jersey: the greatest of the islands remaining to the crown of England of the ancient duchy of Normandy: with an appendix of records, &c. an accurate map of the island and a prospect of Elizabeth-castle.* London:Newton

Finlaison, M. 1974. *A Preliminary Archaeological Survey for the town of St Helier.* A report prepared for La Société Jersiaise by M.B. Finlaison, Director of Excavations

Finlaison, M. 1976 Archaeological; section report for 1975. *BSJ* **21:4**, 451-3

Finlaison, M. 1976a. Excavations at 13 and 13a Old Street, St Helier. *BSJ* **21:4**, 477-494

Finlaison, M. 1977. Archaeological Section Report for 1976. *BSJ* **22:1**, 18-21

Finlaison, M. 1978. Two Romano-British bowls from Le Pinacle, Jersey. *BSJ* **22:2**, 181-5

Finlaison, M. 1980. Archaeological Section report for 1979. *BSJ* **22:3**, 74

Finlaison, M. 1981. An account of the finding of the Clos de Blanche Pierre hoard. *BSJ* **23:1**, 124-128

Finlaison, M. 1986. A thirteenth-Century Aisled Hall from St Helier, Jersey. In P. Johnston (ed.) (1986) *The Archaeology of the Channel Islands.* Chichester: Phillimore

Finlaison, M. 1997. Excavations in the Lower Room of the southwest Keep Tower of Mont Orgueil castle. *BSJ* **27: 1**, 825-895

Finlaison M. 1998. Traces of the Early Norman Cemetery at St Lawrence Church. *BSJ* **27:2**, 292–302

Finlaison, M. 2001. Excavations in the Lower Room of the southwest Keep Tower of Mont Orgueil castle. Part 2 The wall paintings. *BSJ* **28**, 178-87

Finlaison, M. & Holdsworth, P. 1979. Excavations on the Îles Agois, Jersey. *BSJ* **22:3**, 322-346

Fitzpatrick, A. & Megaw, J.V.S. 1987. Further Finds from the Le Câtillon Hoard. *PPS* **53**, 433-444

Galliou P. 1986 Wine and the Atlantic Trade in the Late Iron Age. In P. Johnston (ed.) *The Archaeology of the Channel Islands.* Chichester: Phillimore, 75-88

Galliou, P. & Jones, M. 1991. *The Bretons.* Oxford: Blackwell

Gavey, E. 1997. *A Guide to German Fortifications on Guernsey.* Guernsey: Guernsey Armouries

Ghesquière E., Lefèvre, P. Marcigny, C., Souffi, B., 2000. Le Mésolithique Moyen du Nord-Cotentin, Basse-Normandie, France. *BAR International Series* 856

Girard, P.J. 1981. Excavation of the Long House at Le Feugré, Cobo. *TSG* **21:1**, 94-98

Godfray, A.D.B. 1931. Archaeological Section Report. *BSJ* **11**, 234-5

Godfray, A.D.B. & Burdo, C. 1949. Excavations at Le Pinacle, Parish of St Ouen, Jersey. 1930-36. *BSJ* **15**, 2, 165-238

Gosselin, J. 1812. An Account of some Druidicial remains in the Island of Guernsey. *Archaeologia.* **17**, 254

Green, M.C. 1973. Archaeological Section, In *Société Jersiaise Special Bulletin. 1873-1973.* Jersey: La Société Jersiaise

Grimsley, E. J. 1988. *The Historical development of the Martello Tower in the Channel Islands.* Guernsey: Sarnian Publications

Grose, F. 1785. *The Antiquities of England and Wales.* London. Printed for Hooper

Hamon, G. forthcoming. The prehistoric pottery. In H.R. Sebire (forthcoming) Excavations at the former Royal Hotel site, Guernsey, 1998-2001

Hawkes, J. 1937. *The Archaeology of the Channel Islands. Vol. 11 The Bailiwick of Jersey.* Jersey: La Société Jersiaise

Hazelden, J. 1992. *Soils of Part of Alderney.* Bedford: Soil Survey and Landscape Research Centre

Henig, M. & Wood A.M. 1990. A Cast Bronze Figure from Jersey. *Oxford Journal of Archaeology.* **9:2**, 237-240

Henig, M. 1999. *Intaglio from the Bonded Store, Guernsey.* Unpublished paper. Guernsey Museum

Heylyn, P. 1656. *A Full Relation of two journeys: the one into the mainland of France. The other into the adjacent Ilands.* London: Seile

Hibbs, J. 1985. Little Mister Stonehenge. *BSJ* **24:1**, 49-74

Hibbs, J. & Shute, D. 1984. A re-examination of the La Sergenté passage grave, St. Brelade, Jersey. *BSJ* **23**, 525-531

Hill, M. 1990. The Excavation on La Hougue Catelain, 1982 and 1983. *TSG* **22:5**, 827-870

Hocart, R. 1995. The Channel Islands: a note from the editor. *TSG* **24:1**, 9

Hocart, R. 1998. The Preservation of Megalithic Monuments in Guernsey. In H. Sebire (ed.) *Guernsey Connections: Archaeological and Historical Papers in Honour of Bob Burns.* Guernsey. La Société Guernesiaise

Holdsworth, P. 1986. An Eremitic Settlement on the Ile Agois. In P. Johnston (ed) *The Archaeology of the Channel Islands.* Chichester: Phillimore

Hugo, V. 1883. *L'Archipel de La Manche.* Paris: Calmann Lévy

Jamieson, A.G. 1986. *A People of the sea. The Maritime History of the Channel Islands.* Methuen: London

Jee, N. 1977. Fauna and Flora. In V. Coysh (ed.) *The Channel Islands: a New Study.* Devon: David & Charles

Jee, N. 1968. Archaeological Report for 1967. *TSG* **28**, 138-9

Jenkinson, R., Dillon, P., James. L. & Lowe, V. 1991. A Report on the Stone artefacts in Alderney Museum. *ASB* **26**, 70-78

Johnston, D.E. 1972. Re-excavation of the Beauport Dolmen *BSJ* **20:4,** 405-417

Johnston, D.E. 1973. The Dolmen of Les Porciaux South, Alderney. *TSG* **19**, 301-312

Johnston, D.E. 1974. The excavation of the Tourgis Dolmen, Alderney. *TSG* **19**, 462- 468

Johnston, D.E. 1981. *The Channel Islands: An Archaeological Guide.* Chichester, Phillimore

Johnston, P. (ed.) 1986. *The Archaeology of the Channel Islands.* Chichester: Phillimore

Johnston, P. 1994. *A Short History of Guernsey.* Guernsey, Guernsey Press Company

Jones, R.L., Keen, D.H., Birnie, J.F. & Waton, P.V. 1990. *Past Landscapes of Jersey. Environmental changes during the last ten thousand years.* Jersey: La Société Jersiaise

Jossaume, R. 1985. *Dolmens for the Dead. Megalith-building throughout the world.* London: Batsford

Keen, D.H. 1976. *The Distribution of Flint-working sites in the Bailiwick of Guernsey.* Lanchester Polytechnic Privately circulated paper

Keen, D.H. 1978. Pleistocene deposits of the Channel Islands. *Report of the Institute of Geological Sciences* 78/26. London: HMSO

Keen, D.H. 1978a. A Palaeolithic flake from Noirmont Point. *BSJ* **22**, 205-8

Keith, A. & Knowles F.H.S. 1912. A description of the teeth of Palaeolithic man from Jersey. *BSJ* **37**, 223-40

Kendrick, T.D. 1928. *The Archaeology of the Channel Islands. Vol. 1: The Bailiwick of Guernsey.* London: Methuen

Kinnes, I.A. 1980. The art of the exceptional: the statue menhirs of Guernsey in context. *Archaeologia Antlantica*, 39-33

Kinnes, I.A. 1982. Les Fouaillages and megalithic origins. *Antiquity* **56:216**, 24-30

Kinnes, I.A. 1986. Le Néolithisation de Îles Anglo-Normandes. *Revue Archaeologique de L'Ouest* Supplement **1**, 9-12

Kinnes, I.A. 1988. Megaliths in Action: Some aspects of the Neolithic period in the Channel Islands. *Arch.J.* **145**, 13-59

Kinnes, I.A. 1995. Statue-menhirs and allied representations in Northern France and the Channel Islands. Notizie Archeologiche Bergomensi 3, 131-141

Kinnes, I.A. 1998. This is the Place Where Time Meets Space. In H. Sebire (ed.) *Guernsey Connections.* Guernsey: La Société Guernesiaise

Kinnes, I.A. 2004. Context not Circumstance: a distant view of Scottish Monuments. In I.A.G.Shepherd & G.J. Barclay (eds.). *Scotland in Ancient Europe.* Edinburgh: Society of Antiquaries of Scotland, 139-143

Kinnes, I.A. 2004a. Trans-manche: l'entente cordiale or vive la différence. In J. Cotton & D. Field *Towards a new Stone Age: aspects of the Neolithic in south-east England. CBA Research Report* 137

Kinnes, I.A. & Grant, J. 1983. *Les Fouaillages and the Megalithic Monuments of Guernsey.* Guernsey: Ampersand Press

Kinnes, I.A. & Hibbs, J. 1988. *The Dolmens of Jersey.* Jersey; La Haule Books

Langouët, L. 1973. *Fouilles sous la Cathedral du Xéme siecle.* Dossiers du Centre Regional Archeologie du Alet

Langouët, L. 1986. Les Iles Anglo-Normandes a L'Epoque Gallo-Romaine in P. Johnston (ed.) *The Archaeology of the Channel Islands.* Chichester: Phillimore

Le Patourel, J. 1954. Excavations Castle Cornet, Guernsey. *TSG* **16,** 350-361

Le Patourel, J. 1958. *The Building of Castle Cornet. Part 1: Documents relating to the Tudor reconstruction.* The Royal Court of Guernsey

Le Roux, C T. 1984. New excavations at Gavrinis. *Antiquity* **59:227**, 183-187

Lukis, F.C. 1843. *Bircham Barrows.* Guernsey: Barbet

Lukis, F.C. 1850. *Collectanea Antiqua.* Unpublished Mss held at Guernsey Museum

Lukis, F.C. 1851. Observations on the Celtic Megaliths. *Archaeologia* **35**, 232-258

MacCulloch, E. 1903. *Guernsey Folklore.* London: Clarke

Malone, C. 2001. *Neolithic Britain and Ireland.* Stroud: Tempus

Marett, R.R. 1912. Pleistocene man in Jersey. *Archaeologia.* **62**, 2 450-80

Marett, R.R. 1941. *A Jerseyman at Oxford.* Oxford: Oxford University Press

Marsden, P. 1994. *Ships of the Port of Roman London. First to Eleventh centuries* London: English Heritage

McCammon, A.L.T. 1984. *Currencies of the Anglo-Norman Isles.* London: Spink

McCormack, J. 1986. *Channel Island Chuches.* Chichester: Phillimore

McGrail, S. 1983. Cross Channel seamanship and navigation in the Late First Millennium BC. *Oxford Journal of Archaeology* **2:3**, 299-339

McGrail, S. & Roberts, O. 1999. Romano-British boat from the shores of the Severn Estuary. *Mariners Mirror* **85**, 133-46

McGrail, S. 2001. *Boats of the World. From the Stone Age to Medieval Times.* Oxford: Oxford University Press

Messervy, G. 1913. St Clement's Church. *BSJ* **7**, 345-9

Mohen, J-P. 1998. *Les Mégalithes: Pierres de mémoire.* Trieste: Gallimard

Morzadec-Kerfourn M.-T. 1974. *Variations de La Ligne de rivage Armoricaine au Quaternaire: Analyses Polliniques de Dépôts Orgainques Littoraux.* Memoires de la Société Géologique et Minéralogique de Bretagne 17. Rennes: La Société Géologique et Minéralogique de Bretagne

Mourant, A.E. 1933. *Dolmen at La Hougue Bie: nature and provenance of materials. BSJ* **12**, 217-220

Monaghan, J. 1988. The Guernsey Maritime Trust Gazeteer, 1984-88. *TSG.* **22:3**, 453-465

Monaghan, J. & Bound, M. *A ship cast away about Alderney.* Alderney: the Alderney Maritime Trust

Nicolle, E.T. 1912. Notice sur le torque d'or trouvé à Jersey et sur les torques hélicoïdaux. *BSJ* **7:3**, 247-58

Nicolle, E.T. 1921. *Mont Orgueil Castle. Its History and Description.* Jersey: Beresford Library

Nicolle, E.T. 1924. *The discovery of a beehive hut at La Sergenté, St.Brelade. BSJ* **10**, 67-71

Nicolle, E.T. 1924a. La Hougue Bie. *BSJ.* **10**, 179-194

Nicolle, E.T. & Sinel, J. 1910. Report of the work done at Le Dolmen of La Pouquelaie, Faldouet St Martin. *BSJ* **7**, 67-68

Nicolle, E.T. & Sinel J. 1911. Report on the exploration of the Palaeolithic cave-dwelling known as La Cotte de St Brelade, Jersey. *BSJ.* **36**, 69-74

Nicolle, E.T. & Sinel, J. 1912. *Archaeological researches at La Motte. BSJ* **7**, 241-245

Nicolle, E.T, Warton, R.G. & Sinel, J. 1913. *Report on the exploration of the dolmen at Les Monts Grantez. BSJ* **7**, 314-325

Nicolle, W. (ed.) 1889. *Caeserea or A Discourse of the Island of Jersey par Le Lieutenant-Bailli Jean Poingdestre.* Jersey: La Société Jersiaise

Northover, J.P. 1987. Analysis of the Bronze hoard from Clos de La Blanche Pierre, *BSJ* **24:3**, 363-379

Northover, J.P. 1989. The gold torc from St Helier, Jersey. *BSJ* **25:1**, 112-137

O'Brien 1996. *Bronze Age Copper Mining in Britain and Ireland.* Princes Risborough: Shire

Ogier, D.M. 1998. Lihou Priory: A preliminary essay in H. Sebire (ed.) *Guernsey Connections. Archaeological and Historical Papers in Honour of Bob Burns.* Guernsey: La Société Guernesiaise

Oliver, S.P. 1870. Report on the Present State and Condition of Prehistoric Remains in the Channel Islands. *Journal of the Ethnographical Society of London*, N.S. **11**, 45-73

Oliver, S.P. 1870a. (April) Megalithic Structures of the Channel Islands : Their History and Analogues. *Quarterly Journal of Science* **26**, 1-17

Owen, E. & Frost, M. 2000. *The Dover Bronze Age Boat Gallery Guide*. Dover: The Dover Bronze Age Boat Trust

Ovenden, J. & Shayer, D. 2003. *Wrecks of the Channel Islands*. Guernsey: Howitt Offshore

Parker-Pearson, M . 2005. *Bronze Age Britain*. London: Batsford

Partridge, C. 1991. The Fortifications of Guernsey. *States of Guernsey*. Billet D' État, 13

Patton, M. 1984. Excavation of a Bronze Age enclosure system at La Moye. *BSJ* **23**, 532-538

Patton, M. 1987. *Jersey in Prehistory*. Jersey: La Haule Books

Patton, M. 1991. Stone Axes of the Channel Islands: Neolithic exchange in an insular Context. *Oxford Journal of Archaeology* **10,** 33-42

Patton, M.A. 1993. The Mesolithic of the Channel Islands: Economy and settlement in a Changing Landscape. *Oxford Journal* **12:1,** 9-17

Patton, M .A. 1994. The Mesolithic Site of Canal du Squez, St Ouen. *BSJ* **26**, 274-281

Patton, M. 1995. *Neolithic Communities of the Channel Islands*. Oxford: BAR, 240

Patton, M. A. 1996. Prehistoric Pottery. In W. Rodwell. *Les Écréhous, Jersey*. La Société Jersiaise

Patton, M. 2001. Le Pinacle, Jersey: a Reassessment of the Neolithic, Chalcolithic and Bronze Age horizons. *Arch. J.* **158**, 1-61

Patton, M. & Finlaison, M. 2001. *Patterns in a Prehistoric Landscape*. Jersey: La Société Jersiaise

Patton, M., Rodwell, R. & Finch, O. 1999. *La Hougue Bie Jersey. A Study of the Neolithic Tomb, Medieval Chapel and Prince's Tower*. Jersey: La Société Jersiaise

Pécquart, M., Pécquart, S.J., Boule, M. & Vallois, H.V. 1937. *Téviec: Station-nécropole mésolithique du Morbihan*. Paris: Archives de L'Institut de Paléontologie humaine, 18

Percival, S.T. 1947. Report of the Antiquarian Section. *TSG* **13**, 117-119

Pindar, *Olympian Odes* 1997. Trans. W.H. Race. Loeb: Harvard University Press

Platt, C. 2001. *Mont Orgueil and the Defence of Jersey 1540-1630*. Bognor Regis: Woodfield Publishing

Platt, C. 2003. *The Mont Orgueil Dossier: or Who built the Somerset Tower?* Bognor Regis: Woodfield Publishing

Podger, A. 2001. Jersey Harbours. *BSJ* **28:1**, 118-133

Powicke, M. 1960. *The Loss of Normandy 1189-1204*. Manchester: Manchester University Press

Price, J. 2002. Roman glass from the Channel Islands. Unpublished report for Guernsey Museum

Rault, S. & Forest, S. 1992. La Hougue de Geonnais, Jersey, Channel Islands: an interim report on the 1985-9 seasons of excavation. *BSJ* **25:4**, 691-710

Renfrew, C. 1996. Foreword in P. Bahn (ed.) *The Cambridge Illustrated History of Archaeology*. Cambridge: Cambridge University Press

Renfrew, C. & Bahn, P.'1996. *Archaeology Theories Methods and Practice*. London: Thames and Hudson

Renfrew. C. 1976. Megaliths Territories and Populations. In S.J. de Laet (ed.) Acculturation and Continuity in Atlantic Europe, cited in Scarre, C. 2002 *Monuments And Landscape in Atlantic Europe*. London: Routledge

Renouf, J. 1974. The Gold Torque. *BSJ* **21:2**, 294-5

Renouf, J. & Urry J. 1976. *The First Farmers in the Channel Islands*. Jersey: Education Department

Renouf, J. 1977. Geology. In V. Coysh (ed.) *The Channel Islands a New Study*, Devon: David & Charles

Renouf, J.T. & Sebire, H.R. forthcoming. The Earliest Neolithic in Guernsey. *Oxford Committee for Archaeology: Oxford Journal*

Richards, M.P., Schulting, R. & Hedges, R.E.M. 2003. Sharp shift in diet at the onset of the Neolithic. *Nature* **425**, 366

Roach, R.A., Topley, C.G., Brown, M., Bland, A.M. & R.S, D'Lemos 1991. *Outline and Guide to the Geology of Guernsey*. Guernsey: Guernsey Museum Monogaph No 3

Rodwell, W. 1996. *Les Écréhous Jersey*. Jersey: La Société Jersiaise

Rodwell, W. forthcoming 2006. *Mont Orgueil Castle, Jersey. History and Architecture*. Jersey: Jersey Heritage Trust

Rule, M. and Monaghan, J. 1993. *A Gallo-Roman Trading Vessel from Guernsey*. Guernsey Museum Monograph 5. Guernsey: Guernsey Museum

Rushton, N.S. 2003. The Historical eveidence for the Sixteenth century Structural re-modelling of Mont Orgueil Castle. *BSJ* **28**, 351-375

Rybot, N.V.L. 1930. Report on the reparations and investigations in Mont Orgueil Castle 1921-1929 *BSJ* **11**, 274-367

Rybot, N.V.L. 1932. The dolmen of Faldouet. *BSJ* **12**, 73-89

Rybot, N.V.L. 1934. The surviving menhirs of Jersey. *BSJ* **12**, 337-345

Rybot, N.V.L. 1947. *The Islet of St Helier and Elizabeth Castle, Jersey.* Jersey: States of Jersey

Rybot, N.V.L. 1949. Archaeological Section report for 1948. *BSJ* **15:1**, 11

Rybot, N.V.L. 1950. Report on the excavations made in the north-east outer slopes of Mont Orgueil Castle 1921-1929. *BSJ* **15**, 239-48

Salway, P. 2000. *Roman Britain. A very short introduction.* Oxford: Oxford University Press

Scarre, C. 2002. *Monuments and Landscape in Atlantic Europe.* London: Routledge

Schadla-Hall, R.T. 2002. Interim report on GU582, Lihou Island. Guernsey Museum. Privately circulated paper

Schadla-Hall, R.T. 2001. Excavations and investigations at GU582, Lihou Island, August 2001. Institute of Archaeology, London. Privately circulated paper

Schulting, R.J. & Richards M.P. 2000. The use of stable isotopes in studies of subsistence and seasonality in the British Mesolithic. In R. Young (ed.) *Mesolithic Lifeways: Current Resesarch from Britain and Ireland*: 55-65 Leicester: Leicester University Mongraphs

Schulting, R.J. & Richards, M.P. 2001 Dating Women and Becoming Farmers: New Palaeodietary and AMS Dating Evidence from the Breton Mesolithic Cemeteries of Téviec and Hoëdic. *Journal of Anthropological Archaeology* **20**, 314-344

Sebire, H.R. (ed.) 1998. *Guernsey Connections. Archaeological and Historical Papers in Honour of Bob Burns.* Guernsey: La Société Guernesiaise

Sebire, H.R. 2001. Excavations in Guernsey in 2000. Guernsey *TSG* **25:1**, 12-17

Sebire, H.R. 2002. Excavations in Guernsey in 2001. *TSG* **25:2**, 228-232

Sebire, H.R. 2003. *Frederick Corbin Lukis, a remarkable archaeologist and polymath.* Unpublished PhD Thesis, University of Southampton

Sebire, H.R. forthcoming 1998-2001. Excavations at the former Royal Hotel site, Guernsey

Sharp, E.W. 1959. The Harbours and Shipping of Guernsey in the 19th century. *TSG* **16** Part 1

Sharp, E.W. 1967. Wrecks of the Bailiwick of Guernsey. *TSG* **28**, 206-25

Sheridan, A. 2004 '…beads which gave rise to so much dogmatism, controversy and rash speculation': faience in Early Bronze Age Britain and Ireland. In I. Shepherd and G.J. Barclay (eds.) *Scotland in Ancient Europe.* Edinburgh: Society of Antiquaries of Scotland

Sherratt, A. 1991. Sacred and Profane substances: The Ritual use of narcotics in Later Neolithic Europe. In P. Garwood, D Jennings, R. Skeates and J. Tomes (eds.) *Sacred and Profane: proceedings of a conference on Archaeology, Ritual and Religion.* Oxford 1989. Oxford University Comm. for Arch. Mon. **32** 50-54

Sinel, J. 1911. The Prehistoric Cave Dwelling 'Cotte à La Chèvre', St Ouen. *BSJ* **7**, 209-13

Sinel, J. 1912. Prehistoric Times and Men of the Channel Islands. Jersey: States of Jersey

Smith, B.D. 1998. *The Emergence of Agriculture.* New York: Scientific American

Stevens, C. 2002. *Short Report on the Charred hazelnuts Remains from Site GU582, Lihou Island.* Unpublished Report. Institute of Archaeology, London

Stevens-Cox, G. 1969 *The Channel Islands in the 16th Century, As seen by William Camden.* Toucan Press: Guernsey

Stringer, C.B. & Currant, A.P. 1986. Hominid specimens from La Cotte de Saint Brelade. in P. Callow, J.M. & Cornford. (eds.). *La Cotte de St Brelade 1961-78. Excavations by C.B.M. McBurney.* Geo Books: Cambridge

Symons, A.N. 1946. Out-going President's Address *TSG* **14**, 8

Tanguy, J. 1987. Archaeological Section report for 1986. *BSJ* **24.3**, 303-6

Thomson, R. 1980. The Medieval Pottery. In K.J. Barton. Excavations at the Château des Marais. *TSG* **20**, **5**, 673-7

Thorpe, A. 1999. *From the Neanderthal.* London: Jonathan Cape

Timms 1980. *Flint Implements of the Old Stone Age.* Princes Risborough: Shire

Toynbee, A. 1958. *East to West. A journey around the world.* Oxford: Oxford University Press

Verron. 2000. *Prehistoire de la Normandie.* Rennes: Editions Ouest-France

Walkington, H., Renouf, J.T., James, H.C.L. & Sebire, H.R. 2001. *A Raised Beach in Western Guernsey: Its Archaeological and Geological Significance.* Proceedings of the Usher Society

Wessex 2004. *Castle Cornet, St Peter Port, Guernsey. Integrated works to repair the foul sewer running between the 201 Squadron Museum and the Maritime Museum Report on the Archaeological and Landscape Works.* Wessex Archaeology Report 50712.03

Williams, D. 1996. The Roman Amphora. In R. Burns, B. Cunliffe, and H. Sebire *Guernsey. An Island Community of the Atlantic Iron Age.* Guernsey Museum Monograph No 7: Oxford Monograph No 47

Winder, N. 1995 No further skeletons … Von Hugels excavations in Alderney 1889-90. *TSG,* **23** V, 901-903

Wiseman, A. & Wiseman, P. 1980. *Julius Caesar: The Battle for Gaul.* London: Chatto & Windus

Worsaae J.J.A. 1843. *Danmarks oldtid oplyst ved oldsager.* Copenhagen; Klein

Wood, M. 1989. Romano-British and Roman pottery from Jersey. *BSJ* **25:1**, 175-9

Wood, A.M. 1996. Briquetage, Roman and Dark Age Pottery. In W. Rodwell *Les Écréhous Jersey* 230-233. Jersey: La Société Jersiaise

Wood, A.M. 2000. *The Context and Significance of Roman Guernsey.* Privately Circulated Paper

Wood, A.M. 2002. *Roman Guernsey and the context of the pottery from the Bonded stores.* Guernsey Museum Unpublished Report

Wood, A.M. forthcoming. *Roman pottery from La Plaiderie, the Bonded Stores and other sites in Guernsey.* Report for Guernsey Museum

Wood, M. & Sebire, H. 2002. Report of the Archaeological investigation at the Nunnery, Alderney, Channel Islands. *ASB* **37**, 57-65

INDEX